D1616737

REFUGE OF THE HONORED

REFUGE OF
THE HONORED

Social Organization

in a Japanese

Retirement Community

Yasuhito Kinoshita
Christie W. Kiefer

HQ
1063.2
.J3
K56
1992
West

University of California Press
Berkeley · Los Angeles · Oxford

University of California Press
Berkeley and Los Angeles, California

University of California Press, Ltd.
Oxford, England

© 1992 by
The Regents of the University of California

Library of Congress Cataloging-in-Publication Data

Kinoshita, Yasuhito, 1953–
    Refuge of the honored : social organization in a
Japanese retirement community / Yasuhito Kinoshita,
Christie W. Kiefer.
      p.   cm.
    Includes bibliographical references and index.
    ISBN 0-520-07595-1 (alk. paper)
    1. Retirement communities—Japan—Case studies.
2. Retirees—Japan—Attitudes—Case studies.
3. Aged—Japan—Attitudes—Case studies.   I. Kiefer,
Christie W. II. Title.
HQ1063.2.J3K56 1992
305.26'0952—dc20   91-29107

Printed in the United States of America
9 8 7 6 5 4 3 2 1

The paper used in this publication meets the minimum
requirements of American National Standard for
Information Sciences—Permanence of Paper for Printed
Library Materials, ANSI Z39.48-1984. ∞

Contents

List of Tables and Figures   vii
Preface   ix

1. Introduction   1
2. The Scholarly Context of the Study   16

PART ONE.   AGING IN JAPAN: AN OVERVIEW   35

3. Demography and Income   37
4. Consequences of Social Change   46
5. Welfare Homes for the Aged and Emerging
   Retirement Communities   62

PART TWO.   FUJI-NO-SATO   81

6. The Setting and the System   83
7. The Residents   107

PART THREE.   SOCIAL INTEGRATION   119

8. Management and Residents:
   Communication Failure   121
9. The Residents Association   139
10. Group and Individual Activities   154
11. Patterns of Social Interaction   169
12. Conclusions   199

Bibliography   211
Index   215

Tables and Figures

TABLES

3-1. Estimated Increase in Four Elderly Age Groups   38

3-2. Population Trends and Projections for
Four Age Groups   40

3-3. International Comparison of Statutory
Pension Plans   44

4-1. Adult Children's Views of Desirable Living
Arrangements for Parents, after Marriage,
by Residential Area and Education   58

4-2. Elderly Parents' Views of Desirable Living
Arrangements with Married Children, by
Age, Health, and Actual Living Arrangements   59

5-1. Number of Homes for the Aged and
Residents by Type, 1963–1989   66

7-1. Family Status and Residential Patterns   108

7-2. Men's Occupations   112

7-3. Women's Occupations, by Marital Status   113

10-1. Hobby Groups   155

10-2. Male and Female Memberships
in Hobby Groups   158

11-1. Extent of Men's and Women's Acquaintances   193

11-2. Bases of Men's and Women's Friendships   194

FIGURES

2-1. Depth Model of Japanese Interpersonal
Relationships   28

2-2. Analytical Model of This Study   30

3-1. Life Expectancy at Birth, Years Left
to Live for Sixty-five-Year-Olds   39

3-2. Growth in Aged Population from 7 to 14 Percent,
Comparison of Six Nations   42

3-3. Income Sources of Elderly Households   43

4-1. Living Arrangements of Those Over Sixty-five 53

4-2. Future Estimates of Elderly Households   56

4-3. Trends Among Three Types of Households
with at Least One Member Over Sixty-five   57

4-4. Trends in Co-living for Three Age Groups   60

5-1. Number of Retirement Facilities, 1982–1989   75

5-2. Number of Residents in Retirement Facilities,
1982–1989   75

6-1. Building Arrangements at Fuji-no-Sato   88

6-2. Four Types of Residential Units   90

Preface

This book is an ethnographic study and as such carries the strengths and weaknesses of intensive, descriptive, cross-cultural work. We hope the strengths will speak for themselves. One of the weaknesses, much discussed among method-conscious cultural anthropologists, is the difficulty of creating a narrative that is both recognizable by the people on whom we report and comprehensible to those for whom we write it. We have sought to deal with this difficulty through the collaboration of an American anthropologist with experience in Japan and a Japanese gerontologist with experience in America and training in sociology and anthropology.

This report is the result of research conducted in Japan by Kinoshita for his doctoral dissertation in human development and aging at the University of California, San Francisco. Almost all the descriptive content and most of the analysis are his. Kiefer edited the work for style, made several suggestions about the analysis, and wrote much of the introductory and concluding chapters.

Since 1984, when the dissertation was completed, Kinoshita has been living in Japan, where he is now the director of the Gerontology Center of the Japan Senior Citizen's Welfare Organization (Nihon Rōjin Fukushi Zaidan), a large nonprofit builder of retirement housing. Between 1985 and the present, he has had many opportunities to continue observing the development of the community discussed in this book (Fuji-no-Sato), as well as that of Japan's retirement housing industry as a whole. The results of these observations have been included here. Kiefer, a cultural anthropologist with experience in the scholarly fields of gerontology and Japanology, supervised the original research as Kinoshita's faculty advisor and visited the site in 1983.

ix

Kinoshita has continuously observed the community about which we have written here, Fuji-no-Sato, from 1982 to 1991. He has also directed research on four sister communities run by the same organization, using an interview schedule essentially identical to the one used at Fuji-no-Sato. These include (1) 323 residents of a community in another resort area not far from Tokyo, interviewed in 1984, when that community was in its fourth year; (2) 384 residents of a community in a new suburb of Kobe, in its fifth year in 1985; (3) 188 residents of the oldest community of all, in central Japan, in its tenth year in 1986; and (4) 176 residents of an urban community in Osaka in 1989. All these communities have been observed continuously, and Kinoshita plans to do a thorough restudy of Fuji-no-Sato starting in 1992, ten years from the start of the original fieldwork.

This book focuses on the formative years of Fuji-no-Sato. The phenomenon of retirement housing is still in a formative stage in Japan, and the problems we saw there are being experienced in many other places. It is also important to document a baseline for understanding and evaluating later stages in the evolution of such communities, not only in Japan, but in other developing societies that will face similar demographic problems in coming years.

Looking back now, we can see that the research period of 1982–1983 was especially crucial for both the community and the managing organization. We were lucky to have been there because most of the residents who appear in these pages have died, and the events we describe are only faded memories for the remaining ones.

Recognizing that there is a potential for confusing our report with the current state of affairs, we have taken care to note changes since the formal fieldwork ended in 1984. However, the retrospective report that results creates some stylistic headaches as we strive to make clear which observations and analytic statements belong to the reporting period and which to the present. We have chosen to deal with this by referring to the fieldwork period, 1982–1984, in the past tense and everything else (other than historical background) in the present tense.

The collaborative writing project has been personally rewarding for both of us, although each of us occasionally wonders how he ended up saying exactly what this book says. Perhaps this is a healthy sign that two distinct minds are clearly represented here.

1

Introduction

This is an ethnographic study of social life in Japan. Our purpose is to describe the process of community creation by aged residents in a Japanese setting. The theoretical focus is on the issue of social integration, but this is first and foremost a study of how the elderly Japanese residents approach a type of environment that is new in their culture.

Although our method is descriptive, our aim is not so much to grasp and convey the consciousness of the people at Fuji-no-Sato as to explain to Western gerontologists and Japanologists how the historical, cultural, and material settings of Japanese retirement housing render the social results unique. In contrast to those ethnographies that strive to speak for the "other"—to tackle the gulf of inner experience that separates observer from observed—we are dealing with very large social issues from a comparatively remote perspective. Even from this distant vantage point, we can see numerous troubling mysteries created by the massive scale and speed of the phenomenon we are watching.

We agree with those anthropologists who question the value of the old unself-conscious ethnography, in which a neutral "expert" offered his heavily worked observations as though they represented some transparent truth about the way of life under study. We have tried to deal with this by giving the reader a perspective "over our shoulders," that is, by describing what we did and by giving concrete examples from field notes to draw attention to the material from which we generalize.

The problem of authority in ethnography is also complicated by the effects of the reporter's value biases. We can scarcely be accused of colonialism in describing an industrial giant like Japan, and yet the attitude of the social planner does have an element of elitism in it. To be honest, we can only do our best to keep an eye on our own attitudes and to announce them when we think their effect on our vision is especially refractory. To this end, the collaboration of two very different writers has been especially useful.

For example, fieldwork unavoidably produces some strong relationships, and it should become clear to the reader that Kinoshita grew close to some of the administrators of Fuji-no-Sato's parent corporation. A leader of the Fuji-no-Sato Residents Association probably would have described the conflict with management differently than we have. Knowing this, we have simply done our best to be fair.

We do not claim greater overall objectivity or accuracy of reporting on account of Kinoshita's status as a "native observer"; but we do think it gives us a check on how common a given behavior is within Japanese society, as well as how a "typical" Japanese might be likely to interpret the more common occurrences.

Perception cannot be separated from interest; different interests unavoidably produce different and often irreconcilable descriptions. In the long run, the consensus of interests among users and the practical outcomes of applications produce consensual judgments about the "truth" of an ethnography. This can be clearly seen in the recent dramatic loss of credit suffered by much painstaking anthropological writing done before the postmodern revolt of the 1970s. We therefore submit our work to be tested against the interests of its users without any claim that its veracity goes beyond its practicality.

THE MESSAGE OF JAPAN'S AGED

There are few cross-cultural, descriptive studies of the social life of the aged in age-homogeneous settings. To our knowledge, this constitutes the second cross-cultural study of old people in such a setting outside the United States, the only other being a study of an apartment complex for working-class retirees in France (Ross, 1977). Ours is the first study of the phenomenon in a non-Western society. Theory building in this subfield of gerontology should arise from the accumulation of careful descriptions of the phenomenon in a variety of cultures, and this study is intended as a contribution to that effort.

Although the graying of Japan is now a fairly well known fact, little is known about Japanese retirement communities. Such communities are new in Japan, having emerged during the last twenty years, and their number has grown quickly—to about 155 in 1989. They are, therefore, in the experimental stage, and many communities are planning for the future without systematic knowledge appropriate to their culture and society. Yet there are strong indications that retirement communities are about to emerge in Japan in great number.

Because there was no previous study on a Japanese retirement community, even by Japanese researchers, we began with very general questions. What would happen when a group of old people who had lived in a traditionally family-centered society in which human relationships are hierarchically organized came to live together in a Western-style, age-homogeneous, and peer-group-oriented residential setting? Who were the residents of Fuji-no-Sato? What were their demographic characteristics? Why and how did they come to live there? What were the governing principles of their social interactions? To what extent was social integration possible? We also wondered what Fuji-no-Sato would be like as an environment; how it operated; and most important, what social significance it was likely to have in Japan.

We will not ask whether retirement communities are good or bad for the Japanese aged—a question that is simply unanswerable at this point. Not only can it not be answered by a single study of a retirement community, but any attempt to answer this question involves value judgments that we are not ready to make. It is true that most Japanese still believe that family care is the most desirable arrangement for the well-being of the aged and that it is basically wrong to segregate old people. The Japanese are far more suspicious than Americans of any form of congregate residential arrangements for the elderly. But a growing number of Japanese, young as well as old, are now searching for new alternatives to the traditional family care system, which demographic and social changes since World War II have rendered increasingly problematic.

Fundamentally, we take the value-laden position that it is desirable for a society to provide as many living alternatives as possible for its aged members so they can choose those that best fulfill their needs. As for what those needs are, we are struck by the fact that aging is (among other things) a process of losing individual physical and mental function, ultimately leading to death. It is usually too much to ask that an old person bear this shadow side of a lengthening life span alone. If we put this together with the fact that the work of caring for the elderly unavoidably involves intergenerational relations, we can understand the basic need for a certain kind of social environment. The old need to feel secure that they are and will continue to be listened to, understood, and supported—by both their peers and the next generation—through this difficult process of decline. They need hope not only for tomorrow (beyond their days on earth), but for the immediate day-to-day struggle to live meaningfully. For us, this is the ethical basis of a scientific interest in communities of and for the aged.

In short, this is a descriptive study of the social life of the residents in one retirement community in Japan; as such, it is limited in time (the current generation of Japanese elderly during a single year) as well as in space. Future generations of the Japanese aged will be different in many ways from the present generation, and the social life of the residents at Fuji-no-Sato will probably change as time goes on. The present residents will establish experienced relationships. They will get older and more frail. The natural process of aging and death will alter the social environment. Different people will manage these processes differently.

Mass longevity is a gift of industrialization. For the first time in human history, the average person can expect to attain nearly the full span of life allotted to our species. This fact has led to a major social problem in all postindustrial societies in the West and, as we will see in Part I, in Japan as well. Although there are differences in history, culture, and socioeconomic conditions among aging societies, particularly between the Western societies and Japan, aging tends to pose similar social problems for all (the need to provide sufficient income, adequate housing, and cost-effective, quality health care services), problems that can be solved only through well-coordinated and sensitive social policies. The Japanese have long considered the democratic socialist societies of Great Britain and Sweden the models to emulate in social policy. However, it has become apparent in recent years that these and other advanced welfare nations in the West are having serious problems remaining solvent while maintaining a high standard of public services for

their citizens. If the aging of populations is an inevitable consequence of industrialization, it is a challenge that all societies of our
time may have to face. No one nation can provide *the* model answer, and aging is now a global problem that requires international
collaboration.

The increase of the older population creates similar problems in
different societies, but how each copes with them will be uniquely
shaped by its sociocultural characteristics. Only parts of the knowledge gained by a given society in this process may be transferable
to other societies.

Aging in Japan attracts our scientific attention for several reasons: (1) Japan is the first non-Western society to experience an explosion of its aged population. (2) It has achieved a high level of
industrialization and political stability. (3) It has developed high
standards of health care. (4) Japanese culture appears to encourage
old people to be socially responsible and to venerate the aged themselves. (5) Japan is traditionally a family-centered society in which
the elderly members appear to be better socially integrated than
their counterparts in the West. Thus, the study of how Japan is coping with the problems of aging may reveal dynamic interactions between a society's unique sociocultural characteristics on one hand
and the imperative impact of industrialization and concomitant social change on the other. Here is a nation that has accomplished an
economic miracle in this century. Will it be able to achieve another
miracle, this time conquering the massive social problems result-
ing from its economic success—especially the problem of an aging
population?

However, a strategic and pragmatic approach to the immediate
social problems of aging may leave the really crucial problems unsolved. This does not mean that we underrate the significance of
such an approach, for the immediate practical problems are enormously difficult themselves and must be solved. A more serious
problem in the long run is that neither Japan nor the United States
has a viable philosophy on which to base social policies for the
aged. Put another way, today we need a new philosophy of human
values, for the era of mass longevity is also the era of the mass dependency of the aged. The rationalism that was the propelling philosophy of industrialization in Japan as well as America appears,

with all its benefits, to be dysfunctional when it comes to coping with the mass of dependent elderly. It is a philosophy that judges individuals on the basis of their productive capabilities.

The end of a historical era is often contained unforeseen in its beginning. As Max Weber (1904) demonstrated, the religiously motivated economic activities of the stoic early Protestants contributed to the primitive accumulation of capital, a process from which an intrinsically secular and materialistic culture was born. Similarly, the growing number of unproductive elderly whose presence results from an industrialized living standard now acts as a brake on the continued rise of that standard. Wealth cannot increase indefinitely. Therefore, failure to acquire a new philosophy of human values may result in an intensified generational conflict over shares of social wealth. Rosow (1962) was aware of this problem in the United States nearly thirty years ago and called it the moral dilemma of an affluent society. In the meantime, the prospects of the industrial world have darkened. Rosow's problem is now a major one in all postindustrial societies.

The question seems simple: Is it right (and if so, how can we convince ourselves) that the value of an individual should not be based on his independence or productivity, and that human existence itself is of the utmost importance even if it means heavy sacrifice on the part of the socially productive? Throughout human history, and particularly in this century, the prolongation of human life has been regarded as a yardstick of a society's level of maturity. The extension of life expectancy has validated our boast that our societies are continuously progressing. But we are now at a stage to pause and ask ourselves what the quality of human existence or the meaning of prolonged life should be. The questions are simple, but the answers are not ready in our minds.

A new philosophy of human values should embody the possibility of equality for the dependent old. Whether it is in the macrocontext of American or Japanese society or in the microcontext of the individual retirement community, the essential effect of our philosophy should be the same, for modern civilization itself is being tested by the growth of the dependent aged population.

In this regard, the United States may be in a much more difficult position than Japan because the notion of equality for the socially weak and dependent may be inherently incompatible with American culture, which is based on the mutually contradictory ideals of equality and individual self-determination. This contradiction drives disadvantaged members to marginal positions and blames them for their failure (cf. Henry, 1963; Slater, 1970). To understand this, one need not look at such extreme examples as the fate of the Native Americans, the history of institutionalized slavery, or discrimination against racial and ethnic minorities, but only at the treatment that the once-productive aged are receiving (cf. Butler, 1975; Henry, 1963; Kayser-Jones, 1981; Laird, 1979; Mendelson, 1975; Vladeck, 1980).

The task may be no easier for Japan, however. Although the degree of compatibility between the nature of the culture and the demand for a new philosophy appears to be greater in Japan than in the United States, in the process of industrialization, Japan has adopted many core values of American culture. Industrialization has disrupted Japan's traditional culture, and today's aged are caught in the midst of this disruption.

The issue of housing for the elderly not only represents an urgent and critical problem for Japanese society; it also epitomizes dynamic interactions between the growth of the aged population and various other postwar social changes. With this in mind, we undertook this study of a new style of living for the aged, a style stimulated by the changes we are discussing.

SELECTION OF THE STUDY SITE

Japan has only two types of congregate housing for the aged: welfare homes and emerging retirement communities (see Chapter 5). There is no public housing for low-income elderly, no Sun City–type large-scale developments or mobile home parks, as in the United States.

The selection of Fuji-no-Sato as the setting of this study was based on six considerations:

1. Type of service and type of payment
2. Attitude toward community creation
3. Size
4. Newness of the community

5. Size and philosophy of the management organization
6. Visibility as a model for other communities

When we began this study, there were only thirty-one retirement communities in all of Japan, but both the number and the variety have since grown rapidly and will continue to do so. Fuji-no-Sato is a life-care retirement community, the most common and, for now, the most promising type. A life-care community is defined here as a facility that provides, through contract, both age-appropriate living accommodations and at least some skilled nursing care as needed for the duration of the resident's life. The other two types of retirement communities in Japan are the "life-guarantee" type (of which there are only a few) and the condominium. The vast majority of elderly live either independently or with children, or they are confined to hospitals if chronically ill. When the study began, there was a great vacuum in housing options between these extremes; now many new age-specific communities are established yearly. We discuss the Japanese retirement housing environment in detail in Chapter 5.

The life-care type and the life-guarantee type offer similar services, but differ in payment method. The residents in the former pay a monthly fee in addition to an entrance fee; those in the latter make a one-time lump sum payment intended to cover expenses until they die. As one would expect, the life-guarantee type is vulnerable to unexpected costs, and the Ministry of Health and Welfare has discouraged them since one went into bankruptcy.

Condominiums are essentially residential facilities for independent elderly and provide only minimal medical and health care services; residents have to leave when they become frail and cannot maintain independent living.

Life care is increasingly important because it seems to address effectively the two main problems that have led to the emergence of retirement communities in the first place: (1) societal changes in the living arrangements of the aged and in consciousness regarding filial expectations and filial responsibilities and (2) the insufficiency of the long-term care system for the dependent aged.

The social dynamics of this type of community are the focus of our study. It is particularly significant that Fuji-no-Sato was the only retirement community in Japan that placed strong emphasis on community creation by the residents. This was an explicit goal from its planning stage and is expressed in the architectural design of the community (see Chapter 6).

In terms of size, Fuji-no-Sato has an average full-time population of two hundred thirty to two hundred fifty. Thus, it is a face-to-face community and appears to be an appropriate size for the residents to get to know one another.

The timing of the study was also crucial. Fuji-no-Sato opened in May 1979 and had been in operation for three years and four months when Kinoshita began fieldwork. It achieved full occupancy at the end of the first year. The research was well timed to focus on the process of community creation.

We deliberately chose a nonprofit community, feeling that the various financial positions of the variety of for-profit builders would complicate our study. Fuji-no-Sato was built and is managed by the largest nonprofit organization in this industry, having six large-scale life-care retirement communities. In 1982, when the study began, the corporation had four communities, whose combined population accounted for about 20 percent of the total in Japanese retirement communities.

What we did not realize at the outset was that this company has a unique philosophy, which turned out to have major consequences for the social dynamics of its communities. The builders were advocating something called "new welfare for the middle-income elderly."

The word "welfare" has an ambiguous meaning in Japan today that reflects changing and uncertain social attitudes. On the one hand, welfare still retains the idea, held over from the preprosperity era, of public support for the needy—those who cannot take care of themselves. Strong stigma is attached to those "on welfare"— low-income people who receive financial support. On the other hand, welfare also has the newer, more general, and less pejorative meaning of "public well-being"—people's right to receive various social services. The government has been successful in providing many such services.

Against this background, the builders of Fuji-no-Sato advocate "welfare" in the newer sense for the middle-income elderly, a welfare essentially based on contract. (See also Chapter 8.) Their philosophy, however, contains two important innovations: a greater role for the nonprofit private sector in supplying essential services and the introduction of individual payments for these services. The idea superficially resembles the familiar American practice of *buying* essential services in an open market; but in the Japanese context, the nature of this contract is quite different.

In planning Fuji-no-Sato, a guideline set the amount of the entrance fee within the range of the lump sum retirement payment the average middle-income worker would receive and the monthly fee within the average monthly retirement pension. Particularly important for this study was the fact that Fuji-no-Sato was intended to house not the affluent, but the middle-income elderly.

Lastly, Fuji-no-Sato is still one of the most successful and best known retirement communities in Japan. It has full occupancy, with sixty to eighty people constantly on the waiting list. Many other retirement communities are suffering from low occupancy rates. The development organization has a highly sophisticated long-term fiscal management scheme and has established itself as a leader in this industry by providing management know-how to new developers. Furthermore, Fuji-no-Sato has been covered extensively in the press and electronic media, including foreign newspapers such as the *New York Times*.

THE STUDY

Kinoshita, his wife, and children lived at Fuji-no-Sato between September 1982 and October 1983 while he did the research. His main methods were participant observation and semistructured interviews; but a third method—unobtrusive measures—was used to verify and refine the material that emerged from the main methods.

The participant observation technique was originally developed in anthropology to study small communities, usually in preliterate and little-known cultures. It is based on a holistic approach in which, instead of focusing on specific preconceived issues, the researcher moves into a small community and shares the way of living of the people there. He tries to interpret and understand their life in its totality, as an integrated whole, and as an adaptation to a particular environment, with a particular history. As such, anthropological fieldwork is first and foremost an attempt to understand behavior as the subjects themselves understand it—an "emic" approach—and only secondarily an attempt to test preconceived models or theories—the "etic" approach. Fieldwork often lasts at least a year, as this project did, so the researcher can observe infrequent as well as frequent events. Kinoshita discovered, for example, that the Fuji-no-Sato clinic is extremely busy with serious cases, including some deaths, only during winter months. In a new community like this one, a year is also enough time to see some historical evolution: The role of the residents association changed significantly toward the end of the study.

Until recently (Hochschild, 1973; Johnson, 1971; Kayser-Jones, 1981; Kiefer, 1974; Meyerhoff, 1978; Perkinson, 1980; Ross, 1977), there were few participant observation studies of the aged. We feel this is a deficiency that needs correcting. As Keith (1980b) points out, there are four common problems in gerontology for which participant observation is a good solution: (1) a setting and/or a specific problem that is little known, (2) particularly complex and sensitive issues, (3) informants who are unable or unwilling to report accurately, and (4) collective or emergent realities that must be understood in their own terms. A study of a retirement community in Japan addresses the first and fourth problems and to some extent the second as well.

Kinoshita participated in and observed both daily routine and occasional and unscheduled events in the community. He and his family lived much the same as the residents at Fuji-no-Sato, using the same services and suffering the same inconveniences. During the first three months, he experienced almost every kind of daily activity in order to become familiar with the community and the residents; thereafter, as he became aware of the more significant issues, he focused on those. Kinoshita also participated in seasonal festivities and helped plan events like trips. Participant observer roles even included working at the clinic (day and night shifts) and riding in the community's ambulance. Interactions between the staff and residents and among staff were also observed. Kinoshita attended regular staff meetings and spent quite a bit of time with the staff informally. In August 1983, Kiefer spent ten days at Fuji-no-Sato, talking with staff and getting a feel for the setting.

The other major method, interviewing, was part of the initial plan as well. In order to assure that interviews focused on live issues, Kinoshita spent three months at Fuji-no-Sato before drawing up the semistructured questionnaire from which statistical norms could be drawn. This allowed him to use the interviews to probe emerging significant issues in some depth. This second function required that the questionnaire be partly open-ended. There is a strong tendency to suppress open dissent in this community, and the open-ended interviews gave residents a rare opportunity to vent private feelings about common issues—feelings that might well have led to conflict had they become public. For example, opinions on issues such as problems at the clinic or management policies were generally suppressed if they disagreed with the public position of the residents association. (See also Chapter 11.) Although they were usually cautious in public, the residents disclosed dissenting views quite freely in the interviews.

The interviews served another function as well: Not all full-time residents joined group activities, and little was known about the "loners" from participant observation.

Interview sessions took an average of two and a half hours each. For some residents, these became emotional or social counseling sessions, and in such cases, it was not unusual for Kinoshita to spend four or five hours with the respondent. He kept tabs on these "problem" residents throughout the research period. In most cases, residents were interviewed during visits to their apartments—a significant departure from the usual pattern of social contact in this community. Interview sampling reflected residential patterns and marital statuses. One hundred forty-three residents were asked for interviews, and all but six agreed.

Unobtrusive measures, or nonreactive measures, as they are sometimes called, were also important in this research. The absence of this useful technique in ethnographic research may reflect the difficulty for researchers to know in advance whether they will have access to unobtrusive data. For instance, Kinoshita discovered that various records kept by the staff revealed a great deal about the life of the residents only after he had become familiar with Fuji-no-Sato.

THE ETHNOGRAPHIC EXPERIENCE

Kinoshita moved to Fuji-no-Sato with his wife (who was seven months pregnant) and sixteen-month-old daughter in August 1982.

They were given a "type B" (small, one-bedroom) unit. (For types of residential units, see Chapter 6.) They later found out that their unit had been tried and rejected by a series of residents because of its inconvenient location and high humidity. Work space was provided in a corner of a large conference room in the administrative building, a room used for the monthly staff meeting and occasionally to host large groups of visitors. Kinoshita had to accommodate these other functions (an average of a couple of times per month) but was allowed to use it as his office, keeping books, field data, and other materials there. This was the room to which he returned to take notes after observations and where he usually worked and spent time when not occupied elsewhere in the community. As it turned out, this was a strategically good location; Kinoshita could not only get news about the community quickly here—who was sick, in the clinic, or transferred to outside hospitals or the identities and arrivals of new residents—but could mingle with the staff and listen informally to their views on their work and on general management issues.

In the first weeks, Kinoshita tried to make his stay as visible as possible. He spent extensive time with his daughter outdoors and at the community center, meeting residents and trying to memorize their names and faces. The Kinoshitas had their meals at the dining hall, took baths in the hot spring bath at the community center, and took the shuttle bus to nearby supermarkets, meanwhile explaining to each new acquaintance their purpose in the community. It was the end of the busy summer season, and many residents at first thought the strangers were someone's guests.

To increase his visibility, Kinoshita put a self-introductory notice on the bulletin board at the community center, a method that turned out to be highly effective. New acquaintances soon began to look on him with recognition, saying that they had seen his greeting message and understood some details about his presence. The method was effective again four months later when he announced the beginning of his interview contacts and explained their purpose. The interviewing went smoothly because people knew what to expect and why.

From the start, Kinoshita was careful to present himself in a slightly ambiguous role in order to keep options for interaction open. Initially, he had been asked by a senior official at the head office in Tokyo to take the roles of staff-consultant and counselor. But these roles would have defined his relationships with both the staff and the residents in a very limited way. He decided not to take these roles, particularly after he realized that relations between management and residents were often somewhat tense. Instead, he presented himself consistently as a graduate student from the University of California who would be at Fuji-no-Sato to collect data for his Ph.D. dissertation, which was, of course, exactly true. One senior official at the Tokyo office of the management organization was aware of the communication problem and advised Kinoshita not to worry about his ambiguous role, but simply to look at things through the eyes of the residents and offer constructive criticism of the management when it seemed appropriate.

The residents appeared to be ready to accept the student researcher. With few exceptions, their reactions were favorable; and several facts about this community might have made the research role particularly easy. First, because Fuji-no-Sato was well covered in the mass media and professional journalists visited the place occasionally, Kinoshita may have been seen as a similar visitor, though his stay was much longer. Second, the educational and intellectual levels of the residents, both men and women, were very high for their generation. Many men had been business executives, high-ranking government officials, teachers, or professors; many of the women were retired teachers. The residents therefore had a clear image of this student role, and Kinoshita was able to fit his behavior to their expectations. Finally, Japan as a society places a high value on education, so being a student is a distinct social status. This status is basically a positive one, but it also has a flavor of the half-fledged, and therefore not fully responsible, about it. A student is able to remain neutral in potential conflict situations, free to express his mind rather than act as a decision maker.

There was no such ready acceptance among the staff. Their initial reactions were varied, some being impressed by the doctoral student from an American university, some appearing distinctly unimpressed, and still others not knowing how to respond, keeping formal distance. If the residents represented the middle to upper-middle class, the staff, especially the older ones, represented the lower-middle class; and this difference may have been responsible for their reactions. Only after Kinoshita spent considerable time chatting, drinking, and joining recreational activities with the staff did they begin to trust him.

By the time we selected Fuji-no-Sato as a research site, we thought we knew what kind of community we wanted to study and why. But like anyone trying to understand an unfamiliar community, Kinoshita soon learned that our original assumptions had been far too simple. The portrait of Fuji-no-Sato that emerged during that year yielded far fewer concrete answers than we had hoped. This study gave us a great appreciation for the complexity of the social dimensions of aging. The original questions are still very much alive for us, and we have added a long list of equally urgent new ones in our continuing search for answers.

2

The Scholarly Context of the Study

As an ethnography of an age-homogeneous community in an East Asian culture, this study of Fuji-no-Sato addresses three principal bodies of literature in the West: Asian studies, cultural gerontology, and social change. In the field of Asian studies, it takes its place among many other community ethnographies, each of which reveals a facet of the evolving contemporary culture of Japan. As contributors to this literature, we have sought to clarify some things about the role of the elderly in Japanese society and about the changing meaning of concepts like "community" and "welfare" in the Japanese cultural idiom.

Much has been written about whether Japan serves as a counterexample to Western societies in which age is disparaged (Kiefer, 1990; Palmore, 1975; Palmore and Maeda, 1985; Plath, 1972). The question is a subtle one, and the example of Fuji-no-Sato is instructive on many counts. For one thing, it demonstrates that there are important subgroups of the aged in Japanese society. The residents are upper-middle class in education and income. Perhaps partly for this reason, many of them are either childless or unusually distant from their children and seem to identify more with their achieved occupations and statuses (teacher, executive, public official, minister) than with their more traditional ties (home, neighborhood, friends, extended kin). Our study underlines the relative lack of scholarship on the social implications of such social distinctions among the Japanese aged.

This study also draws attention to the fact that simple comparisons cannot be made between Western and Japanese indicators of status and prestige, at least as applied to the elderly. Public and private assistance programs in advanced societies develop out of native ideas about the rights and obligations of the interest groups involved—government (both local and national), neighborhood, the aged, families, industry. These groups themselves are defined

16

by custom. What is a "neighborhood," for example, who is a "member," and under what circumstances does a member have "rights" to services shared by other members? Simply showing the distribution of services by age group bypasses such questions and often misses the point. It is the strength of ethnography that it brings such problems of definition into focus.

Much has been written about the group centeredness of Japanese life (DeVos, 1973b; Nakane, 1972). It is now clear that "neighborhood" is no more (or not *much* more) synonymous with "community" in Japan than it is in any other society where people are as diverse, mobile, and career oriented as the Japanese. Fuji-no-Sato is an example of this fact. Still, the memory (real or imagined) of a less individualistic and alienated society seems to be relatively fresh in the collective Japanese mind. Although some of the residents of Fuji-no-Sato seemed comfortable enough with their privacy and anonymity, many clearly felt that something was missing in neighborhood relations. Their image of community may not have been a realistic one, but it was *different* from the image held by typical Western elders. The study of attitudes toward community in Fuji-no-Sato provides a close-up of the image that word conjures in the minds of the residents and the planners. As such, it helps clarify what "group centeredness" means to the Japanese themselves, at the same time noting that such images are not uniform or static. The dynamic study of the strain toward community formation should help us understand the unfolding of new definitions and expectations made possible by the untested and unstructured society created in places like Fuji-no-Sato.

Using words and concepts that have become familiar in the social science literature on a particular culture, like Japan, although unavoidable, often creates the unwelcome impression that the writer has simply absorbed cliches about his subject rather than search for fresh ideas. But cliches often express important realities succinctly, and sometimes their use in a new context can even create fresh insights. Most of our use of culture-specific words familiar to the Japan scholar (*amae,* filial piety, etc.) are taken directly from the speech of the residents themselves and therefore convey something about their attempt to express their own reality (cf. Glaser and Strauss, 1969).

AN AGE-HOMOGENEOUS
COMMUNITY

In contributing to cultural gerontology (as we have chosen to call the ethnological study of the aged), we have an agenda different from the usual. We find a growing number of ethnographies, from a variety of countries and settings, of age-homogeneous living arrangements for old people. This literature has grown out of the mid-twentieth-century Western preoccupation with the aged as a "problem" population; as such, it tends to focus on how society provides, or fails to provide, its various over-sixty populations with a safe, comfortable, and agreeable life. These are appropriate questions, given Western values, and we shall examine Fuji-no-Sato as an example of how the answers are affected by culture.

In this vein, Fuji-no-Sato appears particularly relevant to two important issues that, along with the issue of the relative status and prestige of the elderly, provide the thematic structure to much of cultural gerontology: (1) How can society meet equitably the special economic and health care needs of an increasingly frail and post-productive population? Here, equity is usually understood to include not only equality of access to services like housing and medical help, but also the preservation of values like autonomy and self-esteem that make life worth living. (2) Are the elderly "isolated" from meaningful participation in society, or are they "integrated"? If the latter, how is this integration achieved?

Fuji-no-Sato clearly represents, among other things, an attempt by a Japanese institution to address the first question. We could scarcely tell the story of the community without saying something about the successes and failures of that attempt, and there is much the West can learn from this example. The architectural strategies of the community are a case in point, illustrating some fairly successful solutions to cost and quality problems (for example, the provision of outdoor space for gardening and the use of integrated telephone and safety systems), and some rather unsuccessful ones (the plumbing design and the first attempt to provide nursing home care).

Still, a detailed analysis of the cost and quality issues is beyond the scope of this study. Some attention is paid to the place of this community within the Japanese system of geriatric health and welfare, but it is an enormously complex system, nested within an even more complex political and economic matrix, with many features that require careful explication for a Western audience. We have thus chosen to focus this study on the *social* description of Fuji-no-Sato at the expense of its economic and political implications, and we have more to say about the question of integration/isolation than the question of technical success or failure.

A CHANGING COMMUNITY

All the industrial societies, including Japan, have absorbed vast changes in the living habits and values of their members and will continue to do so. It is obviously a stressful process that often produces political unrest and individual pathology; but it is as much a product of industrial technology as is material abundance or population growth. We mentioned that Fuji-no-Sato is not only an example of a kind of *place* (an age-homogeneous community in an East Asian culture), but also an example of the *process* by which new forms of social life are created and take their place in a complex, rapidly changing culture.

We are not interested in the broad question of major historical change—how it happens, its inevitable stages, or its distorting effects on social organization. Rather, we are interested in the micro-process of how a particular solution (the age-homogeneous retirement community) to a socioeconomic problem results in a particular set of interpersonal relations. We have tried to avoid imposing on Fuji-no-Sato our own value judgments about what community relationships ought to look like and to be sensitive to the ideals of the actors themselves—the planners, the administrators, and the residents.

It is not surprising, then, that we have found the most useful concepts to be those that have grown out of the close study of small interpersonal situations: the concepts of symbolic interactionism. In the study that follows, we repeatedly refer to the various actors' *definitions of situations,* and we seek to show how these definitions (1) differ among the various reference groups involved, (2) are selected from the range of possible meanings offered by the macro-culture, and (3) produce dynamic results (conflict, cooperation, alienation, and social bonding). Understanding larger scale historical processes depends to some extent on the careful study of such microprocesses.

SOCIAL INTEGRATION
AS SEEN FROM THE WEST

One is unlikely to find a coherent perception of "old people" throughout American society, much less throughout the wider Western world. Individual perceptions tend to be colored by personal experience, which varies according to the age composition of one's family and community, the nature and extent of one's contact with older people, and so on. However, the profession of social gerontologist does expose the professional to a more or less coherent body of observation, with an implicit set of views. Growing as it did from the needs of health and social welfare professionals in Western industrial nations (Quadagno, 1982), gerontology tends to view the aged in terms of the problems they pose for public policy in such nations.

Many of the caretaking functions earlier performed by families and communities have been taken over by public institutions in Western societies. One result has been a growing professional awareness of and sensitivity to the dissatisfactions of the old. Another probably has been a growing sense of loneliness and insecurity on the part of many elderly, who perceive their great dependence on impersonal institutions and unpredictable regulations. Clients' feelings of isolation and insecurity have themselves become a major problem for the geriatric social service provider; and this problem has generated a lively literature on the social integration of the aged—the conditions that inhibit or promote it and its effect on health and well-being.

In such an atmosphere, Western social gerontologists are often surprised to find communities of old people who appear to have a full and rewarding social life somewhat independently of the ministrations of family, social worker, or activities director. Writing about her experience in such a community in the United States, Hochschild (1973: xiv) says, "One reason I have written this book is that these forty-three people were not isolated or lonely. They are part of a community I did not expect to find." Ross (1977:xi), reporting on a retirement home in Paris, concludes, "Probably the most surprising finding of my study was that, except for their being old, little about these old people was surprising. Their friendships, fights, and love affairs, their in-jokes and strategies for coping with common problems are only striking because we don't expect old people to go on living like everyone else."

This issue of social integration pervades all descriptive studies in social gerontology, and it has been relatively well treated in theory development. The beginning gerontologist will be familiar with Cumming and Henry's social psychological "disengagement theory" (Cumming and Henry, 1961), which suggests that a certain pattern of social disintegration is natural and often beneficial in old age. The disengagement model provides one of the few examples of an empirically studyable theory in social gerontology and has therefore attracted a great deal of attention, albeit mostly negative (see Maddox, 1964).

We make no attempt to test social psychological models like disengagement theory, but we are keenly aware of the bearing of our work on the sociological problem of integration. Among Western sociologists, Irving Rosow has given us the most comprehensive discussion of this problem, and we follow the outline of his argument in exploring the issue in the context of Fuji-no-Sato.

Having described a type of integrated elderly community in his landmark study, *Social Integration of the Aged* (1967), Rosow turned to the theoretical question of the conditions of social integration in *Socialization to Old Age* (1974). Taking the viewpoint of the individual rather than the social system, he argued that integration can be understood through the use of three common sociological concepts: social values, social roles, and group membership. Each concept generates a set of independent factors, and together these "provide the ties that bind social norms into institutions, structure social intercourse, place a person in society and order his relation to others. Thereby, they provide the means and substance of integration" (Rosow, 1974:29).

Values, in other words, can be seen as the affective potentials that are embodied in institutional goals and rules and that in turn legitimize institutional arrangements. Roles provide the sets of mutual expectations that give predictability and worth to structured interpersonal relationships, and group memberships help determine one's role partners and select a certain repertoire of roles from the available cultural inventory.

As individuals learn values and role behaviors and acquire group memberships through socialization, "socialization becomes one major mechanism of integration" (Rosow, 1974:28). Turning his attention to the socialization of the aged in the United States, Rosow concludes that our society does not provide viable roles or norms for its aged members and that no consistent, effective socialization to age-appropriate values, roles, and memberships takes place. Rather, youth-oriented age norms assure that most elderly remain alienated from mainstream American society.

Assuming that socialization to age-appropriate roles is desirable and noting that age-homogeneous communities often seem to provide the possibility of such socialization, Rosow proposes the promotion of semisegregated communities of elderly to deal with the problem. If the aged are to generate new norms and roles that will allow adequate socialization—albeit within a circumscribed community—Rosow notes that two conditions are especially favorable: "first, when the [aged] members are also *socially homogeneous on factors other than age,* notably social class, race, ethnicity, and marital status. . . in other words, the factors that normally govern voluntary social groupings and spontaneous association. . . . The second condition favorable to such groups is *large concentration* of similar elderly" (1974:160–161, original emphasis).

The conditions Rosow describes, and the outcome of strong social bonding and high interaction rates, have been found in a variety of studies of age-concentrated living situations, including a small apartment building in California (Hoschschild, 1973), a mobile home park in California (Johnson, 1971), a large retirement community in Missouri (Perkinson, 1980), a neighborhood Jewish "network" in California (Myerhoff, 1978), and a retirement home in France (Ross, 1977). The French ethnography is particularly relevant here, both because it was a study by a cultural anthropologist of social integration outside the United States and because it focused on the internal social organization of the community.

Unlike the typical ethnography, with its innocence of theoretical perspective, Ross's study was designed to test a specific set of hypotheses about internal social integration or "community creation," a set of concepts derived from a review of the literature. As measures of community formation, she chose (1) physical distinctness, (2) "we" feeling (a "sense of distinctiveness, or shared fate, of things in common, in short, a feeling that 'we' is the right word to describe a collectivity of individuals") (Ross, 1977:3), and (3) social organization (a term she left undefined). She hypothesized that these factors would be strengthened by seven "background factors" describing the residents before they entered the community—homogeneity, lack of alternative, financial investment (amount and irreversibility), material distinctness, social exclusivity, leadership, and size—and six "emergent factors"—participation in communitywide events and decision making, proportions of certain kinds of contact among residents, interdependence, unpaid communal work, threat from outside, and the formation of community-specific symbols. Ross found that her French retirees had indeed forged a rather strong community and that the explanatory model made sense. Later, she surveyed other studies to substantiate the point (Keith, 1980a).

SOCIAL INTEGRATION
FROM A JAPANESE PERSPECTIVE

We are eager to maximize the usefulness of the Fuji-no-Sato example for Western cultural gerontology, but we believe it would be unwise simply to transfer the concepts of Rosow and Ross to the Japanese setting without noting that basic Japanese assumptions about the relationship between individual and society are often at odds with those of Westerners and that the difference renders many of the Western concepts problematic in our context.

All three of Rosow's key terms, "norm," "role," and "group," as they are used in the West, contain assumptions that do not easily fit the Japanese case. Americans use "norms" to refer to social standards that give values to social behaviors, and these values are supposed to be universally accepted, at least within one's reference group. Americans are embarrassed to be reminded that they change values when they change social settings, but Japanese culture has relatively less need for universal norms. Rather, different social situations easily call forth different sets of *context-specific* norms, and the Japanese have little trouble accepting the value incongruity of situated behaviors.

The term "role" presents similar difficulties. The American drive toward consistency among situated norms derives in part from the American perception that the actor is first and foremost a *person*, an individual with a personality distinct from his role performances. The Japanese, although able to distinguish between person and role, place a positive value on the total psychological identity of actor and performance. Kiefer has made this point in earlier work on Japanese Americans: "The psychological process of disengagement requires a perception of one's social roles—a perception that is alien to the issei. Behind the Westerner's perception of himself as purposefully engaged in, and thus potentially disengaged from, his intimate social relations lies a long history of philosophic individualism. . . . The issei, however, cannot disengage from his social roles because he is those roles" (Kiefer, 1974:207). DeVos has used the term "role narcissism" to characterize the importance of formal roles for the Japanese: "For some Japanese the occupational role completely takes the place of any meaningful spontaneous social interaction. A tradition of role dedication still can lead to what appears to be an extraordinary capacity for self-sacrifice, such as, in the very recent past, that of soldiers going to certain death. . . . Role dedication can be viewed as the core of the two chief Japanese traditional virtues of loyalty and endurance" (DeVos, 1973:13).

This indicates, among other things, the relative meaninglessness of informal roles for the Japanese. They have some difficulty establishing social relationships that are not governed by formal, institutional roles, whether these be familial, occupational, or communal. Formal roles, where they are operative, tend to take over and dominate Japanese self-perceptions. This is an especially important point in newly created communities like retirement homes, where there may be a scarcity of community-relevant formal roles available to replace the largely irrelevant ones belonging to family and work contexts and to structure and lubricate community social interaction. The informality of social behavior at Fuji-no-Sato, far from providing the comfort that seems to draw American retirees to similar settings, is a source of consternation to many Japanese residents. It is not enough to say that Americans are more skillful at informal interaction; one must realize that Japanese elders lack the automatic perception of themselves that underlies the development of such a skill: a perception of self as an *unconnected personality, ne-*

gotiating roles. Consequently, as David Reynolds (1976) has shown, when things do not go smoothly in interpersonal relations, Americans tend to seek some action that will correct the situation, but Japanese tend to redefine their role as one in which the situation is acceptable.

These considerations have already clarified some of the differences between Japanese and American definitions of the concept of a "group." In America, almost any perception of shared characteristics—age, for example—can provide the basis for an emergence of group identity or "we" feeling. This is not so in Japan, where social roles tend to fall into hierarchical patterns and where horizontally organized groups, as among age peers, tend to be small, to develop early in life, and to command intense loyalty and careful lifelong preservation. A collection of same-age neighbors is simply not a "group" in any real sense in Japan, even if they share other characteristics like social class or political orientation.

The term "socialization" transfers less awkwardly from American to Japanese culture, but socialization in East Asia has unique dynamics. In America, familial roles tend to be rather loosely defined, and many elderly, unable to draw personal satisfaction from grandparenting and the like, struggle to maintain the extrafamilial roles they occupied when younger. In Japan, by contrast, familial roles tend to be well defined and rather all-encompassing for the elderly, especially women. Although the normlessness and rolelessness of the aged typical of American society seems less serious in Japan as a whole, it is probably more serious for those elderly who lack family roles: the never married, the divorced, and those who have no children or who are estranged from them. For these people, there are few groups that can serve as socializing agents and few meaningful normative behaviors that can be learned. Moreover, as families become more geographically dispersed and less economically interdependent, socialization to the all-important familial roles also becomes more difficult.

As a result, Japanese society may appear on the surface to be undergoing Americanization in many ways (for example, the dwindling rate of three-generation households, the growth of nursing homes and retirement communities), but the meaning of these changes is different in the two cultures. Given the American tendency to emphasize *ad hoc* relationships among peers in forming group identities and defining norms, Rosow may be correct about the usefulness of age-homogeneous environments in the social integration of the aged in America. Given the Japanese preference for familial and hierarchical relationships, we doubt that the same principles apply here.

In view of these differences, the study of Fuji-no-Sato assumes great theoretical and practical importance in cultural gerontology. We find ourselves at odds with much of what has been written about social integration in the West, especially with claims that Western models may have universal applicability. Consider one researcher's statement on this point:

> Although I did my homework about aging in France, my research focus was not on French old people, but on the possible development of a community by old people in an age-homogeneous residence. There is an atmosphere of Frenchness about the descriptions which follow. . . . However, my central conclusion about patterns of community creation and of individual socialization are intended to be distinct from this ambience, to provide a basis for general hypotheses about community, old people, and communities of old people in other settings. (Ross, 1977:4)

Although we found Ross's method—the close observation and classification of interactions among residents—highly useful, we have had to reject her notion that these interactions can be understood or explained without explicit reference to culture. For example, although it is natural for Westerners to talk about "creating a community," the phrase sounds oxymoronic in Japanese. To the extent that the Japanese individual is closely identified with his social roles, to the extent that most Japanese roles are ascribed, not created or achieved, and to the extent that ascribed roles assume some sort of community to begin with, it is difficult to imagine how one could simply create a Japanese community where none existed before. Indeed, this has been a serious problem in other planned living environments in Japan (Kiefer, 1976).

A MODEL OF JAPANESE
INTERPERSONAL RELATIONS

The significance for our purpose of these East-West differences in social expectations can be clarified through the use of a model. We have noted the relative importance of formal roles as opposed to informal ones in Japan and the relative importance of familial and other long-standing, intimate relationships as opposed to casual or recent ones. These traits, of course, go together: Close, long-standing relationships tend to be *functionally diffuse,* to provide partners with a variety of choices, and to meet a variety of their needs. Once we get "close" to someone, we can ask him or her for all sorts of things, and vice versa, in contrast to relative strangers or people we have a limited or distant relationship with. For this reason, we are most comfortable with family and old friends, although there may be many important functions they cannot perform for us, such as granting honor or prestige, providing technical services, paying money, or offering the excitement of new experiences.

The formality of Japanese social relations puts a special premium on these long-standing, intimate relationships because it is relatively difficult to contract new relationships, and once they have been contracted, they are relatively demanding. As a result, it is usually impolite, for example, to introduce strangers to one another unless one has been specifically asked to do so for the purpose of beginning an association that is sure to benefit one or both of them.

The result of such rules is that one's social contacts tend to be divided into sharply defined types, each of which is governed by distinct sets of rules. You want to keep casual acquaintances and strangers at a distance in order to avoid heavy obligations, and you want to keep your intimate relations strong in order to be sure of having your needs met.

Consider Figure 2–1. Each sphere represents a different level of social importance for a hypothetical actor, the most important at the center and the least important at the periphery. The first level contains the most socially and psychologically significant others, such as family members, close friends, and long-term colleagues—in a word, confidantes. Level three represents the world of strangers, people with whom one has at most only fleeting, mutually anonymous contacts, such as people on the same train, waiters, casual customers, or shopkeepers. One need not be overly formal or ritualistic in these relationships. Lying in between, level two contains a broader range of people, from those who are almost strangers to the vast number of people with whom one is regularly but not intimately socially engaged. Here one's identity is known, and one's actions may have long-term repercussions. Behavior is accordingly

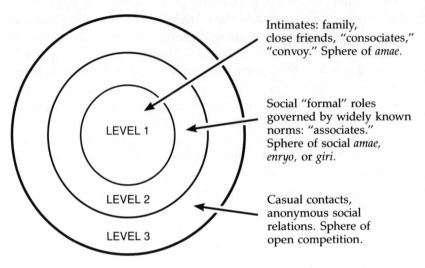

Intimates: family, close friends, "consociates," "convoy." Sphere of *amae*.

Social "formal" roles governed by widely known norms: "associates." Sphere of social *amae*, *enryo*, or *giri*.

Casual contacts, anonymous social relations. Sphere of open competition.

LEVEL 1

LEVEL 2

LEVEL 3

Figure 2-1.   Depth Model of Japanese Interpersonal Relationships

regulated by role-specific norms, which in Japan are comparatively inflexible and well defined.

Any complex society can be conceived in terms of a model of "circles of intimacy" like this. But if you think of the boundaries between the circles as being relatively durable, easy to see, and difficult to cross, you can understand the Japanese difference. If the social spheres in Western cultures are thought of as separated by flower beds, the Japanese spheres might be seen as separated by fences.

There are also some culturally specific ideas that are useful in characterizing interaction at each level. In the first level, for example, one can indulge in one's need to be humored, nurtured, or spoiled—the complex made famous by Takeo Doi as *amae* (Doi, 1973). The prototype of the *amae* relationship is the parent-child role set, and such a relationship may be so close as to be symbiotic and unique, almost unfettered by normal social expectations. Intimate friendships can be included here if they are of long standing.

Second-level relationships are those wherein one has to wear one's social clothes. Here the key concept is *enryo*, restraint or holding back, which is chiefly used as "a negative yardstick in measuring the intimacy of human relationships" (Doi, 1973:38). Because this is the level in which formal role relationships dominate, one must carefully control one's behavior, continuously assessing the quality of the relationship and keeping an appropriate distance. *Amae* also comes into play at this level, but in a different sense. The parties continuously "read" each other's needs and reactions to assess the changing quality of the relationship. Relationships that are close enough to avoid the need for *enryo* are ideal, but such closeness is often impossible. *Enryo* need not be used in either first-level or third-level relations, both of which are more casual, although for different reasons.

Looking at this model from the standpoint of social support, level one relationships are the strongest. People tend to refrain from seeking help from those at level two. Having received help from second-level people, one will feel *giri*, or psychosocial indebtedness, a need to repay the favor quickly. Third-level relationships are not part of one's support network, and help can be sought there only in extreme emergency.

This model is not static. Although the basic structure of social relations may be stable, the real value of this model is that it can also be used to clarify the process of life span social development. Relationships can develop in either direction; a stranger can move into the second level, then gradually into the first as time goes on. Likewise, even a parent-child relationship can grow cold and distant, losing the meaningfulness of first-level relations. Relationships must be defined mutually; it is essential that the parties share a similar perception of their quality and depth. The Japanese are socialized beginning in childhood and continuing at school and at work to be skillful at this kind of perceptual bargaining.

This perspective is a theoretical backbone of Plath's work on the life cycle: "Growth then becomes in part a property of others, particularly of those who are one's *consociates*. The term may be an unfamiliar one, but it is apt here. It derives from the work of Alfred Schutz and the phenomenologists. If 'associates' are persons you happen to encounter somewhere, sometime, 'consociates' are people you relate with across time and in some degree of intimacy. They are friends, lovers, kinsmen, colleagues, classmates" (Plath, 1980:8). Consociates, then, are essentially the people in the first (and occasionally second) level of our model; associates are most of those in the second level and a few in the third.

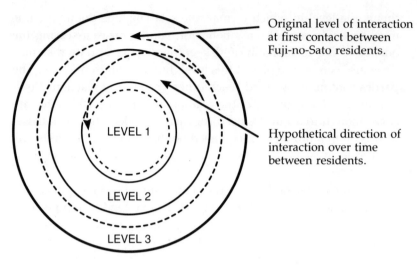

Figure 2-2.   Analytical Model of This Study

Plath's use of the term "convoys" to describe groups of consociates, whose personalities, life circumstances, and relationships
evolve slowly over many years, can also be understood with the
help of this model. First-level relationships are extremely durable;
and when they grow out of second- and third-level ones, their evolution usually takes many years as well (Plath, 1980:224–226).

THE MODEL AND FUJI-NO-SATO

The model, then, helps us visualize the *evolution of social relationships*
at Fuji-no-Sato. Our purpose in using it is analytical. Given that the
residents are mutual strangers until they move to the community, it
can be theorized that their relationship will develop, as shown in
Figure 2-2, from the outer edge of level two toward, and possibly
into, level one. How and how far their relationships move in this
direction is the focus of our analysis. Our initial intuition is that, at
the beginning, the residents employ outer second-level norms and
maintain distance appropriate to that mutually perceived relationship. As they get to know one another, they will adjust the application of norms and the perception of distance while changing the
definition of their relationship.

We take this as an "emic" analytical model of social integration at Fuji-no-Sato. We do not try to operationalize the concept of "community" as a dependent variable, but simply assume that Fuji-no-Sato functions as a socially defined context, limiting the kinds of possible relationships among its members. Viewing Fuji-no-Sato as an independent social system, then, and following Rosow's definition, we define social integration as the locating of individuals in the system and the patterning of their relationships with others. Likewise, "socialization" is defined as an important mechanism of integration—the process of development of patterned social interaction. "Norms" refer to social standards against which one's behavior is to be evaluated. "Roles" generally mean constellations of rights and duties—meaning both formally recognized roles, like elected offices in the residents association (which are very limited) and the much more important informal roles of neighboring, friendship, and so on.

There are five interrelated factors that render relatively problematic any attempt to develop "deep" interpersonal relations on the part of the residents at Fuji-no-Sato. (1) Although American relationships seem to the Japanese to be too shallow and ephemeral, it is nonetheless true that when Americans meet each other for the first time, they handle the establishment of relationships better than the Japanese do in similar situations. (2) It is difficult in Japanese interpersonal relations to differentiate conceptually feelings from other social values. The Japanese generally expect both emotional and instrumental needs to be met in their relationships with others. It is necessary, then, for acquaintances to keep both perspectives on their developing relationships. Although the Japanese may be less skillful than Americans in building new relationships, they expect and often attain deeper and more sensitive relationships. (3) As Plath pointed out, it takes considerable time for the Japanese to develop solid first-level relationships. The depth of relationships generally correlates with their duration. This is a serious obstacle to the rapid development of deeply meaningful relationships among Japanese. At Fuji-no-Sato, however, this time factor is mitigated by at least two of the "background factors" identified by Ross: the physical distinctness of the community (which intensifies "we" feeling among residents) and its limited size (which concentrates opportunities for interaction). Both factors tend to accelerate the intimacy process. (4) First-level relationships, with the exception of family, are usually informal outgrowths of second-level relations, which are formal and role-specific. In other words, the Japanese develop new first-level relations only with people in the second level who share some basis for sustained, frequent interaction—an attraction or a natural tendency to be together over long periods. (5) Fuji-no-Sato is very unusual as a Japanese setting because the residents' relationships do not begin with the performance of ascribed roles. The residents lack preexisting structural reasons for regular interaction that would naturally lead to the development of first-level relations.

LIMITS OF THE MODEL

The model we have just presented seems to us to make fair sense out of the actual impression we got from the people at Fuji-no-Sato. Often they seemed to be struggling, against considerable cultural barriers, to find their way to a secure and socially comfortable way of life. However, in the process of explaining their struggle, the model does not give much scope to the positive aspects of their lives. In fact, the residents were able to act cooperatively to solve certain common problems and thereby to enhance their feelings of both individual effectiveness and collective "we-ness" vis-à-vis the management. They controlled tension among themselves to some extent through formal channels of communication and representation; and they were able to sustain a modest level of polite interaction that might, in the long run, lead to deeper and more satisfying relationships for many.

To some extent, the model we have presented helps explain these positive features of social life as well. Level two, the circle of *giri*, demands attention to the things that keep conflict within bounds and sustain instrumental exchange—politeness, respect, return of value received, anticipation of one another's instrumental needs. But there is certainly more to social life at Fuji-no-Sato (or anywhere else) than these.

When the collective behaviors constrained by rules of prescription and proscription are subtracted from the whole round of communal life, what is left is a considerable "free zone"—the area where humor, whimsy, and appreciation of the eccentric and unique come into play. We have been saying (and we believe it is true) that this area is not large in Japanese society compared with some others. But it is there, and it is important. In fact, without it no society could deal effectively with the novel and the unexpected, a failing that rarely can be attributed to Japanese society.

The description of Fuji-no-Sato contains many important incidents that are not clarified by our model. The "rulefulness" of human behavior is limited.

PART I

AGING IN JAPAN:
AN OVERVIEW

3

Demography and Income

Two centuries ago, the manufacturing techniques we call "industrial" began to transform the agricultural and handicraft societies of northwestern Europe. This familiar transformation is still going on in many parts of the world. Greater production meant better nutrition, housing, and sanitation, with the result that life expectancy began to increase. At first, high birth rates led to a population boom; then birth rates fell, and the age structure of the industrial populations began to change dramatically.

The combination of a mature industrial technology and a non-Western cultural history makes Japan sociologically interesting in a number of ways, not the least of which is the problem of population dynamics. Where the veneration of parents is combined with a huge and growing population of aged, how does the society react? Fuji-no-Sato is an attempted solution to the problem these demographic and economic processes produced: caring for one of the world's most venerable populations.

THE GRAYING OF JAPANESE SOCIETY

The aging of Japanese society has three distinct features. First, because their industrialization began late, the Japanese were able to borrow methods and materials that the West had taken a century to perfect. Wealth and health accordingly grew rapidly, leading to a dramatic drop in death rates. The growth of the aged population therefore has been recent and rapid. Second, the proportion of the elderly is projected to reach a higher level than in any other nation, probably as a result of complex social, genetic, and environmental conditions. This need not concern us so much as the consequences. Third, an unusually large proportion is expected to be over seventy-five and therefore more frail.

Table 3-1.   Estimated Increase in Four Elderly Age Groups
(thousands of people)

	65–69	70–74	75–79	80+
1985	4,193 (100%)	3,563 (100%)	2,493 (100%)	2,218 (100%)
2005	7,245 (173%)	6,479 (182%)	5,016 (201%)	5,456 (246%)
2025	6,820 (163%)	7,728 (204%)	7,586 (304%)	9,782 (441%)

Source: Ministry of Health and Welfare, 1986.

The proportion of over-sixty-five members in the total population is the usual index for the aging of a given nation. This proportion was fairly stable in Japan in the pre–World War II era: 5.3 percent in 1920, when the first national census was taken, 4.8 percent in 1930, and 4.7 percent in 1940. Although the first postwar census in 1950 reported 4.9 percent over sixty-five, just a decade later the rate was 5.7 percent. The new, sharp increase has continued with accelerating speed; it reached 7.1 percent in 1970, 9.1 percent in 1980, and 12.0 percent in 1990. It is projected to reach 16.3 percent in the year 2000, continuing to a high of 23.6 percent in 2020, exceeding the projected highest levels of the Western nations. Table 3–1 illustrates these increases, showing the growing numbers of those in several age groups. One can clearly see from these figures that Japan is now on the threshold of a gray population explosion. Figure 3–1 shows the problem from another angle: the prolonged life expectancy at birth and the average years left to live for those reaching sixty-five in selected years. Note that over a forty-year period, life expectancy rose by almost twenty-five years for women and over twenty-four years for men, giving Japan the world's highest life expectancy at birth. In the same period, the average years left to live for women aged sixty-five stretched by 6.8 years, from 12.2 to 19.0, and for men by 5 years, from 10.6 to 15.6.

The percentage of "old old"—those over seventy-five—in the total aged population was stable at about 25 percent from 1920 until 1950, when it began to grow. By 1960, it was 30.4 percent, and it is projected to reach 55 percent by 2025 (Table 3–2). The impact of this increase of a relatively frail and dependent group will be enormous for Japanese society. The speed of Japan's aging can be appreciated when it is compared with that of major Western nations. The rise of the aged sector from 7 percent to 14 percent in France took one

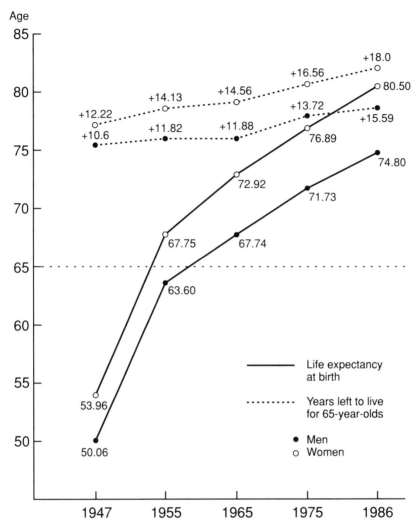

Figure 3-1.   Life Expectancy at Birth, Years Left to Live for
Sixty-five-Year-Olds (Ministry of Health and Welfare, 1986).

hundred thirty years, in Sweden eighty-five years, in West Germany and Great Britain, forty-five years. In Japan, it has taken only
twenty-five years (Figure 3–2).

That these demographic changes have consequences for both social planning and personal experience hardly needs to be said. The
nation must develop social services for the aged with an urgency

Table 3-2.   Population Trends and Projections for Four Age Groups
(thousands of people)

	0–14 Years	15–64 Years	Age 65 and Over	Age 75 and Over	Total	Avera Ag
1920	20,416 (36.5%)	32,605 (58.3%)	2,941 (5.3%)	732 (1.3%)	55,963 (100%)	26.
1925	21,924 (36.7%)	34,792 (58.2%)	3,021 (5.1%)	808 (1.4%)	59,737 (100%)	26.
1930	23,579 (36.6%)	37,807 (58.7%)	3,064 (4.8%)	881 (1.4%)	64,450 (100%)	26.
1935	25,545 (36.9%)	40,484 (58.5%)	3,225 (4.7%)	924 (1.3%)	69,254 (100%)	26.
1940	26,369 (36.1%)	43,252 (59.2%)	3,454 (4.7%)	904 (1.2%)	73,075 (100%)	26.
1950	29,786 (35.4%)	50,168 (59.6%)	4,155 (4.9%)	1,069 (1.3%)	84,115 (100%)	26.
1955	30,123 (33.4%)	55,167 (61.2%)	4,786 (5.3%)	1,411 (1.6%)	90,077 (100%)	27.
1960	28,434 (30.2%)	60,469 (64.1%)	5,398 (5.7%)	1,642 (1.7%)	94,302 (100%)	29.
1965	25,529 (25.7%)	67,444 (68.0%)	6,236 (6.3%)	1,894 (1.9%)	99,209 (100%)	30.
1970	25,153 (24.0%)	72,119 (68.9%)	7,393 (7.1%)	2,237 (2.1%)	104,665 (100%)	31.
1975	27,221 (24.3%)	75,807 (67.7%)	8,865 (7.9%)	2,841 (2.5%)	111,940 (100%)	32.
1980	27,507 (23.5%)	78,835 (67.3%)	10,647 (9.1%)	3,660 (3.1%)	117,060 (100%)	34.
1985	26,033 (21.5%)	82,506 (68.2%)	12,468 (10.3%)	4,712 (3.9%)	121,049 (100%)	35.
1990	23,132 (18.6%)	86,274 (69.4%)	14,819 (11.9%)	5,917 (4.8%)	124,225 (100%)	37.
1995	22,387 (17.5%)	87,168 (68.3%)	18,009 (14.1%)	6,986 (5.5%)	127,565 (100%)	38.
2000	23,591 (18.0%)	86,263 (65.8%)	21,338 (16.3%)	8,452 (6.4%)	131,192 (100%)	39.
2005	25,164 (18.7%)	84,888 (63.2%)	24,195 (18.0%)	10,472 (7.8%)	134,247 (100%)	40.
2010	25,301 (18.6%)	83,418 (61.4%)	27,104 (20.0%)	12,456 (9.2%)	135,823 (100%)	41.
2015	23,876 (17.6%)	81,419 (59.9%)	30,643 (22.5%)	13,894 (10.2%)	135,938 (100%)	42.
2020	22,327 (16.5%)	81,097 (59.9%)	31,880 (23.6%)	15,313 (11.3%)	135,304 (100%)	43.
2025	22,075 (16.4%)	81,102 (60.2%)	31,465 (23.4%)	17,367 (12.9%)	134,642 (100%)	43.
2050	21,967 (17.1%)	76,433 (59.4%)	30,281 (23.5%)	17,005 (13.2%)	128,681 (100%)	43.
2075	22,466 (18.0%)	73,739 (59.0%)	28,685 (23.0%)	14,826 (11.9%)	124,890 (100%)	42.

Sources: Up to 1985: "National Census," "Population Estimates" Statistics Bureau, Manageme
and Coordination Agency. *From 1990: Future Population Estimates for Japan,* Institute for Pop
lation Problems, Kōseishō.
Note: Figures are as of October 1 for each year.

that allows little time to plan. Some of the many programs that have
been instituted already have failed. New strategies are constantly
being sought, and some that appear successful from the clients'
view are being curtailed because they cost too much. No one knows
where such trial and error will lead Japan, but everyone is aware
that aging has become a serious social problem, and the media are
preoccupied with it.

Meanwhile, the demographic changes are a challenge to the aged
themselves, within whose lifetimes expectations of late life have
been revised. They were born and grew up in a period when aging
was not a significant problem. They survived several wars, only to
grow older at a time when their society is seriously disrupted by
their age group.

INCOME

Japan has become one of the strongest economic powers in the world, with a gross national product second only to that of the United States; this situation both exacerbates the older-population problem and helps relieve it. The standard of living for the Japanese has greatly improved in recent decades, but here let us examine how the nation's wealth affects the income structures of the aged, particularly the middle class, with whom we are most closely concerned. The people we are writing about are, after all, those who have most contributed not only to the reconstruction of postwar Japan but also to its current economic strength.

The main sources of income and their changing importance are illustrated in Figure 3–3. This is the nationwide average of so-called "elderly" households—that is, households consisting of either a man over sixty-five and his wife over sixty or of such a couple with unmarried children under eighteen years old. This is the most reliable official information we could get; the financial situation of the aged in three-generation households is difficult to assess because incomes are given per household. It is evident that the average elderly household has become more financially independent since the 1960s. The contribution of earned income nearly tripled from 16.6 percent in 1963 to 44.3 percent in 1981, and, even more dramatically, the role of retirement pensions rose from only 9.1 percent in 1963 to 47.2 percent in 1985. In contrast, the proportion received from children and other relatives fell in the same period from 64.5 percent to 2.5 percent while public welfare support has remained fairly low. Now earned income and retirement pensions together are the dominant sources of support for elderly households, jointly accounting for 86.8 percent of the total income in 1985. However, households of this type are still the minority because the majority of the Japanese aged are living with families of their children (see Chapter 4). However, the separate living arrangement has been growing in popularity and is expected to keep doing so.

The pension system has become an important source of income for the aged and deserves a closer look. Due to the relatively short history of the system, most elderly do not live solely on their pensions (Figure 3–3, Table 3–3). This may be a major reason why the Japanese tend to keep working after their first retirement and may also contribute to the very high rate of co-residence with children.

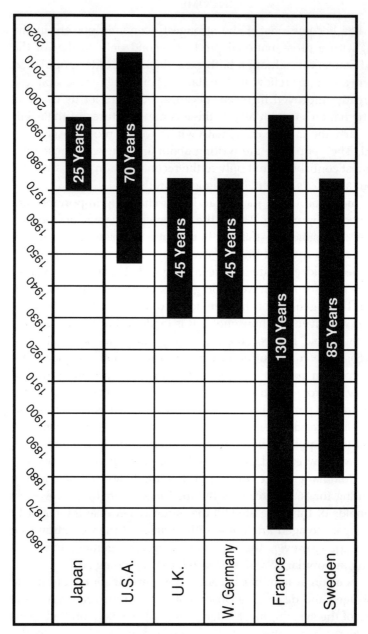

Figure 3-2. Growth in Aged Population from 7 to 14 Percent, Comparison of Six Nations (Ushio, 1989: 4).

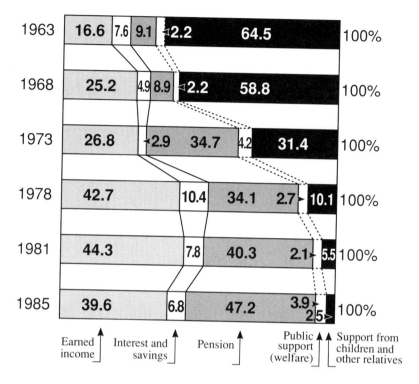

Figure 3-3. Income Sources of Elderly Households
(Ministry of Health and Welfare, 1990).

Figure 3–3 shows a dramatic improvement in pension coverage in 1973. This was the year automatic indexing of benefits to inflation was introduced. The nationwide figure glosses over a complex pension structure composed of a variety of systems with different rules and rates. To get an idea of this complexity, we compare the average monthly amounts of retirement pensions in four major pension systems. As of March 1981, retirees from municipal government were getting the highest amount, $613, followed by $575 for retired national government workers; the average rate was $421 for retired workers in private industry. The amount of the national pension is small, only $92 that year, which reflects the government's tendency to respond to claims of critical need rather than to those of simple equity. If both husband and wife are on the national pension system, their combined amount will be twice the single figure ($184 in 1981), still a far smaller amount than in the other three systems.

Table 3-3. International Comparison of Statutory Pension Plans

	West Germany	Sweden	United Kingdom	United States	Japan
Name of plan	Wage Earner's P.I., Salaried Employees' P.I.	National Basic Pension (AFP)	National Insurance	O.A.S.D.I.	Employees' Pension Insurance
Coverage	Employees in general	All residents	All residents	Employees in general, self-employed persons	Employees in general
Pensionable age	65	65	Males: 65, females: 60	65	Males: 60, females: 55
Average monthly old-age (retirement) benefit (A)	Average of two schemes: $633	(July 1985) Single: $357, couple: $585	(Jan. 1985) Single: $380, couple: $610	(Nov. 1985) Single: $820, couple: $1,241	(Jan. and Mar. 1985) $860
Average monthly manufacturer's wage, 1983 (B)	$1,730	$1,623	$1,422	$2,887	$2,165
(A)/(B)	38.2%	36.1%	42.9%	43.0%	39.8%
Contribution rate	192.0/1,000 (shared equally by employees and employers)	94.5/1,000 (employers, self-employed persons)	194.5/1,000 (total), 90.0/1,000 (employees), 104.5/1,000 (employer)	114.0/1,000 (shared equally by employees and employers)	95.4/1,000 of all income, 124.0/1,000 of average contribution (shared equally by employees and employers)
National subsidy	Any deficit (about 18.5% of cost in 1983)	Any deficit (about 32% of cost in 1984)	9% of all revenue contribution	None (in principle)	1/3 of cost for basic benefits (in principle)

The average monthly amount of a worker's pension in 1981 was about 44.2 percent of the average monthly salary at retirement, which appears virtually the same as the 44 percent given by Social Security in the United States in 1980. However, it is not clear that the figures are really comparable. "Retirement" is likely to occur in a series of downward steps for Japanese workers, so the replacement rate may not reflect the *highest* salary, as it usually does in the United States. Table 3–3 shows the average 1985 industrial pension in Japan at about $860 which was 39.8 percent of the average 1983 industrial wage, still close to the U.S. ratio of 43 percent.

Japanese workers may receive a lump sum payment in lieu of a pension upon retirement. Although the company pension system is being developed gradually, particularly among larger corporations, the traditional retirement payment is still widely prevalent. According to a study by the Ministry of Labor, a college graduate who had worked for twenty-five consecutive years for a company (one thousand or more employees) received an average $84,896 in 1979 (still using 135Y/$). This was approximately twenty-nine times his monthly salary. Here, too, public workers receive larger retirement payments than other workers. For instance, Musashino City in Tokyo is known to pay the highest retirement bonus in Japan. A low-rank, nonmanagerial worker in this city in 1984 could receive, after thirty years' work, $296,297. However, even an enviable interest rate of 10 percent on this amount would still provide a meager pension in today's expensive Japan. Still, the retirement bonus is an important factor in one's preparation for economic security in old age.

Today's Japanese aged, then, are getting a share of the nation's great wealth. Whether or not that share is adequate is in part a political question, and we cannot answer it objectively. More important for our purposes is the fact that now, for the first time, many Japanese elderly, particularly those in the middle class, can be financially independent of their children. This is taking place when the traditional system of family care of the aged is becoming increasingly problematic, and financial independence may give the aged more control over their options for care and security.

4

Consequences of Social Change

Few generations anywhere have had to cope with social changes as massive as those that have unfolded in the lives of the current Japanese elderly. War was part of daily life among the Japanese, ending in massive destruction and devastating defeat. Equally disorienting was Japan's reconstruction and rise to economic leadership in the forty years following the war. A seventy-five-year-old man in 1990 would have been thirty years old when Japan was defeated in 1945; his generation not only fought the wars but also did the main work of reconstruction. War also produced a large number of young widows and never-married women, and these women without families have now reached old age.

Beneath the technological and political changes, fundamental change occurred in the core social institution of Japanese society, the family. The shift from empire to democracy meant a change in the support system for the elderly. This chapter discusses the impact of that change.

THE *IE* SYSTEM

Modern Japanese history began in 1868 when the Tokugawa shogunate collapsed and was replaced by the Meiji imperial government. Pressed by the fear that Japan would be subjugated by the Western powers as China and many other Asian nations had been, the new regime had to unite the nation and establish its internal sovereignty quickly. For this purpose, the patriarchical family, or *ie*, system was formalized and strengthened. In fact, imperial rule would not have been possible without the family system—a system in which support of aged parents was firmly institutionalized.

In 1871, the imperial government issued an order that required every Japanese to be registered in the family record, and this order provided the basis for the 1899 Meiji Civil Code, which formally established the family system. The household, the official unit of family registration, was defined as the group of lineal related members sharing communal living. Each household head was legally required to report to local agencies such family events as birth, death, marriage, divorce, and adoption. Despite official abolishment of the family system in 1945, the family registration system was maintained and is currently enforced, with the result that every Japanese still has his or her family record. The family registration record (*koseki*) is one's documented social identity, a copy of which must be submitted when one applies for school or a job. Even today the household is the basic unit in the Japanese census, which explains why most major demographic surveys are based on a sampling of household units.

This was not a completely new policy. The Tokugawa shogunate had developed a similar system in the seventeenth century through the local branch temples of the major Buddhist sects. The earlier system had other aims, to be sure, such as suppressing Christianity and keeping tax records. But the system was centralized, improved, and given new legal consequences by the Meiji government.

The prototype of the new national family system was that of the ruling *bushi* or warrior class of the feudal era, which was strongly patriarchal. By carefully enforcing family registration and by legally institutionalizing the patriarchal system across Japan, the imperial government sought to gain tighter control over the people.

Under the *ie* system, the household head was granted unusually strong legal power and authority over his family members, particularly his wife and children. For instance, he could punish his children by expulsion from the family, a sanction that not only stigmatized the children but also erased records of their family ties. Only outlaws and social dropouts had no such records. A son younger than thirty years and a daughter younger than twenty-five years could not marry without the approval of the household head. In such a patriarchal system, wives too had a very vulnerable status. Because it was essential to have a male successor, barren wives were apt to be sent back to their native families, and the divorce rate in the pre-1945 era was comparatively high for its time.

However, it appears that the household head rarely exercised these prerogatives and did so only under extreme circumstances because he was, at the same time, held liable for the well-being of his family members. Public disclosure of one's family problems was the last thing the head of a household wanted. When legal power was used, it was not so much due to the wishes of the head as to mounting pressure from kin or neighbors to enforce sanctions. The family system functioned not only as a political unit but also as a welfare unit and protector of household members.

Ideologically, imperial Japan was a family state. The family of the emperor was idealized as a model for other families and used as a metaphor for the state as a whole. The family system was idealized as a model for other institutions. The authoritarian relationship between the household head and his family members was parallel to the absolute relationship between the emperor and his people. The nation was conceptualized as an organized mass of families with the emperor as the ultimate head of all families. Indeed, the Japanese word for nation, *kokka*, is made up of two words, "nation" and "family," and it was taught that all Japanese were literally the emperor's functional children (*sekishi*).

Throughout the pre-1945 period, the imperial government launched a massive moral campaign to consolidate the family system. For this purpose, Confucian teachings that had been the ideological backbone of the feudal warrior family were emphasized. Two key Confucian concepts, *kō* and *chū*, were singled out as core concepts for a campaign of moral indoctrination, mainly through compulsory school education and military training. *Kō* is filial duty, and *chū* is complete devotion to the emperor. This set of beliefs was the ideological side of the institutional relationship between the family system and the imperial rule.

Kō prescribed four distinct duties for childen (Kawashima, 1957): to show and feel respect toward one's parents, to promote the honor of one's family through achievements, to support one's parents in their old age, and to worship one's ancestors. For ordinary people, however, today as then, *kō* was taken to mean *oya-kō kō*, meaning the third duty. The highest praise of an old person was to say that he or she had a dutiful son (*kō kō-musuko*); of an adult child it could be said that he or she showed *oya-kō kō*. The worst criticism was to be labeled *oya-fukō*, lacking filial duty—expressions that are commonly used even today.

When *kō* was transposed onto one's role as a citizen, it became *chū*, unconditional devotion to the emperor. This concept was a vital principle in many areas of citizenship, such as in army service, where one was taught that all orders were given or approved by the emperor himself and were therefore unquestionable.

The legitimacy of the family (*ie*) system was supported not only through Confucian moral indoctrination, but also by the civil and criminal codes. The toughest penalties (for example, death or life imprisonment without parole) applied to parricide.

More important for our discussion, however, are the rights and duties regarding support of aged parents in the civil code. Let us compare the old Meiji civil code and the current democratic civil code with regard to the support of old parents.

The Meiji Civil Code (1899)

Article 954:   Lineal kin and brothers and sisters have a duty to support one another. It is the same for lineal ascendants of the household head and those of his wife who were in the same household.

Article 956:   When there is more than one person who has a duty to provide support, it is divided according to their respective capacities. However, the supporter living in the same household should provide support first.

Article 957:   When there is more than one person who needs support and when all of them cannot be supported, the support should be given in the following order:
1.   lineal ascendants
2.   lineal descendants
3.   spouse
4.   lineal ascendants of the spouse, who are in the same household
5.   brothers and sisters
6.   others

Article 954 defined the extent of family support, article 956, the duty to provide support, and article 957, the right to receive support. The ideology of the patriarchal family system is clearly stated in these articles. Priority was given parents of the household head over his wife and children, his children over his wife, and his co-resident parents-in-law (a deviant household form) before his own brothers and sisters.

In the *ie* system, the oldest son ideally succeeded his father and eventually became the household head. His younger brothers were expected to establish "branch" families and his sisters to marry into other *ie* households. If one had only daughters, one of them, usually the oldest, remained at her natal household, and when she got married, her husband became a *muko-yōshi*, an adopted son who took the family name and eventually became the household head in the family registration. If a couple had no children, the usual practice was to adopt a young kinsman and raise him as the eldest son. These practices assured the continuity of the family line, as well as the support of the aged.

The duty of the eldest son to support his aged parents was usually compensated by the passing to him of the largest share of the family inheritance; younger brothers received less and sisters even less than brothers. Despite the strictness of these legal prescriptions, there were very few filial support lawsuits in the pre-1945 period. Yuzawa (1970) attributed this to the effectiveness of moral indoctrination by the imperial government; at any rate, it suggests the prevalence and solidity of the family ethic.

Japan's defeat in World War II changed practically everything about the society in some way or other. The postwar reconstruction started with the dismantling of imperial rule. The old constitution, which had given the emperor absolute power, was completely rewritten, as was the old civil code. A sudden fascination with the idea of democracy brought traditional morality and custom under vehement attack. Because of its crucial role in imperial Japan, the family system was labeled feudalistic and became the target of a new moral campaign. It was under these circumstances that the present civil code was written. Let us look at the articles most relevant to support of aged parents:

The Present Civil Code (1948)

Article 877:   Lineal kin and brothers and sisters have a duty to support one another.

Article 878:   When there is more than one person who has the duty to provide support, its order should be determined by mutual consultation. When this is not possible, the Family Court makes the decision. Likewise, when there is more than one person who needs to be supported and when all of them cannot be supported, the order to receive support should be determined by mutual consultation. When this is not possible, the Family Court makes the decision.

Here we see the new democracy in its essence. These articles of the new code are highly ambiguous on almost every point at issue, including the support of the aged. They simply do not prescribe anything in this respect. This often leaves it up to the children to decide who should support aged parents and to what extent. The change is from strict legal prescriptions to legal ambiguities. In other articles, democracy is seen to permeate the heirship as well; a widow can now receive half of her husband's inheritance; the other half should be equally divided by his children. The undemocratic prewar system functioned to support aged parents because the duty of filial support by the eldest son was reciprocated by his almost exclusive rights of inheritance, a reciprocity whose basic structure has been lost in postwar Japan.

Still, the law tells us little about how the *ie* system actually functions in modern Japan. On the whole, the Japanese are not a litigious people, and they still dislike exposing their family problems in public. The facts that the imperial government had to engage in a massive, nationwide moral campaign and that it had legally to formalize the *ie* system indicate that there existed a gap between custom and law. The prototype of the *ie* system was the patriarchal family system of the feudal warrior class, a ruling class that represented only a tiny portion of the predominantly peasant population. The most significant difference between this law and preexisting custom was this: The heads of peasant households had little authority either within or beyond their families; legal power was in the hands of the warrior class; and few peasants had the financial means to control their heirs anyway. Peasant families in feudal Japan were pretty much like peasants in other premodern societies. Differences between peasant and aristocrat continued after the formal propagation of the *ie* system because the living situation of the majority of the Japanese was not improved much by the change of governments. The imperial government had to launch the Confucian ethics campaign and to establish the legal code in order to consolidate the *ie* system in all social classes.

There were, of course, great similarities between the *ie* system and the indigenous family practice. For centuries, the Japanese have placed a strong value on caring for aged parents, not so much because of the influence of Confucianism, but because of ancestor worship, the core of Japanese religious life throughout their history (Smith, 1974). In fact, ancestor worship is so fundamental to Japanese life that it may have been the chief determinant of the treatment that the aged received. The existence of aged parents itself was a symbol of the continuity of one's family line. There was a readiness among the Japanese to absorb the emphasis on support of aged parents and ancestor worship in the *ie* ideology.

Today's aged spent their formative and early adult years under imperial rule; hence they were subject to massive moral indoctrination in filial duty, and many of them actually lived up to it. When they themselves reached old age, the mechanism of reciprocity that had guaranteed filial support under the old civil code was lost, and they had to face uncertainty about whether, and from whom, they could count on sustenance. In this sense, the present older generation may be said to have reaped the worst of both worlds.

CHANGING LIVING ARRANGEMENTS

Given the equivalence of co-residence and caring for aged parents under the *ie* system, a look at changing residence patterns will help us understand the impact of family democracy. Are the elderly still living with their adult children, particularly with the eldest son's family, as tradition would demand? One approach to this problem is to focus on the "lag" phenomenon. Despite the change in the formal social institutions, the old system and its ideology have remained an important, if not the only, frame of reference for many people. This "cultural lag" phenomenon is particularly evident in postwar Japan because clear-cut new norms are not available.

In the pre-1945 period, the aged had scarcely any choice but to live with their own (natural or adopted) son's family. Interestingly, though, the first national census in 1920 reported a high proportion (54.3 percent) of nuclear households: a couple with or without children or a single parent with unmarried children (Yuzawa, 1970). Two reasons may be offered to explain this result. First, life expectancy was low, and the proportion of the aged was quite small, which shortened the duration of the three-generation phase of household composition. Second, the *ie* system functioned in such a way that only the eldest son remained in the parents' household— sisters married out, and brothers who established branch nuclear families were more numerous than oldest sons.

Rates of three types of living arrangements of the elderly (sixty-five or older) are shown for the period 1960–1985 in Figure 4–1. The term "subhousehold" in the figure means those elderly who are in

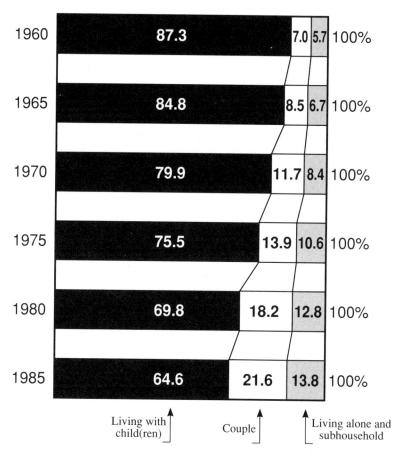

Figure 4-1.   Living Arrangements of Those Over Sixty-five
(Soda and Miura, 1982: 73; Ministry of Health and Welfare, 1990).

institutions or living with relatives other than children. In 1960, 87.3 percent of those over sixty-five lived with children, 7.0 percent with a spouse, and 5.7 percent either alone or in subhouseholds. The traditional living arrangement decreased from 87.3 percent in 1960 to 64.6 percent in 1985. Elderly couple households increased from 7.0 percent to 21.6 percent while single-person and other households increased from 5.7 percent to 13.8 percent. Although the rate of co-residence with children continues to fall, this has to be interpreted with caution. First, note that the rate of co-residence is still about four and a half times the American rate. Second, the *rate* decrease is more than offset numerically by the increase in the over-sixty-five population, so the actual *number* of co-resident households continues to increase, as shown in Figures 4–2 and 4–3. Figure 4–2 illustrates the increase of elderly households as a percentage of the 1970 total. Between 1965 and 1986, elderly households grew by 315 percent while the total of all types grew by 45 percent (Ushio, 1989:11). Figure 4–3 shows the growth in numbers of various types of households having at least one member over sixty-five. The co-resident type grew by a half million between 1980 and 1985.

The democratization of the family, then, in conjunction with the growing number—and the growing financial independence—of the aged, has been a major factor contributing to the increase in elderly-only households.

The impact of this trend upon people's thinking is of great interest to us, but it is difficult to assess. Whether people favor co-residence or not, for example, is clearly affected by their perceptions of the alternatives and of the costs and benefits of various life-styles. Such perceptions are too complex to be included in the usual surveys, but they are bound to be affected by economic trends, health trends, changing technologies, and a variety of social attitudes. Since 1973, the prime minister's office has been conducting annual nationwide surveys on aging; the 1974 survey focused on the support of aged parents. The results are worth presenting in detail for three reasons. First, this is the most thorough survey on filial support available today. Second, it has two appropriate samples: married men and women in their thirties and forties, who may be in a position to support their aged parents, and men and women who are between sixty and seventy-four years old. Third, the results of this survey have been replicated by other, smaller scale surveys.

Here we would like to introduce two words that are so commonly used that familiarity with them is important in understanding Japanese perceptions. One is *dōkyo*, which literally means co-living; but when this word is used by the Japanese, it essentially means co-residence between aged parents and a family of their child, which generally means the three-generation household. That is, *dōkyo* is the word used to describe the traditional living arrangement of the aged. The other word is *bekkyo*, literally separate living. This word denotes the nontraditional living arrangement of the aged.

Table 4–1 presents the thinking of adult children as a group re-garding the desirability of living with their parents after they marry. Because it is fairly common in Japan for unmarried children to re-main at the parents' house until their marriage and because *dōkyo* after marriage generally means the child's commitment to the tra-ditional support pattern, the "after children marry" clause was added to the question.

First, looking at the overall results, 49 percent of the adult chil-dren would prefer living together as much as possible. We call this type the *dōkyo* type. Twenty-five percent would prefer separate liv-ing while their parents are healthy but living together when they become frail and dependent. We call this the modified *dōkyo* type. Seventeen percent thought that they should live separately if they could maintain high interaction, what may be called the conditional *bekkyo* type. Finally, 7 percent would prefer to live separately as much as possible (the *bekkyo* type). The differences between city, town, and country are quite noticeable in that rural residents are the most traditional—62 percent *dōkyo* type versus 33 percent *dōkyo* type in big cities, with town populations falling in between. In the rural-urban continuum, the impact of factors such as the abolish-ment of the *ie* system and housing and labor patterns is clearly seen.

The same trend is discerned with educational differences. The higher the education the respondents received, the less traditional they are in their opinion about desirable living arrangements of aged parents. Because urbanization and educational trends are highly correlated, these two factors reinforce each other. Although the rural residents are still strongly oriented toward the traditional *dōkyo* type, the metropolitan residents now have three main alter-natives (the *dōkyo* type, the modified *dōkyo* type, and the conditional *bekkyo* type).

The elderly respondents were men and women sixty to seventy-four years old. Of the total 7,863 subjects, 95 percent had at least one child. Of the 7,471 parents, 75 percent were living *dōkyo*, and 25 percent were living *bekkyo*. Of the *dōkyo* elderly, 63 percent were living with a son's family, 26 percent with unmarried children, and 11 percent with a daughter's family.

Table 4–2 presents the opinions of the elderly about living ar-rangements. The answers were precoded as in Table 4–1, but the *bekkyo* type is composed of an active type ("should live separately as much as possible") and a passive type ("to live separately cannot

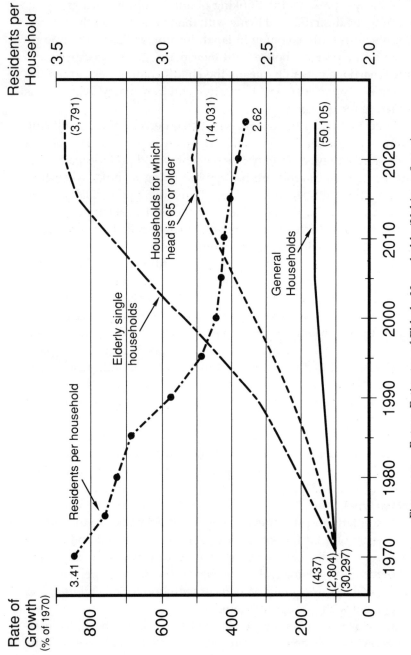

Figure 4-2. Future Estimates of Elderly Households (Ushio, 1989: 11).

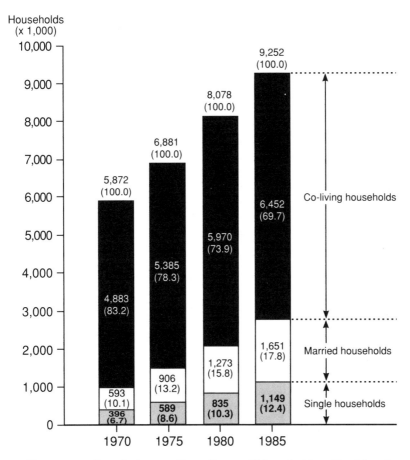

Figure 4-3. Trends Among Three Types of Households with at Least One Member Over Sixty-five (Ministry of Health and Welfare, 1990: 22).

be helped"). Overall, 59 percent selected the *dōkyo* type as the most desirable living arrangement, 17 percent the modified *dōkyo* type, 8 percent the conditional *bekkyo* type, and 14 percent the *bekkyo* type (5 percent active *bekkyo* and 9 percent passive *bekkyo*).

In terms of age differences—sixty to sixty-four, sixty-five to sixty-nine, seventy to seventy-four—the older respondents were, the stronger their *dōkyo* orientation became, although differences were small. Similarly, there are wide age differences in the other three types of arrangement. Next, regarding the health status of the respondents, which were divided into four categories (healthy, not so

Table 4-1. Adult Children's Views of Desirable Living Arrangements for
Parents, after Marriage, by Residential Area and Education

	Number of Subjects	Desirable Living Arrangements (%)				
		Dōkyo	Modified Dōkyo	Conditional Bekkyo	Bekkyo	Others or Unknown
Area of residence						
Metropolis	1,206	33	27	24	11	5
City (>150,000)	1,118	45	28	18	6	3
City (<150,000)	1,195	53	26	14	5	2
Rural	1,376	62	20	10	5	2
Total	4,895	49	25	17	7	2
Education received						
High (14–16 years)	657	35	29	24	8	4
Middle (12 years)	2,058	45	27	19	7	2
Low (9 years)	2,119	57	23	12	6	2

Source: National Welfare Association, 1982, p. 26.
Dōkyo: to live together as much as possible.
Modified *dōkyo*: to live separately while parents are independent, but to live
    together when they become dependent.
Conditional *bekkyo*: to live separately if high contact is possible.
Bekkyo: to live separately as much as possible.

healthy, occasionally bedridden, and bedridden for more than six
months), the more dependent the health status was, the stronger
the *dōkyo* orientation became. For instance, in terms of their actual
living arrangements, *dōkyo* versus *bekkyo*, 72 percent of the *dōkyo*
respondents chose the *dōkyo* type, whereas the opinions varied
more among the *bekkyo* respondents: 25 percent *dōkyo*, 36 percent
modified *dōkyo*, 13 percent conditional *bekkyo*, and 24 percent *bekkyo*
(of which 16 percent was passive and 8 percent active).

Tables 4–1 and 4–2 are both subject to various interpretations.
For one thing, *bekkyo* can mean living in the same neighborhood as
one's children, or it can mean living across the country—very different choices in terms of family dynamics. The overall point is that,
in comparison with the pre-1945 period in which *dōkyo* was not only
normatively prescribed but for nearly everyone a practical necessity

Table 4-2. Elderly Parents' Views of Desirable Living Arrangements with
Married Children, by Age, Health, and Actual Living Arrangements

		Desirable Living Arrangements (%)				
	Number of Subjects	Dōkyo	Modified Dōkyo	Conditional Bekkyo	Bekkyo	Others or Unknown
Age						
60–64	2,969	56	19	8	15	2
65–69	2,723	60	17	8	13	2
70–74	2,171	65	15	5	13	2
Total	7,863	59	17	8	14	2
Health status						
Healthy	4,666	59	18	8	13	2
Not so healthy	2,753	58	17	8	15	2
On and off in bed	363	66	12	4	15	3
In bed for over 6 months	73	76	13	—	6	5
Actual living arrangement						
Dōkyo (75%)	5,584	72	10	5	11	2
Bekkyo (25%)	1,887	25	36	13	24	2

Source: National Welfare Association, 1982, p. 36.
Dōkyo: to live together as much as possible.
Modified dōkyo: to live separately while parents are independent, but to live
    together when they become dependent.
Conditional bekkyo: to live separately if high contact is possible.
Bekkyo: to live separately as much as possible or cannot be helped to live separately.

as well, there is now a variety of possible living arrangements for
the elderly. The survey we have been discussing cast attitudes in
terms of four common alternatives, showing that there is a great
deal more to the question than simply whether or not the generations should share a household. Despite the growing complexity of
alternatives, however, options for the dependent elderly are still
very limited, and many must count on the close support of children
when they become frail.

In the end, decisions about where to live, and with whom, are
affected not just by the preferences of children and elderly parents,
but by many other factors that are rapidly changing in Japan, such
as income, cost of housing, health of the elderly, employment of

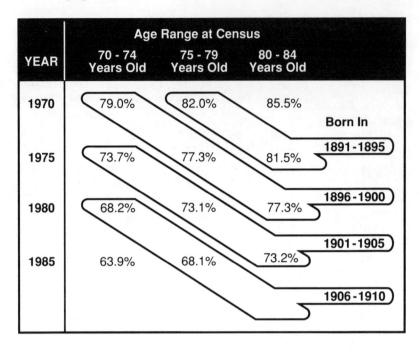

Figure 4-4.   Trends in Co-living for Three Age Groups
(Ministry of Health and Welfare, 1990: 23).

women (the usual caretakers of old parents), geographic mobility of workers, availability of professional homemaking and home health services, and the range and desirability of living styles.

To illustrate the complexity of the situation, consider Figure 4–4, which shows trends in parent-child co-residence for various age cohorts over time. At first glance, there appears to be a remarkable consistency for each cohort over time, suggesting that the end results are primarily an outcome of preference. But this interpretation would rest on several assumptions that seem unlikely under examination. It assumes that co-residence is unaffected by (1) the growing frailty that accompanies advanced age, (2) the rising pensions and living standards and changing life-styles, (3) the rising cost of housing in cities, (4) the increasing employment of women, (5) the declining fertility rate, (6) the growth of the retirement housing industry, (7) the locally variable improvements in professional support for independent living, and (8) the possible differences in longevity of co-resident versus independent-living elderly.

The rate of co-residence for a given cohort should increase as that cohort gets older and frailer, but this increase may be canceled out by lower death rates among the independent-living, and/or by financial pressures against co-residence, and/or by rising living standards and pensions that allow the elderly more choice in where to live. Pondering the effects of these and other factors, we have to admit that we simply cannot interpret Figure 4–4 with any confidence, nor can we predict what numbers will be added to it in future censuses.

5

Welfare Homes for the Aged and Emerging Retirement Communities

Following the democratization of the family, Japanese society has begun to develop new living options for the elderly; but the process is so far slow and uncertain. Without confidence in the wisdom and justice of the newer options, the aged, their caretakers, and the "experts" who would replace the old system seem equally hesitant. Long-term living and care environments for the old are developing to meet a growing demand. This is the social climate in which retirement communities are beginning to emerge.

WELFARE HOMES FOR THE AGED

Under the current Japanese welfare system, all homes for the aged are public and nonproprietary. They are welfare facilities providing basic living necessities, rather than medical facilities providing extensive treatment. The modern welfare facilities started in the 1890s as sporadic philanthropic activities sponsored by Buddhist and Christian organizations devoted to saving the destitute and family-less elderly. Such houses were called *yōrōin*, literally support houses for the aged. The imperial government was reluctant to develop welfare services for its people, particularly for the aged, partly because of the cost and the unfamiliarity of the notion of public welfare, but mainly because of the ideological threat to the *ie* system that such services implied. The *ie* system was an integral element of imperial rule, a system under which welfare could in no sense become a public issue. The family was the welfare unit in those days, and the well-being of its members was a private problem for which each household head was held liable. The very existence of destitute and familyless aged was unwelcome evidence of a weakness in the patriarchal system and therefore in the government itself. Public support for them was a contradiction of the ruling ideology. Put otherwise, the degree to which the aged were cared for by their families was a barometer of *ie* ideology and consequently of the soundness of imperial rule.

The familyless old, then, in addition to poverty and insecurity, bore the stigma of political and ideological deviance. Contempt for the residents of *yōrōin* was actively encouraged as part of the indoctrination of filial duty.

Information on *yōrōin* is scarce, as is often the case with stigmatized activities. In 1913 (the last year of the Meiji era), there seems to have been only twenty-three *yōrōin* throughout Japan, whose occupancy ranged from "several" to thirty residents. Between 1913 and 1926 (the Taisho era), thirty-two *yōrōin* were reported to be in existence (Ogasawara, 1982:26). It was in 1932, following the impact of the Great Depression, that the government enacted the first law to provide public support for the destitute, but the law was limited in scope. One hundred thirty *yōrōin* are believed to have been in existence in 1941—apparently the largest number before the end of World War II. As the war escalated, it became increasingly difficult to maintain their operation; so in 1945, only seventy-five were still open.

In 1950, under the postwar democratic constitution, a law was passed that articulated for the first time in Japanese history the citizen's right to live and the government's responsibility to provide minimal support. With this law, *yōrōin* were reclassified as public welfare facilities. In 1950, the number of such facilities in Japan was 170, and it increased steadily to 607 in 1960 (Ogasawara, 1982:34).

June 1963, the date of the Welfare Act for the Aged (Rōjin Fukushi Hō), was a turning point in the care of the elderly. The significance of this act resembles that of the Older Americans Act in the United States; both have served as basic frameworks for welfare services to the elderly. The Japanese law has shaped the current system of homes for the aged. Previous *yōrōin* were incorporated into the new system under a new name, *rōjin hōmu*, or home for the aged. The change of names was calculated to remove some of the stigma of institutionalization, but this was not a particularly successful strategy.

THREE TYPES OF HOMES
FOR THE AGED

The Welfare Act for the Aged established three types of homes, as well as community-based senior centers. Although *yōrōin* had served only the destitute elderly who had no supporting family, the new system took into account the need for physical care of the dependent aged as well as their economic needs. This was a remarkable departure from traditional welfare services in Japan, which were essentially designed for low-income people.

The first of the three new types of facilities, then, the *yōgo rōjin hōmu*, or elderly care home, is a welfare facility that provides light to intermediate care for those over sixty-five who cannot remain independent for physical, mental, environmental, and/or financial reasons. The old *yōrōin* were all reclassified as *yōgo* homes. Having been originally designed as residential and not intermediate care facilities, they took on a new function that often conflicted with the old one.

Tokubetsu yōgo rōjin hōmu, commonly shortened to *toku-yō hōmu*, are "special elderly homes," similar to what Americans call skilled nursing facilities, for those over sixty-five who require constant care due to marked physical and/or mental impairments and who cannot be cared for at home. Unlike *yōgo* homes, financial necessity is not a condition of admission to *toku-yō* homes. Officially, they are open to middle-class families with severely dependent elderly, although priority tends to be given to low-income applications if other conditions are equal and space is limited.

The third type is the *keihi rōjin hōmu*, or "limited fee home for the elderly," a type of boarding facility providing those over sixty with services for daily living for a small fee. *Keihi* homes are divided into two subtypes: type A and type B. The former offers accommodations to those over sixty who do not have families or who are unable to live with their own family and whose monthly income is less than one and a half times the average monthly operating cost per resident. The type B *keihi* homes waive the strict income requirement and accept those capable of independent living who have other legitimate financial reasons to request housing.

In short, the three types of homes are designed to deal with two types of dependency: economic and physical. Financial necessity is required for admission to *yōgo* and *keihi* homes, which are designed primarily for lower-income elderly. *Toku-yō* homes are designed to be available for severely dependent elderly regardless of their financial situation. *Toku-yō* homes are the only specially designed long-term care facilities for the aged in Japan, although acute hospitals often serve this function (Kiefer, 1987). The underlying philosophy of the Welfare Act for the Aged is still that family care is the most desirable arrangement for the aged, and it restricts subsidized residential care to those who for some reason cannot be cared for by their families.

Eighty percent of the total operating cost of *yōgo* and *toku-yō* homes is covered by the national government and 20 percent by the prefectural and local government. Fiscal support goes directly to the homes rather than to the individual residents, and it is not a cost-reimbursement system. Each home operates within a budget set by the Ministry of Health and Welfare. In the 1983 fiscal year, the monthly operating cost per resident in a fifty-bed *toku-yō* home in Tokyo—where the cost was higher than the national average—was about $780, that of a *yōgo* home in Tokyo, about $479 (Health and Welfare Statistics Association, 1983:167). The residents of *keihi* homes are in principle required to pay for their own living expenses. The government supports administrative costs because the homes are designated as welfare facilities by the 1963 act.

Admission to *yōgo* and *toku-yō* homes is arranged through the municipal offices of the Social Welfare Agency, offices also set up by the act. These offices decide whether the applicant should be admitted and, if so, to which type of home. The applicants or their families cannot choose the type of home or its location, and physicians have no official role in the process of admission or assignment. In this sense, admission to a *yōgo* or *toku-yō* home amounts to institutionalization. Admission to a *keihi* home is different, being based on a direct contact between the director of the home and the applicant.

RECENT GROWTH OF
TOKU-YŌ HOMES

The recent growth of *toku-yō* homes, shown in Table 5–1, is considerable, rising from only 1 home in 1963, the year the Welfare Act for

Table 5-1.   Number of Homes for the Aged and Residents
by Type, 1963–1989

	Toku-yō Homes		Yōgo Homes		Keihi Homes	
	Number of Facilities	Resident Population	Number of Facilities	Resident Population	Number of Facilities	Resident Population
1963	1	80	673	47,024	16	1,082
1965	27	1,921	702	51,569	36	2,259
1967	62	4,592	750	55,711	44	2,840
1969	109	7,819	790	59,382	48	3,082
1971	197	14,751	839	63,306	60	3,880
1973	350	26,503	890	67,770	82	5,352
1975	539	41,606	934	71,031	121	7,527
1977	714	55,482	938	71,352	143	8,952
1979	903	71,481	942	70,844	187	11,405
1981	1,165	89,510	945	70,218	229	13,831
1983	1,410	105,887	945	69,724	259	15,341
1987	1,855	138,125	945	68,436	288	16,941
1988	1,995	144,673	945	68,156	288	16,917
1989	2,125	152,988	949	68,113	290	17,021

Sources: Health and Welfare Statistics Association, 1983 and 1990; Miyajima, 1986.

the Aged took effect, to 2,125 homes in 1989. Since 1970, about 100 new toku-yō homes have been built annually, amounting to a new bed for every forty-five new elderly added to the population each year.

In sharp contrast, Table 5–1 shows that the number of yōgo home beds grew slowly from 1963 to 1975, then began to decline. The 673 yōgo homes in 1963 were old yōrōin that had been reclassified by the new law. Thus, yōgo homes inherited problems such as old, poorly constructed buildings and multibed rooms with minimal privacy. Also, despite the official redefinition of yōgo homes as intermediate-care facilities, they have continued to function as residential facilities. As a result, relatively healthy and moderately impaired residents live together, a fact that complicates administration. The Ministry of Health and Welfare decided that yōgo homes built since 1973 should have single- or double-occupancy rooms, which greatly increased their cost. After 1976, new yōgo homes were not to be built except under special circumstances; rather, efforts should be made to remodel the old multibed wards into single or double rooms at many *yōgo* homes. These facts explain the decline of *yōgo* home beds.

Growth in the number of *keihi* homes has been steady but slow—about 660 beds per year, or one bed per 400 elderly—since 1963. Their role remains minor compared with *toku-yō* and *yōgo* homes. The combined total of residents in the three types of homes in 1989 was 238,122, approximately 1.7 percent of the total over-sixty-five population. During the same time, the rate of acute hospitalization in this age group has been stable at about 4 percent. All the homes have high occupancy rates (Soda and Miura, 1982:229). Despite the increase of *toku-yō* homes, they are still in short supply, and their occupancy rate is virtually 100 percent, the highest of all three types.

The various processes by which people are institutionalized in *toku-yō* homes are not well studied. One survey (TMIG, 1981) yielded the following results: In 1980, ten out of the total of forty-nine *toku-yō* homes in Tokyo were chosen, representing a range of different sized institutions. Of 1,442 residents, 36.2 percent came from general hospitals, 32.1 percent from *yōgo* homes, and 25.3 percent from their own residences. The socioeconomic background of the residents from general hospitals and private residences was not reported, so it is not certain how many of them were middle class. Apparently, when residents of *yōgo* homes become more frail, they are admitted to *toku-yō* homes for the same reason they were admitted to *yōgo* homes: the lack or inability of families to care for them in the first place.

The Japanese government has made strenuous efforts to build *toku-yō* homes since 1963, but the need for more persists. For instance, in 1980, there were an estimated 438,000 *netakiri* (bedridden) elderly in Japan *excluding* those in *toku-yō* homes (Health and Welfare Statistics Association, 1983:161). In general usage, the word *netakiri* applies only to the aged whose health is so deteriorated that they need extensive care, usually around the clock. Of these *netakiri* elderly nationwide, approximately 74 percent had been disabled for more than six months at the time of the survey.

As pointed out, *toku-yō* homes are the only specially designed long-term care facilities that provide skilled nursing care for the aged in Japan. There are no proprietary nursing homes. One way to cope with the increasing demand for long-term care is to keep building *toku-yō* homes, but this would be an expensive solution. The Japanese government suffers from huge fiscal deficits and has been enforcing stringent constraints on all social programs, and those for the aged are the most drastically affected. In order to build more *toku-yō* homes, individual payments probably would have to be greatly increased. This would be difficult because it would mean a drastic departure from the traditional view of welfare. Welfare, for the Japanese, has meant social services for low-income people, which should be in principle free of charge. In this sense, the very existence of *toku-yō* homes is contradictory to the Japanese welfare system because financial necessity is not the primary admission requirement. There is wide agreement that individual payments should be maintained at a minimum level. The introduction of even partial payments by *toku-yō* residents was possible only after public protests and political struggles between the ruling Liberal Democratic party and the opposition parties. The more populist parties opposed the policy, fearing that such payments by "welfare" beneficiaries would be a foot in the door for a more general rollback of welfare benefits. If the present Japanese political climate holds, these fears may be justified. The individual payment system may eventually be widened to include recipients of other social services as well.

Victims of the policy debates, families with severely dependent aged, are and will continue to be left pretty much on their own. At best, they can get moral support from others in the same predicament. Many middle-class families, or their aged parents themselves, are now able to pay for care at *toku-yō* homes even if it means paying substantially more than the current maximum payment. It may be a serious financial burden for them, but it may in some cases be preferable to the stress of having bedfast or disoriented parents at home.

ACUTE HOSPITALS

Until recently, the only institutional alternative to *toku-yō* homes was acute hospitalization. Japanese medical insurance systems include full coverage for those over seventy years old. This, together with the shortage of nursing facilities, helps account for the extremely long stays of elderly in acute hospitals. In 1984, the average stay of the over-sixty-five was eighty-eight days (compared with eleven days in the United States). Even with the relatively low staffing patterns and cost of Japanese acute hospitals, the cost per day for the average over-sixty-five patient in 1978 was $51 (versus $400 for U.S. Medicare patients that year). This is an unacceptably expensive solution. In 1984, there were 820,000 elderly in Japan's acute and geriatric hospitals. Indeed, 131,000 or 30 percent of the 438,000 *netakiri* elderly, were hospitalized at the time of the survey in 1980.

The long acute hospitalization stays of the elderly were possible because (1) the public medical insurance system required very low out-of-pocket payments and (2) the system functioned in such a way that longer hospitalizations and more treatment resulted in more profit for the hospitals. As a consequence, some hospitals, called *rōjin byōin,* or hospitals for the aged, had a high proportion of elderly inpatients. Technically, *rōjin byōin* are simply hospitals wherein the aged exceed 60 percent of the total inpatients, and few have special qualifications for treating the aged. Rather, they are a consequence of the interaction between the shortage of *toku-yō* homes and the special medical insurance system for those over seventy years old.

Since February 1983, however, this use of acute hospitals for what is in effect long-term care has been discouraged by a new law, the Rōjin Hoken Hō, or Law for the Health of the Elderly. Under the new law, acute hospitals are reimbursed on a diminishing schedule—the longer the stay, the lower the rate. More recently, cost ceilings also have been set on specific in-hospital procedures, giving hospitals further incentives to discharge chronically ill patients earlier. Intermediate nursing care, rehabilitation, and other low-cost strategies for continuing support of these discharged patients are being developed and studied, but as yet no one knows how well the 1983 law will work. It seems to have had some effect on the inflation rate of health costs, however. Whereas costs had been increasing at an average annual rate of 23 percent between 1973 and 1983, in 1984, the increase was only 8.9 percent, and in 1985, it dropped to a mere 2.7 percent (Ushio, 1989:9).

COST-EFFICIENT MEASURES

The growth of the frail elderly population, coming as it has during a time when families are shrinking and health care costs growing, has forced the Japanese health authorities to innovate. They have had to look for models of low-cost care, and they have sought such models in Scandinavia and to some extent the United States.

A new overall strategy, based on deinstitutionalization, has developed. The national government now encourages municipalities to create improved rehabilitation and home support for the disabled elderly and improved outpatient services for the ambulatory. Day care, in-home help and home nursing, respite beds in hospitals and nursing homes for those usually confined to bed at home, and intermediate nursing care beds are included in the array of encouraged services. Day-care centers provide meals, medication supervision, and some rehabilitation therapy. Workers from these centers also make home calls to help with bathing, meals, and other needs of the homebound. In 1979, there were only 20 such day-care programs in Japan; by 1986, there were 210, and the growth continues. In the same period, the number of respite beds nationwide grew from 5,840 to 37,346, and the number of home helpers in local agencies from 13,120 to 23,555 (Miyajima, 1986:35–36).

An important component of the move toward deinstitutionalization is a new type of facility geared toward rehabilitation and community support. The first twenty of these *rōjin hoken shisetsu*, or "geriatric health facilities," were completed in 1988, the target being some two hundred thousand beds by the year 2000. The new facilities, to be built by licensed hospitals and welfare organizations, will take as inpatients transferees from geriatric hospitals and will at the same time provide outpatient services to impaired elderly in the communities. Inpatient services would focus on essential medical care, daily living support (meals, dressing, bathing, medications), and rehabilitation (occupational and physical therapy).

One serious problem with the growing care system is that no distinct yardsticks have yet been developed for placement of the frail or ill elderly person. Rather, the emphasis has been on trying to keep as many out of hospitals and nursing homes as possible, without a clear sense of what is most appropriate in a given case. As we write this, the 1983 Law for the Health of the Elderly is about to undergo review, with an eye to adjusting and clarifying its provisions.

In sum, for the middle-class elderly, still healthy and financially independent, or for those in middle age, there are few alternatives but relying on one's own children when it comes to the care they may eventually need. There are the *toku-yō* homes, but they are in short supply, they carry the stigma of welfare and of family failure, and access to them is not controlled by the consumer. In other words, there is little security in this alternative.

Nor is the family a secure source of support, even for the middle class, as dependence upon adult children has grown increasingly problematic in recent decades. *Dōkyo*, the traditional living arrangement for the support of aged parents, has been declining. There is a growing ambiguity about filial responsibilities. At the same time, the elderly themselves are becoming more independent, financially and psychologically. Japanese society has yet to provide a realistic alternative to the traditional *dōkyo* arrangement. It is against this background that retirement communities are now emerging in Japan.

Japan is, on the whole, a tight-knit society. Education is uniformly high; transportation, data processing, and communications technology are efficient; and social values are relatively homogeneous for a modern culture. However, the speed of Japan's aging, and the magnitude of the social changes that have come with it, have brought confusion in their wake. Caring for the elderly has become not only an economic and technical problem, but a communication problem as well. We must begin our discussion of retirement communities with an explanation of the nomenclature—something unclear to the average Japanese as well.

RETIREMENT COMMUNITIES

Confusion Over Names

The three types of homes for the aged just discussed—*yōgo, tokuyō,* and *keihi* homes—are public in the sense that they are designated welfare facilities with fiscal support from national and local government. The welfare act that created them, however, has one minor clause that describes another type of facility—the nonpublic, residential facility for the aged. Such facilities are called *yūryō rōjin hōmu* or *yūryō* homes for the aged. *Yūryō* literally means fee chargeable; residents of these homes must pay all their expenses because there is no public fiscal support.

This clause, which seems to have been an afterthought, defined *yūryō* homes for the aged as "facilities which continuously house more than ten elderly and provide them with necessary services for daily living, including meals, and which are not designated as welfare facilities by the Welfare Act of the Aged." This is a "blanket" clause, added to regulate all types of residential facilities already in existence. As such, it creates a terminological problem to the extent that it designates not a homogeneous group, but a hodgepodge of widely different entities.

Early *yūryō* homes were small-scale homes run by philanthropic individuals, small groups, or nonprofit charity organizations (*shakai fukushi hōjin*), quite different from the retirement communities emerging now. They functioned much like *keihi* homes, charging low fees and catering to those whose income, although small, exceeded the upper limit of eligibility for *keihi* homes.

That these old *yūryō* homes and modern Western-style retirement communities are lumped together and officially classified in one category results in a communication problem. The modern retirement communities have no widely accepted name of their own. This may not sound like a problem to Americans, who have their own profusion of names for retirement housing—"life-care facility," "residential home," "adult community," "senior housing," and so on—but at least these phenomena have existed for a few decades now, and most people are aware of them. The Japanese terminology problem is made worse by the confusing presence of welfare law at the very root of the concept of retirement housing.

The advent of retirement communities was probably not in the minds of the architects of the 1963 act because the first units were not built until the early 1970s. In 1974, the Ministry of Health and Welfare issued revised guidelines on *yūryō* homes to the prefectural governors. In these guidelines, a *yūryō* home was redefined as "a facility that provides residential accommodations for more than fifty residents, age sixty or older, and which also furnishes such services as counseling, leisure activities and health care. Meal services are not necessarily required."

In 1980, a retirement community in Tokyo went into bankruptcy, the first case in this industry. The incident became a major social issue and was highlighted in the mass media because the residents lost much of their investment, which in many cases was probably their life savings. The incident also triggered the formation of a study group on retirement communities within the Ministry of Health and Welfare. Under the ministry's strong leadership, the National Retirement Housing Association (Zenkoku Yūryō Rōjin Hōmu Kyōkai) was established in February 1982. Twenty-five facilities managed by thirteen organizations joined the association at its inception, and many others have joined since. Although the majority are modern retirement communities, the membership includes *yūryō* homes, too. The association is expected to become the watchdog of the industry and to take the lead in developing quality standards for retirement communities. Since 1990, the association has taken the initiative to develop an insurance system protecting the investments of retirement home residents.

Guidelines for the size, design, construction, management, staffing, and services of *yūryō* homes were revised and expanded in 1981, 1986, 1988, and 1991. Now all planned *yūryō* homes must apply to the National Retirement Housing Association, which evaluates the feasibility of the plan and has the power to disapprove it. Local authorities are now also empowered to require the correction of problems in existing facilities. Some prefectures, including Saitama near Tokyo, are trying to enforce tougher regulations than those established by the ministry.

This is a dramatic change since the mid-1980s. As recently as 1985, there were no national guidelines for the construction and operation of *yūryō* homes and no attempt to differentiate the more modern retirement communities from the old style homes. Neither the Retirement Housing Association nor the local governments had authority to regulate retirement housing, and anyone who had the capital could, in theory at least, develop such facilities by simply registering with the local government. The Ministry of Health and Welfare recognized the need for more retirement housing, but it took the attitude that because these were not welfare facilities, they should not be regulated. It is perhaps inevitable that the public is increasingly aware of problems surrounding the construction and operation of such facilities as their number increases, and that regulation follows. Meanwhile, regulation has had the effect of improving the image of retirement housing in the national consciousness. The phrase *yūryō hōmu* has lost its original meaning for most Japanese and has come to stand for the more modern type of facility now being built.

THE "SILVER BUSINESS"

In 1982, when our research began, there was a great unfilled demand for retirement housing, a need for appropriate living conditions for middle-class elderly who were neither sick nor destitute but could not or preferred not to live with children. No official count was available of the number of existing units designed to fill this need because many builders did not belong to the Association of Retirement Housing, and many did not register with their prefectural governments as required by the 1963 Welfare Act (another measure of its ineffectiveness with respect to housing). In 1982, Soda and Miura counted ninety nonwelfare facilities (including both *yūryō* and more modern types), housing 6,813 residents. These ranged in size from 10 residents to 400. The following year Kinoshita attempted a survey of the major retirement housing developments that were fully operative nationwide at that time. He found thirty-one of them, including seventeen of the "life-care" type, with a full range of support services for frail residents, and ten of the "condominium" type, designed for basically healthy people. Nearly all of the thirty-one had been built within the preceding decade (Kinoshita, 1984:108–110).

In 1992, the picture is quite different. Seeing the success of some of the earlier developers, a wide variety of institutions have begun to build an increasingly diverse array of retirement housing styles. Indeed, this is now a booming industry, referred to with characteristic sarcasm by the Japanese press as the "silver business" (*shirubaa bijinesu*). These private ventures now represent a spectrum of cost and living standard options, of financing plans, and of health and supportive service packages, with individual developers tending to specialize in one segment of the market. Figures 5–1 and 5–2 show trends in the numbers of retirement facilities and residents, respectively.

At the most supportive end of the spectrum, one finds many life-care facilities, the type represented by Fuji-no-Sato, which we describe in detail. Here the developer makes a commitment to make

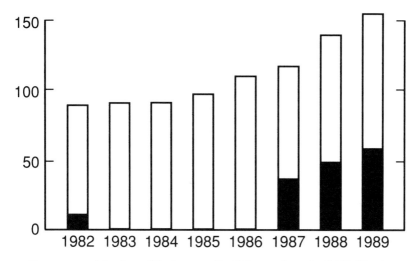

Figure 5-1.   Number of Retirement Facilities, 1982–1989 (*Nikkei Business*, 1991: 196). ■ = For-profit (1983–1986 = no information)

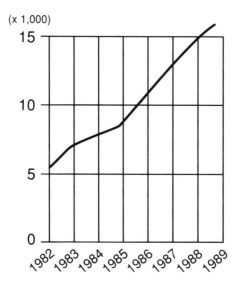

Figure 5-2.   Number of Residents in Retirement Facilities, 1982–1989 (*Nikkei Business*, 1991: 196).

available at the facility the basic health care services needed as long as the resident lives there. The configuration of such services varies from place to place, but the builders of Fuji-no-Sato have actually set the standard for the industry, and many of the features we describe here can be widely found throughout the silver business. In general, these life-care facilities, the oldest of which dates back to 1975, require that entrants be at least sixty years of age and that they are healthy enough upon entrance to live independently in their own apartments. Entrants are required to pay an endowment fee upon moving in, as well as a monthly operating fee during their stay. Since the late 1980s, the growing array of silver business concepts has been further complicated by the emergence of private skilled nursing facilities, confusingly called *yūryō toku-yō*.

At the low end of the support spectrum, one finds congregate housing of the condominium type, with few or no health-related services, although some of these provide a nurse on the premises full time. Accordingly, entrants must sign an agreement that they will move out when they can no longer live independently in their apartments. The minimum age for admission may be as low as forty-five in these facilities, the first of which was built in 1971.

For historical interest, we mention one other type of facility that was popular in the early stages of retirement housing development but proved financially too risky and has not thrived as the other types have: the so-called "life-guarantee" type. These are similar to life-care communities in type of service and design, but the residents pay only an entrance endowment, not a monthly fee. The Tokyo community that went bankrupt was of this type. The life-guarantee system is very vulnerable to inflation and other contingencies in expenditures because the system does not have the flexible financing of the monthly fee. In the case of the oldest life-guarantee community, for example, the management was not prepared for the inflationary oil shock of the 1970s. The facility stopped accepting new residents in 1973, and it is said that it operates with a large deficit (reportedly $13,333 per resident in 1983 alone). Because it is owned by a large life insurance company, it has avoided bankruptcy. The Ministry of Health and Welfare now discourages this system of operation, and no retirement communities begun after 1975 have adopted the life-guarantee system. Many life-care facilities in the United States have suffered a similar fate, partly because the average life span of residents in this type of setting is longer than the national norm.

THE IMAGE PROBLEM

The financial problems of the life-guarantee communities are no longer a serious issue in the silver industry as a whole, but they illustrate a tenacious problem that stalks any effort to provide senior housing in Japan: the historical connection between age-homogeneous communities, on the one hand, and poverty and ill health, on the other.

Because of the history we have sketched, people who can afford senior housing tend to look upon it as an acceptable way of handling *increasing dependency* as they age. Some form of long-term care is therefore expected by the typical potential resident. The only available research to date concerning the level of demand for retirement community space is a 1982 survey of 712 retired business executives and public school teachers in Tokyo (Japan College of Social Work, 1982). As selection criteria, 73.3 percent of these respondents mentioned medical and health care services, 54.2 percent mentioned reliable and safe management, 33.8 percent mentioned comfortable living accommodations, and 28.4 percent mentioned good interpersonal relationships among the residents.

Although the advertising of U.S. retirement communities emphasizes an active way of life, the Japanese focus is on health care services. Even condominium-type communities, which lack all but the most superficial services, make these services their sales point, although potential residents know they will get only minimal health care there. The lack of standards is serious for the life-care and life-guarantee systems precisely because residents expect long-term nursing. Usually, the entrance contract does not make clear what health services are covered by the entrance fee or how much the residents will have to pay out of pocket when they become ill. Furthermore, the type and extent of care varies from one community to another, making it extremely difficult for the potential residents to make realistic financial plans for their declining years.

During the first decade of the silver business, there seemed to be little awareness of these problems on the part of the retirement housing industry. Little attention was paid, even by life-care and life-guarantee facilities, to estimating the future needs of facilities for supportive services and skilled nursing beds as their resident populations declined in health. In the last five years, however, the problem has become clear, and builders of most newer communities are aware of the need for such planning. The builders of Fujino-Sato seem to have evolved a workable model and continue to provide examples of successful planning to the industry as a whole.

We now turn to the "welfare" image problem. As we have said, retirement communities are ordinarily referred to collectively as *yūryō* homes for the aged, a term that originally meant welfare facilities for lower-income elderly. The term *rōjin hōmu* (home for the aged), the generic name for *yūryō, toku-yō, yōgo,* and *keihi* homes, has an even worse image for the average Japanese. A home for the aged is a place where the few unfortunate elderly without family support have to spend their last years. A new social entity should have a new name and image.

Partly for this reason, in spite of a clear need for housing of this kind, the occupancy rates of the early retirement communities averaged about 75 percent in the early 1980s, threatening future financial stability. The life-guarantee community that went bankrupt after one year had an occupancy of only 32 percent.

However, despite this problem, there is an indication that the retirement community is gradually coming to be known as a possible new alternative for old age. Even in 1983, the social demand survey cited earlier reported that among retired business executives and teachers, 97.1 percent were aware of the existence of retirement communities, whereas 61.5 percent were aware of *yōgo* homes, 30.2 percent of *toku-yō* homes, and 20.9 percent of *keihi* homes.

More and more retirees seem to be aware of the benefits of age-homogeneous communities and appear willing to use them. But there is still considerable debate and confusion over the *ethics* of senior housing as a *business venture*. The feeling is still widespread and strong that something is wrong when the elderly are not housed and nursed by their families. It is tragic enough when the government must do this as a service to the destitute, but when even the affluent aged must offer money for their security, the situation borders on the grotesque in the public mind. Massive changes in the demographics, economics, and politics of aging simply have not been absorbed into the ethical norms of the culture. There is a sense that private business should stick to doing what it does best—making profits—and that this is incompatible with the needs of the elderly. The problem is by no means alleviated by the Japanese news media, most of which continue to represent retirement housing as a slightly scurrilous industry.

PART II

FUJI-NO-SATO

6

The Setting and the System

THE SETTING

LOCATION

Fuji-no-Sato is located on the Izu Peninsula about two hours by express train southwest of Tokyo. The peninsula has been developed as a major tourist attraction and resort for Tokyo area residents. Izu was given modern fame by Yasunari Kawabata's first novel, *The Izu Dancer*, which depicts the area around Fuji-no-Sato some seventy years ago. Beautiful mountains lie along the central spine of the peninsula, separating the eastern and western coasts. Because of its proximity to Tokyo, the eastern coast is the one better developed for tourism.

The peninsula has just about every requisite for a resort area. Because of the fine scenery, it is a part of the larger national park that includes Mt. Fuji. There are good natural hot springs here and there, around which tourism started about a century ago, leading to the development of the first major towns. Then, as today, a trip to a hot spring was one of the most popular enjoyments of the Japanese, especially the elderly, because it is believed to be good for relaxation and health, particularly for chronic impairments like arthritis and back pain. Today the peninsula also offers a wide range of leisure and sport facilities for the young and old and for families. Because it is in a national park, development is in general carefully controlled, and nature is well preserved. Every year the unspoiled natural environment attracts thousands of people who flee the stifling heat and smog of Tokyo to enjoy the golf courses, tennis courts, bicycle trails, and amusement parks. National highways trace the scenic coastline and attract motor tourists. Because of the peninsula's volcanic origin, beaches are few, and the coastline is mostly rocky, high cliffs. But the water is clear, and the scattered small beaches attract enormous summer crowds.

Climatically, the name Izu evokes images of a land without winter. Slightly cooler in summer than in the center of Tokyo, it is also much warmer during winter months. In early March, the blooming of wild narcissus at the southern tip of the peninsula marks the beginning of the spring sightseeing season. Although the mild climate makes tourism a yearround business, summer is the busiest season. Extra trains from Tokyo are added on routes to the eastern side. The trains are usually packed, as are the highways. Summer season starts in early July and usually ends in September, when the waves begin to run high, making swimming dangerous. The end of the summer season is generally proclaimed symbolically by a typhoon or two lashing the peninsula with violent wind and rain.

The eastern side of the peninsula, where Fuji-no-Sato is located, is within the range of a day trip from Tokyo. The immediate area is occupied by a small, relatively isolated fishing and farming village, about thirty minutes by car from the nearest city. Compared with other sightseeing spots on the peninsula, the area has an atmosphere of cultured taste, being occupied mostly by homes and small hotels—the result of private development by a railway company. Today there are a great number of these second homes, mostly Western-style cottages owned by wealthy Tokyoites. There are also many elite small hotels and rental cottages, which are leased only in the summer. In recent years, large corporations from Tokyo have built hotel-like facilities for employee recreation and training. Thus, the population of the village multiplies on weekends and in summer when people come from Tokyo to stay there. Prices at local supermarkets are higher than average, almost equivalent to those in Tokyo.

In short, the area has an established social image as an upper-middle-class resort. As such, it combines two distinct levels: the traditional village—a huddle of old houses on low land near the fishing port—and the newly developed spacious resort section on high ground near the railway and highway. The traditional economic structure of the village has disintegrated, and the old-time residents are now dependent on revenues from tourism. Citrus farming was once a booming local industry but is almost dying now. Commercial fishing has dropped sharply in recent years, probably because the local waters have been fished out by modern methods. Many former fishermen now conduct sport fishing trips.

Most of the resort section had already been developed at the time Fuji-no-Sato was planned, but sufficient land was found along the lower edge of this tract, near the village. One cannot see the Pacific Ocean from the community, but it is only about a fifteen-minute walk to the high-cliffed coastline. Fuji-no-Sato is also a fifteen-minute walk from the railway station, or five minutes by the community's shuttle bus. In the immediate neighborhood, resort cottages are scattered throughout the natural woods. There are several coffee shops and a couple of restaurants within walking distance of the community. Streets are wider than the Japanese rural average but short, curved, and without signs, so people unfamiliar with the area often get lost.

BUILDING STRUCTURES

The stringent zoning regulations applied to development in this national park have made Fuji-no-Sato a unique retirement community in Japan. On postcards available at the community shop, an aerial view shows thirteen white buildings embedded in natural green woods. Besides the buildings, the only visible surfaces are the community's wide streets and a utility yard at the back of the community center. Under the yard is hidden a sewage treatment plant. By regulation, the buildings are two-storied and cover no more than 20 percent of the land that the community owns. The woods are so well protected that the management cannot cut a tree on its own land without prior approval from the local office of the Environmental Protection Agency. Fuji-no-Sato is, in fact, the only retirement community in Japan that has no high-rise buildings.

The community is isolated from the main village and secluded by deep woods from the shopping area near the highway and from the railway station, which is also the nearest place where the residents can catch a local bus. Although some residents enjoy walking in the woods and take shortcuts to reach these conveniences, the majority take the community's shuttle bus, which runs three times a day, or call a taxi when the shuttle service is not available. At the time of the research, only 9 of the 372 residents owned cars. Because of their geographical isolation and limited transportation, most spent their days within the grounds of the community.

The structures of Fuji-no-Sato conform to the upper-middle-class social image that the surrounding area seeks. The thirteen buildings, painted white, brighten the community with reflected sunlight. In summer particularly, the contrast between the white buildings and the dark green woods is remarkable. As one crosses the access bridge that leads into the estate, heading toward the center of the spacious community, one finds small gardens everywhere along the wide streets and among the buildings. The gardens, divided into tiny plots by volcanic rocks, are meticulously cared for by the residents. A variety of flowers grows here most of the year, and in winter, the people cultivate plants with colorful leaves.

Gardening was the most important spontaneous activity among the residents. The amount of energy they poured into this art, and the intensity of their interest in it, prompt the question whether there may be more to it than mere hobby activity. We discuss this issue in detail in Chapter 10. For instance, many residents would order seeds by mail through catalogues and plant them first in boxes in their living units, rather than buy seedlings from a nursery. This way they could carefully monitor temperature and moisture until the seedlings were strong enough to transplant outdoors. They also had to buy soil to supplement the poor, rocky earth. Early residents repeated story after story about the hardships of making the gardens, which required, among other things, removing tons of rock by hand. It was as if the gardens were symbols of their contribution to the community or territorial markers announcing their possession of it.

Many first-time visitors, prospective residents and potential developers alike, who have come to see a *yūryō* home for the aged, cannot conceal their astonishment at the unexpected cheerfulness and modernity. Even those who have seen photographs of the place are skeptical until confronted with the reality.

Residents vividly remember their first encounters with the community. Mr. Sonoda, a seventy-three-year-old retired bank executive, illustrates the social image problem that Japanese retirement communities have. To convince his son and daughter-in-law that his decision to move in was reasonable, he invited them to Fuji-no-Sato to see with their own eyes that this was not "one of those awful *rōjin hōmu*." This worked well enough, but Mr. Sonoda complained that his former neighbors and friends who had not seen Fuji-no-

Sato were still skeptical. If he told them it was a *rōjin hōmu*, people immediately suspected that he had been forced by family problems to live in a gloomy institution. Eventually, he decided not to use the word "*rōjin hōmu*" and to tell those who had not seen the community that he was living at a famous resort.

The arrangement of the thirteen buildings is illustrated in Figure 6–1. Ten residential buildings surround the community center. All but three of the residential buildings are connected to the community center by second-floor bridges. The clinic and the administrative building are located near the entrance to the community.

The arrangement of the buildings is calculated to promote community building among the residents. For instance, the separation of the administrative building and the community center is based on the innovative idea that the activities in the two settings are functionally different, and this difference should be symbolized spatially. Also, compared with most other *yūryō* homes, Fuji-no-Sato and its sister communities have much greater, and more functionally diverse, communal activity space, the result of a deliberate attempt by the designers to promote community feeling.

One building on the grounds (not shown) is not part of Fuji-no-Sato. This is a fifty-bed *toku-yō* home at the southeast corner of the estate, which is run by a separate, nonprofit, social welfare organization. Although Fuji-no-Sato has a relatively large clinic of its own, the inclusion of the *toku-yō* home was part of planning for the long-term care of dependent residents. As in other retirement communities that have *toku-yō* homes on their estates, the management intended that the home would be used by their residents.

This was in practice unrealistic. As we discussed in Chapter 5, *toku-yō* homes are public welfare nursing homes for elderly who cannot be cared for by their families, and admission is arranged through the local social welfare agency. Despite the fact that Fuji-no-Sato provided the land for this *toku-yō* home without charge, the home is open to all eligible elderly in the city to which the community belongs. Fuji-no-Sato's residents share with other elderly in the area equal access, and the management has no direct control over the process. That the promotional brochure for Fuji-no-Sato emphasized the presence of the *toku-yō* home ("when residents become bed-ridden, there is a *toku-yō* home just nearby") was misleading, particularly for potential residents who were unfamiliar with the

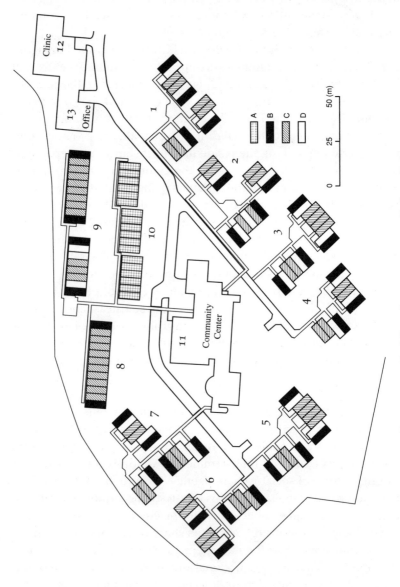

Figure 6-1. Building Arrangements at Fuji-no-Sato

policies of *toku-yō* homes. In fact, some residents who were thus led to believe they would have priority for admission later expressed resentment toward the management when they learned the facts.

Free use of the land by the *toku-yō* home may have been a condition set by the city government for the construction of Fuji-no-Sato. The city, which had no *toku-yō* home until this one was built, has gained the most by this arrangement. There may have been a verbal agreement that the city would allocate some beds for Fuji-no-Sato residents in return for the land; this is a common practice in similar situations in Japan.

However, despite such a possible agreement, all beds of the *toku-yō* home were occupied soon after its opening, and it became very difficult for community residents to gain admission. On the average, only three out of the fifty beds were filled by residents of Fuji-no-Sato.

Although the community buildings and the *toku-yō* home are geographically close, they are separated by woods; so to visit the home from the community, one needs to leave the community, cross a small bridge near the entrance, and then walk about half a mile on a narrow road. Except for a group of volunteers who visited the home every weekday and a physician at Fuji-no-Sato who also served the home, the community and the home had very little interaction.

ACCOMMODATIONS

Fuji-no-Sato has 288 residential units in ten buildings. Four units were occupied by the staff, and two or three units were reserved for guests and other temporary needs. As of October 1, 1982, 281 units were occupied by 372 residents, of whom approximately 230 to 250 lived here full-time.

There are four types of units (Figure 6–2). Type A (36 units) is a studio, type B (66 units) a small one-bedroom, type C (112 units) a large one-bedroom, and type D (66 units) a two-bedroom. Type A is for a single resident, type D is for two, and types B and C can be used as singles or doubles. Each unit has its own balcony, where the residents set potted plants and dry their laundry.

Type A has a large room used as a combined living room and bedroom, and most residents in this type of unit use beds. At the

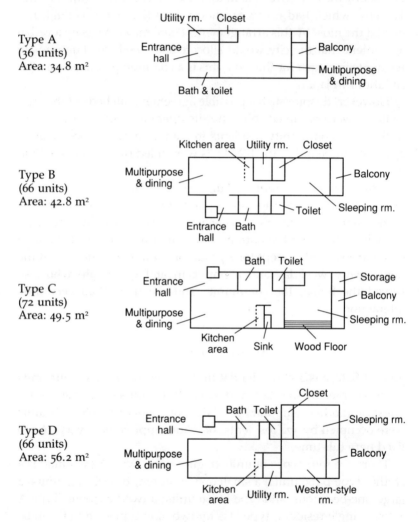

Type A
(36 units)
Area: 34.8 m²

Utility rm.   Closet
Entrance hall
Balcony
Multipurpose & dining
Bath & toilet

Type B
(66 units)
Area: 42.8 m²

Kitchen area   Utility rm.   Closet
Multipurpose & dining
Balcony
Toilet   Sleeping rm.
Entrance hall   Bath

Type C
(72 units)
Area: 49.5 m²

Bath   Toilet
Entrance hall
Storage
Balcony
Multipurpose & dining
Sleeping rm.
Kitchen area   Sink   Wood Floor

Type D
(66 units)
Area: 56.2 m²

Closet
Entrance hall
Bath   Toilet
Sleeping rm.
Multipurpose & dining
Balcony
Kitchen area   Utility rm.   Western-style rm.

Figure 6-2.   Four Types of Residential Units

opposite side from the balcony, all units have a small kitchen. There is a Japanese-style bath, a toilet, a washstand with a large mirror, and space for a washing machine. Each unit has a three-hundred-liter (seventy-nine-gallon) hot water tank, operating on off-peak electrical power. The availability of hot water is far less prevalent in Japanese houses than in the United States, which in turn makes this an attractive feature of Fuji-no-Sato. Electric radiant heat is installed in the living room floor.

Emergency and safety measures are important characteristics of Fuji-no-Sato. Standards far exceed the existing regulations. As pointed out earlier, there are no regulations on retirement communities *per se*, and Fuji-no-Sato has adopted its own standards. For instance, the buildings are of fireproof construction. Because the whole peninsula is known for earthquakes, buildings are also designed to resist tremors stronger than the great Kanto earthquake of 1923. There are no sprinklers, but a heat detector in each unit triggers an alarm in the administration building. Cooking is done with an electromagnetic plate, a safe invention used experimentally at this facility, which heats only the contacting surfaces of pots and pans and presents no fire hazard if accidentally left on. An emergency nurse call button is installed in every room, including the toilets and the baths. These buttons, connected to a warning system in the administration building, are tested every three months. Handrails are installed in the bath and toilet. All incoming calls from outside are received and transferred by a staff operator to the appropriate resident, but the residents can make outgoing calls directly from their telephones. Although having one's own phone is not inexpensive in Japan, under this system, at least residents need not pay for installation, maintenance, and other miscellaneous fees, but only for the calls they make. All calls within the community system are free, and many residents took extensive advantage of this privilege. A third advantage of the system is that the staff takes incoming messages for absent residents.

Units are sold unfurnished. Residents have to bring all their own furniture and appliances except for the cooking plates. In gerontology, it is often argued that familiar furniture and other personal things may soften relocation stress and facilitate adaptation to a new environment, but most residents buy new goods rather than use their old familiar ones. Both practical and cultural explanations can be given for this. Practically, old appliances may be worn out, and old furniture may not fit into the new small space. Culturally, the Japanese tend not to change residence unless their job demands it or unless they acquire a brand-new house. It is not unusual to start one's life at a new place with new furniture and appliances. The residents apparently felt little need for continuity of atmosphere in their quarters, but this itself cannot be taken as a sign of emotional independence.

Although the residents complained of the lack of space in their units, many of them made their rooms quite comfortable. Furniture was small and simple but generally of good quality and relatively expensive. More than half the residents used beds instead of Japanese *futon*. There was also a tendency to separate the kitchen from the living room with furniture or a curtain. Many widows had their deceased husband's photos either on the wall or on a table or dresser, usually with a small *butsudan*, or Buddhist altar. They would offer tea and rice to the altar every morning, and some of them also grew flowers to offer.

Although there is a dining hall and a hot spring bath at the community center, the residents could cook and bathe in their units if they wished to. Newspapers and milk were delivered at the doorstep by nearby stores upon request. However, mail was delivered to the community center, and the staff would sort it into residents' boxes, a strategy that brought residents to the community center frequently.

COMMUNITY CENTER

The community center is located in the middle of Fuji-no-Sato. The location has the symbolic meaning that this building should be the center of the residents' life, and to a great extent, this was true. As the stage of all indoor group activities, the center has five large activity rooms: a craft room for wood-block printing and wood carving groups; a room called the "salon" for singing, record concerts, discussions, knitting, and various Christian meetings; two Japanese *tatami* rooms for traditional Japanese singing and music, Japanese chess, and tea ceremony; and a larger "meeting room" that can seat eighty to ninety people at one time and was used by groups with large memberships. The general meetings of the residents association, meetings between management and residents, and funeral ceremonies were held in the meeting room. The schedule for the use of these rooms was kept by the staff and posted on a blackboard at the center.

The hot spring bath was sexually segregated, and the women's section was the larger, reflecting the community's sex ratio. Thirty men and forty-five women could use the baths at a time. They were open from 3 P.M. to 9 P.M., with the peak use at around 6 P.M. It was rare that more than a dozen people bathed here at a given time. Most residents had their favorite bathing time, usually either before or after dinner. Hot spring water, piped in from a nearby well, is extremely salty; but it is said to be good for arthritis, rheumatism, skin diseases, and gynecological disorders. Although residents' opinions as to the healing effectiveness of bathing varied, all agreed that it relaxed and warmed them, especially in winter. Along with the dining hall, the hot spring baths were settings for the exchange of news and gossip and were the most important settings for social interaction.

The community center also had four guest rooms for families and friends of residents and for other visitors, including prospective residents, who were encouraged to experience a taste of Fuji-no-Sato before making a final decision. Next to the guest room section there was a small room where barber and beauty parlor services were offered once every two weeks; and there was also a laundry room with one washing machine and one dryer.

There was a shop in the community center, run by the management, that sold bathroom tissue, toothpaste, detergent, cooking seasonings, and other assorted nonperishables, including soil and fertilizer for gardening. In a corner of the shop was a small office where two or three staff worked. This office was open for small daily needs of the residents, whereas the main office at the administration building handled other paperwork. The residents reported to the small office for various maintenance problems in their units, made requests for room cleaning, and made reservations for guest rooms and for meals at the dining hall. A local bank provided service there three times a week.

There is a porch in front of the main entrance of the center where the shopping shuttle bus was parked. Three times a day, once in the morning and twice in the afternoon, the bus made its one-hour trip. It was also at this porch that the staff sold fresh produce to the residents every Tuesday and Friday. Because the vegetables and fruits were both fresher and cheaper here than at the local stores, the sale was very popular. Many residents would come out early, wait ten to fifteen minutes, then pounce on the best items when the sale opened. It was a slightly frantic scene, reminiscent of a bargain sale at a department store, and some residents were disgusted by it. A local bakery also brought freshly baked breads and pastries to sell at this twice-a-week event.

A couple of bulletin boards, one for administrative notices and one for the residents association, adorned the wall between the main entrance and the shop. The staff would post announcements such as the names of new residents, funeral schedules, and other service-related messages. The minutes of the monthly executive meeting of the residents association and other important association news, such as negotiations with the management on various issues, were regularly posted on the other board. Although the two boards were equal in size, there was a clear contrast in that the administration's board was generally crowded with messages, and the other one was sparsely used. The office bulletin board was one of the two effective means of communication from the management and figured importantly in Kinoshita's research. The other communication channel was the public address system. Each residential unit had a loudspeaker, and the staff at the administration building would announce important news, such as changes in the hours of the clinic, cancellations of the shuttle bus, or temporary breakdowns of the hot spring bath, over the public address system. This may seem intrusive to Americans, but the public address system is a common method of communication in Japanese neighborhoods, and people were used to it.

As many as two hundred people can eat at one time in the cafeteria-style dining hall on the second floor. However, far fewer than this were present at any given mealtime. The hall was open one hour for breakfast (7:30 A.M.–8:30 A.M.) and one and a half hours for lunch and dinner (noon–1:30 P.M. and 5 P.M.–6:30 P.M.), and the residents tended to leave the hall when they had finished their meals, seldom staying the full period. It is not a Japanese habit to make ordinary mealtimes into social events, as in French or American cultures. Despite this, the dining hall was an important place for the residents to meet one another; if they did not use the dining hall and the hot spring bath, they simply lost some of the limited opportunities to meet other residents and make conversation. A lounge at one end of the dining hall would appear to have made an ideal meeting place because it had several couches, a T.V. set, and newspapers; but only a handful of residents spent time there either before or after meals. Moreover, even though Fuji-no-Sato had full occupancy, not all the residents lived there full-time. Of the permanent residents, a significant number preferred cooking in their own units to using the dining hall.

The residents were required to make reservations for meals at least one day in advance and to purchase coupons, which they dropped in a box when they received their trays. Regular users did not have to make daily reservations, although they were required to pay for the meals they missed unless they had canceled their standing reservation. Some disoriented residents, who often forgot whether or not they had eaten, were excluded from this practice and dealt with tolerantly.

Weekly menus were posted in the dining hall, and anonymous comments on the food were invited via a box provided by the residents association. Comments, more often negative than positive, were summarized in a posting on the association's bulletin board. The association also used the comments to negotiate changes with the director and the head staff of the dining section.

Special foods were prepared on traditional occasions, and these were very popular. On such occasions, dining hall patronage would swell significantly.

ADMINISTRATION

The administration building stands next to the community clinic. Here administrative staff do the paperwork for the community, operate the telephone exchange, manage the various warning systems, and so on. During the night, a male security guard is on duty here.

This is the information center of Fuji-no-Sato. On one wall are three important data boards indicating the daily location of each resident. The "residence" board carries name plates of all the residents, arranged by unit number. Black name plates indicate that a resident is in the community, red ones that he or she is absent. The night guard would arrange the name plates on this board every morning before he left, using the information on the twenty-four-hour warning system.

The second data board is the "hospitalization" board. Here the names of the residents currently hospitalized, either at the community clinic or at outside hospitals, are listed. The third is the "absence board," which lists the names of the residents away from the community for several days or longer. Residents are encouraged to report where they are going and for how long and to leave telephone numbers where they can be reached in an emergency.

Fuji-no-Sato has a very advanced twenty-four-hour technological warning and safety monitoring system, divided into two parts. One part controls the fully automatic building safety warning system, such as heat detectors, machine room, gauges, and so on. The other part is the residential safety system. This device has three main functions. First, it registers residents' nurse calls. On receiving a nurse call, the staff quickly telephone the resident to verify the problem. If the call verifies an emergency or if there is no answer after five or six rings, the staff then calls the clinic to send a nurse to the distressed unit. During the night, this device and a twin device at the clinic are connected, so both the night guard and the duty nurse at the clinic can respond.

The second function of the resident safety unit is the twenty-four-hour warning. When the residents do not leave their units during a twenty-four-hour period, that is, when they do not lock the front door of the unit from outside during this period, a blinking light goes on automatically in the administration building. This alerts the staff to call the resident in that unit to make sure he or she is all right. If the resident is not feeling well or has physical problems, the staff can call the nursing station at the clinic. However, when the resident cannot be reached, things can become rather complicated because the staff must locate the resident and confirm his or her safety. Usually, one of the staff at the administration building would visit the resident's unit, but before that, staff would often call the branch office at the community center to ask if the person had been seen that day. This generally worked because most residents would visit the shop or other parts of the community center during the day. If these measures failed, the search would continue until a staff member confirmed that the resident was all right. Because the twenty-four-hour warning system was regarded as nonemergency by both the staff and the residents, and in most cases the alarms were false, particularly on rainy days, the staff's reaction was routine. They were aware of the habitual repeaters, the residents who often did not lock their doors when they left their units. However, when one of the more conscientious units was involved, the staff responded quickly.

The twenty-four-hour warning system is important because it works as a preventive measure; possible health crises are checked in their early stages by this system. In most cases—other than false alarms, of course—when the residents do not leave their units for one full day, they are very likely not feeling well and not eating properly but do not think they are sick enough to push the emergency button. Detecting this kind of situation through the alarm system, clinic staff can evaluate the seriousness of an illness, give proper advice, and follow the ill resident's condition.

There was one case in which a resident's life was actually saved by the twenty-four-hour warning system during Kinoshita's research. At 11:30 A.M., December 8, the twenty-four-hour alarm flashed, indicating the unit of Mrs. Kaneda, a seventy-five-year-old widow. Because she was one of the false alarm repeaters, a male staff member said, "Oh, it's Mrs. Kaneda. Again!" But a woman staff member quickly called her unit. There was no answer. She then called the office at the community center to ask whether Mrs. Kaneda had been seen there or whether she had had breakfast in the dining hall (which could be easily checked by going through the meal coupons). The answer was no; no one had seen her that morning, and she had not eaten breakfast in the hall. After this, the staff woman went to Mrs. Kaneda's unit herself and found that, although she could hear a sound from the T.V. set, the door was locked from inside, and Mrs. Kaneda did not answer. Feeling that this might be an emergency, she rushed back to the office, got the master key, and returned to the unit. When she opened the door, she saw Mrs. Kaneda lying in her living room with her eyes half open, unable to speak. Using Mrs. Kaneda's phone, the staff person called the nursing station at the clinic. The head nurse and the physician came and checked Mrs. Kaneda's blood pressure. Mrs. Kaneda had apparently had a massive stroke. A later examination of

her room suggested that she may have had it sometime late the previous night.

Mrs. Kaneda was quickly hospitalized at the clinic, and her children were called in the belief that she might die. Although her life
was saved and she later regained her consciousness, she was severely paralyzed and now survives on intravenous nutrition.

The third function of the twenty-four-hour warning system is to
tell the staff instantly whether a given resident is in his or her unit
any time of day. A green light by each unit number of the device
stays on when the unit is locked from the inside, but it goes off
when the door is locked from the outside. Thus, by looking at the
bank of lights, the staff can tell who is home without visiting their
unit. Every night at 10 P.M., the night guard records the presence/
absence of residents in all units by this method. Because night
comes early at Fuji-no-Sato, 10 P.M. is fairly late. The night guard
checks this again at 7 A.M. the following morning to see whether
any resident has come back after 10 P.M., and rearranges the residence board accordingly before he leaves at 9 A.M.

The residents were quite aware of the role of the administration
building as an information center and took advantage of it. When
one called another and got no answer, he would call the office to
find out whether the fellow resident was temporarily out of the unit
or away from the community for some days.

HEALTH CARE

In 1983, Fuji-no-Sato had a clinic with eighteen beds, the largest
retirement community facility in Japan at the time. In addition to
acute care, the clinic also provided a service that was then rare
for retirement communities: twenty-four-hour nursing care. Since
1983, there has been a dramatic improvement in the level of services
provided at Fuji-no-Sato and at newer communities built by the
managing company. Before we describe these, let us look at the
health care system in operation at the time of the study.

Japanese law defines a clinic as a medical facility that has at least
one full-time physician and fewer than twenty beds. A hospital is a
medical facility with at least three full-time physicians and more
than twenty beds. Thus, the medical facility at Fuji-no-Sato was
clearly designed to fall within the legal definition of a clinic.

The clinic was on the ground level of a two-story building, the second floor being taken up by several apartments for single staff. Besides the eight inpatient rooms, ranging in size from a private room to a couple of four-bed wards, the clinic had a waiting room, a small laboratory in which blood and urine samples were tested, a treatment room, a physician's office, a nursing station, a special bathing room for bed-ridden patients, an X-ray room (including a CT scanner), a laundry room with heavy-duty equipment, and a small room for short-term keeping of a corpse. Most of the equipment was very sophisticated. The clinic was also unusual in having its own ambulance. Few small clinics offer this because it is a somewhat overregulated service in Japan.

A seventy-two-year-old woman was the full-time physician at the clinic. She had retired from her private practice in internal medicine, but was hired by Fuji-no-Sato in 1981 as its fourth physician. (Major problems at the clinic, such as hiring physicians, are discussed in Chapter 8.) She was on duty from Monday to Friday and lived in the community on weekdays, but she returned to her home during weekends. On the first and third Saturdays of each month, a geriatric cardiovascular specialist would come to the clinic from another city. On other Saturdays, a part-time physician, a man in his mid seventies, would come in from the neighborhood. He was also a retired physician, a former president of a large public hospital, and he was also on call in emergencies when the full-time physician was not available. No physician was on duty on Sundays.

The outpatient service was open only in the mornings; in the afternoons, the physician made her rounds of inpatients and visited the *toku-yō* home. Although the clinic was open for people in the neighborhood, outpatients were mostly residents of the community. On average, twenty-three residents visited the clinic each morning.

The health care program for the residents had two features: intensive checkups for all residents once a year and monthly physician consultations. Nearly all permanent residents, and even some not yet living at the community, appeared for their annual checkup; but the monthly visit schedule was poorly attended because the residents could visit the clinic whenever they liked. The majority of residents had at least one chronic illness; because Japanese law required them to wait two weeks between prescription refills, in most cases, the residents visited the clinic regularly every two weeks, at which time their blood pressure was measured.

Due to the well-developed medical insurance system for those over seventy, residents' out-of-pocket payments for both outpatient and inpatient services are very small. In 1983, new restrictions were placed on reimbursement for hospitals with more than 60 percent aged inpatients, but these restrictions do not apply to clinics.

In deciding to build a maximum scale, combined inpatient-outpatient clinic, which could also double as a long-term care facility, the management hoped to capitalize on the government-supported medical insurance system, which reimburses clinic services well. Partly for this reason and partly out of their lack of knowledge about the care needs of the elderly, the management considered the eighteen beds, plus twenty-four-hour nursing care, adequate for all the health care needs of its residents—ambulatory, acute, and long-term. After four years of operation, however, it became obvious that the mixture of the "cure" and "care" functions of the clinic was problematic. Nearly all beds were constantly occupied by residents who were either in recovery or chronically physically dependent and/or disoriented. The problem was typified by the need to control disoriented inpatients who roamed the clinic day and night. Subsequently, the management became aware of the need to prepare for cutbacks in the medical insurance system for the elderly. They decided to build a nonpublic nursing home, called the Care Center, in the community for the residents of Fuji-no-Sato. It was completed in 1984.

One of the most important changes at Fuji-no-Sato and subsequent life-care facilities since our ethnographic research has been a far greater commitment to managing an increasingly frail resident population. The sister facilities all have larger clinics and skilled nursing capacity. All of them, including Fuji-no-Sato, now also operate an array of supportive services designed to promote independence among the chronically ill and disabled.

In 1992, the staff at Fuji-no-Sato is organized into six departments, roughly corresponding to six levels of care: general, residential, personal, nursing, medical, and terminal. The general care function has already been described. It is the system whereby staff keep track of relatively healthy residents and attend to their daily needs, both health care and otherwise. Residential care refers to services designed to help slightly impaired residents function in their own units. In this category falls housekeeping help and the close monitoring of levels of well-being so that health problems (and coping problems for the anxious or disoriented residents) can be detected early and their consequences minimized. For example, there is now on duty at the dining room during all meals a staff person whose dual function is to help frail residents get their meals (by carrying trays, etc.) and keep track of which of the regular diners are absent, so that their whereabouts and condition can be quickly learned. If residents are absent, this person will go to their apartment and take appropriate action (deliver their food, refer them to the clinic for medical help, or call a nurse from the clinic to evaluate them at home). Staff is also available to run errands for housebound residents and help them with chores that are beyond their or their spouse's capacity.

Personal care refers to the next highest level of health support, to help with bathing, dressing, eating, managing medicines and accounts, and so on. Staff members sometimes take disabled residents to and from the dining room or the hot spring bath and help them there if they don't want to be cared for strictly in their own apartments. The decision as to what kind of help is appropriate is made in close consultation between the staff and the residents.

Much of the work at these two levels—residential and personal—is done by staff referred to as "helpers." These people, some of them housewives, are usually college educated, and many have considerable backgrounds in social work. They are paid on a level with nurses and are treated as professionals on about the same level. One of the problems faced by the administration at Fuji-no-Sato is how to allocate work between the helpers and the nurses because (as it turns out) most of the work traditionally done by nurses in an institutional setting does not actually require special medical training, but can be done by anyone with some appropriate experience.

In 1988, the Ministry of Health and Welfare passed a new law providing for the professional certification of nonnurse aides of this kind. Helpers with four years of college can take the new national examination for licensure as a social welfare worker (*shakai fuku-shishi*). Those with two years can apply for a credential as a custodial welfare worker (*kaigo fukushishi*).

Nursing care is available not only at the skilled nursing facility on the premises, but in the private units as well. Nurses make rounds of the residents who need regular services and visit other residents on an emergency basis if they cannot come to the clinic. The medical level of care is provided at the clinic, both outpatient and inpatient, and at the skilled nursing facility. Terminal care, resembling hospice treatment in the West, is provided at the nursing facility and in the residential units.

The gerontologist will recognize this as the "continuum of care" model, now gaining popularity in many Western settings. Its effective operation is based on careful tracking of each frail resident's day-to-day level of functioning and preparing a care plan that maximizes his or her autonomy. This system uses a previously untapped potential of retirement housing, a potential more difficult to develop in traditional settings: the availability of a wide range of services under one integrated management system. Residents can be moved from one level of care to another with relative ease because the personnel at each level are familiar with one another and often with the client as well.

But making the most of this potential takes experience and careful planning. At Fuji-no-Sato, a team approach to case management has gradually evolved to complement the six-level, six-department system we've described. Each case is discussed, evaluated, and planned by a team of six to seven professionals representing different skill levels and different areas of expertise. The management tries to assemble case teams that are efficient and knowledgeable without being rigid or insensitive to the individual resident's feelings. The level of success tends to vary according to the personalities of workers and residents, but on the whole, the system seems to work well. It is being studied and imitated by newer life-care facilities throughout Japan.

THE OPERATING SYSTEM

To briefly recapitulate our description of retirement communities in Chapter 1, Fuji-no-Sato is a life-care community, a type we defined as one whose contract provides not only residential accommodations specifically designed for the needs of the elderly but also skilled nursing care for physically or mentally dependent residents.

We also pointed out that, due to a lack of standards, there is great variation throughout the retirement housing industry in the terms of entrance contracts and the type and extent of services. This variability complicates the discussion even of life-care plans, let alone of retirement communities as a whole. But despite the somewhat chaotic situation in the industry, not only have the details of Fuji-no-Sato's health care system been copied widely throughout the silver business; their style of contract and overall operating system also has. This is undoubtedly due largely to the financial success and overall quality of services at Fuji-no-Sato and its sister communities.

The ownership of the property at Fuji-no-Sato resides with the management, not with the residents themselves. The residents purchase, as it were, the right to live in the community throughout their lifetime and the right to receive the promised care and services. In theoretical discussions of the rights of residents, the management uses the term "social property," which is meant to indicate that Fuji-no-Sato combines features traditionally assigned to individual and to governmental property. The notion symbolizes the philosophy that the private nonprofit sector should play a greater role in the area of services to the aged, stepping in where neither the family system nor the public bureaucracy can respond adequately.

There are restrictions on age and health status for membership in the community. One must be sixty years old or older (for a married couple, either husband or wife must meet this requirement) and must be able to care for oneself and live independently. However, no physician's examination is necessary; lay staff at the head office in Tokyo makes judgments after interviews with the applicants.

The application requirements and entrance fees are based on the expected length of an average resident's life and his or her projected care needs. However, the operating system and fiscal management scheme are also based on the premise that residents will help each other, an assumption that lowers the entrance fee. In this nonprofit facility, all fees are assigned to specific budget lines to minimize ambiguity.

After our research, the managing organization began to rely more on interviews with the prospective residents in order to assure that they understood the operating system before deciding to move in and to assure that they were not being unduly influenced by the attitudes of family members. Applicants are encouraged to spend some days in the community before making a final commitment.

There are two types of fees: an entrance fee and a monthly fee. Upon signing the entrance contract, the resident pays the entrance fee, which varies according to the size of the unit and the number of occupants. As of 1983, the entrance fees ranged from a low of $100,964 for a type A unit (single occupancy) up to $201,186 for a type D unit with two people. The corresponding March 1991 fees were $184,667 for the type A and $363,037 for the type D for two. For simplicity's sake, all these figures are at the March 1991 exchange rate of 135 yen per dollar. The entrance fee covers, among other things, the cost of land acquisition, construction, depreciation, various taxes, overall maintenance of the facility, and the long-term care fee, which was $22,222 per person in 1983. The long-term care fee is calculated to cover all future care costs of the average resident as his or her dependency increases, thereby avoiding the need for additional payments for any services. The management estimated that the average length of stay at Fuji-no-Sato would be fifteen years. The entrance fee is partially refunded, pro-rated by the length of stay, if the contract is terminated within ten years by the resident or by his or her death.

The monthly fee in 1983 (again using 135 yen per dollar) was $215 for single occupants and $348 for double occupants, regardless of the size of the unit. By March 1991, these figures had risen to $280 for singles and $447 for doubles. The annual operating cost, more than half of which goes to staff salaries (excluding personal and health care personnel), is covered by the monthly fee. Even though the contract states that the monthly fee may be raised or at least reexamined once every two years in accordance with general price increases, the success of Fuji-no-Sato made it possible for the management to hold to the original fees set by negotiations between the management and representatives of the residents association in 1983 until new negotiations in 1989. (The 1983 negotiations are described in Chapter 9.)

The monthly fee, however, does not include utilities (electricity, water, telephone) or meals. According to the information brochure published by Fuji-no-Sato, the average total expense per month in 1983, including the monthly fee, was $638 for a single occupant and $1,212 for a couple (135 yen per dollar). As of March 1991, these figures were $743 for a single occupant and $1,312 for a couple. These amounts do not include such expenses as clothes, leisure activities, or transportation.

Is it expensive to live at Fuji-no-Sato? This is an extremely sensitive question for the management, whose aim has been to provide services for average elderly people. We have mentioned that the community has been widely covered in the mass media, which have consistently reinforced the image of Fuji-no-Sato as a deluxe place for the wealthy elderly, much to the disappointment of its builders. As far as monthly living expenses are concerned, it does not seem to be particularly expensive. The main debate is whether or not the entrance fee is beyond the reach of most people. In black and white, the figures do look high. But the issue should be judged from the viewpoint of the average person's alternatives in preparing for safety and security in old age and the costs of those alternatives. Then there is the matter of the competition. In spite of the relatively high staffing and quality of care at Fuji-no-Sato, the fees are significantly lower than those of many life-care communities of comparable size as of March 1991.

The value of home ownership in Japan, particularly in the greater Tokyo area, is relevant in this regard. The vast majority of the residents came from the Tokyo area, and many sold their homes to move to Fuji-no-Sato.

The case of Mr. and Mrs. Shirase is a good example of the strategic value of selling a house. Mr. Shirase, seventy, is a retired journalist. After graduating from an elite university, he worked for a large newspaper as a journalist for thirteen years. Then he became a free-lance journalist, writing on politics and social issues. He also made money translating books into Japanese. He perceived his income as somewhat precarious, particularly because in Japan one's financial security and social status are largely determined by the company one works for. After he reached sixty, Mr. Shirase recalls, it was getting harder to earn a living, and he began to worry about his old age. Mrs. Shirase, sixty-six, is a housewife who never worked after marriage. They have no children and never thought of adoption.

Shortly after World War II, the Shirases managed to buy land in a suburb of Tokyo, on which they eventually built a modest house. Soon the postwar reconstruction began, and the price of land in the metropolitan area literally skyrocketed. The former farmland around their house is now an upper-middle-class suburb, and their investment in property obviously turned out to be a lucky one.

The Shirases had modest savings for their old age. However, because Mr. Shirase was self-employed, he got no retirement bonus or pension. He and his wife have a small national pension. When his wife saw an advertisement for Fuji-no-Sato, they discussed it and agreed without much argument to sell the house and move there. It was apparent that if they continued living in their house, their financial woes would get worse as they grew older.

Although Mr. Shirase did not disclose the sale price of their house and land, they were able not only to pay the entrance fee for a type D unit but also to purchase a small one-bedroom condominium in Tokyo, which they rent out, and still keep a comfortable amount in savings. Both Mr. and Mrs. Shirase said that financially they felt more secure than ever and agreed that without selling the house, this could not have been possible.

Of course, it could have been a completely different story if the Shirases had a child, as most Japanese elderly do, and wished to leave the house to the child.

7

The Residents

As of October 1, 1982, 372 residents occupied 281 units at Fuji-no-Sato. There were 134 men (36 percent) and 238 women (64 percent). Although the management tried to maintain a ratio of at least 40 percent men, their actual percentage has been less than this since the second year of the community. This is a "young-old" population. In 1982, the age range was from 51 (a wife whose husband was over 60) to 96 years; the men's mean age was 72.2, the women's 68.8, and the overall 70.0, about four years older than in the community's first year.

Table 7–1 shows the family status and occupancy patterns of the two hundred eighty-one residential units. Eighty-three units (29.5 percent) held married couples; seventy-four units (26.3 percent) widows; thirty-nine units (13.9 percent) never-married women; and twenty-one units (7.5 percent) widowers. Thirteen units (4.6 percent) were occupied by divorced women, eight units (2.5 percent) by divorced men, and four units (1.4 percent) by never-married men. Thirty-one units (4.4 percent) had been signed for by married persons whose spouses had not yet signed.

Of the remaining eight units, four (1.4 percent) were occupied by mother-daughter pairs, two (0.7 percent) by sisters, and one by a married brother and his never-married sister. This last pair did not occupy the unit, but merely took possession of it in order to secure the right of one or the other to occupy it at some future time. In terms of family relationships, there was one pair of sisters who occupied two neighboring units and a trio of a brother and sisters who occupied two more. There was also one case of a never-married woman in one unit with her mother and sister next door.

Overall, one hundred ninety-eight residents (53.2 percent) were married; ninety-nine (26.6 percent) were widowed; fifty-two (14.0 percent) had never been married; and twenty-three (6.2 percent) were divorced. As one would expect, there were distinct gender differences in marital status. Three-quarters of the men were married,

Table 7-1. Family Status and Residential Patterns

Family Status	Units		Full-time		Part-time		Second Home Use		Total
					Residential Pattern				
Married couple	83	(29.5%)	55	(66.3%)	6	(7.2%)	22	(26.5%)	83 (100%)
Widow	74	(26.3%)	57	(77.0%)	3	(4.1%)	14	(18.9%)	74 (100%)
Never-married woman	39	(13.9%)	25	(64.1%)	4	(10.3%)	10	(25.6%)	39 (100%)
Widowers	21	(7.5%)	20	(95.2%)	0	(0.0%)	1	(4.8%)	21 (100%)
Divorced woman	13	(4.6%)	9	(69.2%)	2	(15.4%)	2	(15.4%)	13 (100%)
Divorced man	8	(2.5%)	8	(100.0%)	0	(0.0%)	0	(0.0%)	8 (100%)
Married man	17	(6.4%)	2	(11.8%)	1	(5.9%)	14	(82.3%)	17 (100%)
Married woman	14	(5.0%)	1	(7.1%)	3	(21.4%)	10	(71.5%)	14 (100%)
Never-married man	4	(1.4%)	2	(50.0%)	1	(25.0%)	1	(25.0%)	4 (100%)
Mother-daughter	4	(1.4%)	4	(100.0%)	0	(0.0%)	0	(0.0%)	4 (100%)
Sister	2	(0.7%)	2	(100.0%)	0	(0.0%)	0	(0.0%)	2 (100%)
Friend (woman)	1	(0.4%)	0	(0.0%)	1	(100.0%)	0	(0.0%)	1 (100%)
Married brother and never-married sister	1	(0.4%)	0	(0.0%)	0	(0.0%)	1	(100.0%)	1 (100%)
Total	281	(100.0%)	185	(65.8%)	21	(7.5%)	75	(26.7%)	

and 16 percent were widowed. There were only four never-married and eight divorced men. In sharp contrast, 41 percent of the women were married; 33 percent were widowed; and 20 percent had never married (forty-eight people). There were fifteen divorced women in the community.

To some extent, the unusually large number of never-married women (as well as 10 percent of the widowhood) results from the loss of men, and the sheer social disruption, of World War II. Asked why she never married, one sixty-four-year-old former public employee said, "I was once engaged, but before we were married he was drafted into the army and sent to the Malay Peninsula. Then he was killed there. After the war was over, I once took part in a matchmaking (*omiai*). Not that I wanted to marry, but people around me were concerned about my future, and I felt obliged to accept the *omiai* at least once, so as not to disappoint them."

A sixty-six-year-old former kindergarten principal said,

> There was a time when I thought I might want to marry, in my twenties. When we were young, men were getting to be in short supply, and our parents started pressuring us to find one. Many of my friends gave in to their parents' urging to marry military men, or men soon to be drafted. But so many of them had only a short married life, and then their husbands were killed. What was left after the war was the parents-in-law, and the confusion. One of my friends married three times in ten years; her first husband was drafted after one week of marriage and killed. The second was also drafted and died in China of some illness. The third one was a much older man, so she had to take care of him for many years. Looking back now, it was such a difficult time for me to decide which way I should go.

However, personal illness was also a frequent reason for remaining single. Tuberculosis victims were especially vulnerable because that illness carried great stigma in the days when these women were young. A sixty-seven-year-old primary school teacher said, "The biggest reason [not to marry] for me was that I was not very healthy. I had the problem of tuberculosis, so I gave up the possibility of marrying. Also, there weren't many young men in those days, because of the war. If I had not been a teacher, I might have married someone, but my job gave me economic independence. Now, I think it was just my fate."

The ways the residents used their new homes also varied considerably. Occupancy patterns are listed in Table 7–1 according to full-time, part-time, and second home use. Part-time residents live in the community at least one-third of an average month. Second home users visit their units only occasionally for short periods. Two-thirds of the units were occupied by full-time residents; about a quarter (26.7 percent) were used as second homes; and 7.5 percent were part-time homes. Due to the large number of part-time and occasional residents, the average population of Fuji-no-Sato was in the 230–250 range, not the full complement of 372. Full-time residents accounted for 66.3 percent of the married couples, 77.0 percent of the widows, and 64.1 percent of the never-married women. This was also the predominant pattern among widowers and divorced men and women.

This residential pattern shows that Fuji-no-Sato is not simply a final residence for the elderly, but plays a complex role in creating options for people who can afford some luxuries. The part-time and occasional residents had obtained the right to live in Fuji-no-Sato and to receive long-term care there, thus preparing for the worst; but they had the means to live elsewhere when they so chose. For example, even among those who had sold their houses to pay the entrance fee, there was a tendency to own small condominiums in the Tokyo area. Many part-timers, especially the never married, were relatively young and still working. The second home or vacation home use pattern clearly served many people as a gradual transition to full-time residence in the community. This is important because, as we discuss in Chapter 11, the community did not have effective socialization structures. A gradual transition may have improved some people's eventual adjustment. However, the large number of non-full-time residents may have weakened social cohesion in the community.

Important information about residence choices and life-styles is also gleaned by looking at residents' parental statuses. The fifty-two never-married men and women had no children. Counting each married couple as one parental unit along with widows, widowers, and the divorced, there were eighty-four additional cases of childlessness, one hundred twenty-six (53.2 percent) cases of natural parenthood, and seventeen (7.2 percent) cases of adoptive parenthood. The facts are not known about ten (4.2 percent) cases, most of whom were divorcees who did not answer.

Fuji-no-Sato clearly had an overrepresentation of the childless, over one-third of the cases falling into this category. Of one hundred twenty-six parental pairs, eighty-four (66.6 percent) had at least one son; thirty-eight (30.2 percent) had only daughters; and in four cases (3.2 percent), we did not ascertain the sex of the child(ren).

The traditional *dōkyo* arrangement is a *total* support mechanism for the aged parents in which the financial, social, practical, and emotional needs of the aged are to be met in one family setting. Tradition prescribes that males financially support their dependent parents in the following order: eldest son, younger son, husband of the eldest daughter, husband of a younger daughter, adopted son. Physical care and emotional support fall to the women, so in the absence of a wife, an aged person is usually cared for by either the wife of the responsible male descendant or an unmarried daughter.

Despite social changes and the official abolishment of the family
(*ie*) system, this rule remains an important frame of reference. This
system can involve a great burden for the supporting children, so
great in fact that it is believed that only one's own children should
bear it. The burden is balanced in theory by a reciprocal obligation
of equal weight: the parental responsibility for bringing up the children. Many residents of Fuji-no-Sato appeared to be greatly disadvantaged, lacking children as a resource for old age security. We
have seen that only 30 percent of the units had a son; only 45 percent had any children at all. However, it has become increasingly
difficult for the elderly to practice the traditional pattern even if
they have natural sons and even more difficult when they have only
daughters or adopted sons because no clear new norms of filial support have been established. Childlessness, then, may actually be an
advantage—that is, having children may simply interfere with one's
freedom to sell one's property, usually a necessity for getting into
Fuji-no-Sato. We discuss this further in the last chapter.

SOCIOECONOMIC BACKGROUND

The level of education for both men and women at Fuji-no-Sato was
remarkably high, not only for their generation, but even by today's
standards. More than half the men (56.8 percent) were university
graduates, their degrees disproportionately from the elite handful
of imperial universities. An additional thirty-five men (26.1 percent) had finished various higher schools (about fifteen years of
schooling), another twelve (9.0 percent) had finished middle school
(about eleven years of schooling), and only six (4.5 percent) had the
compulsory six years of primary school alone. We did not ascertain
the education of five of the men. The men were educated under the
old imperial Japanese educational system where the opportunity
for higher education was limited to a tiny portion of young people.
Roughly speaking, the higher schools (fifteen years of schooling)
were equivalent to today's university education (sixteen years) in
terms of social class. Of the men, then, 82.8 percent had university-
level or higher education by current standards. They represented
the elite of their generation as a whole.

The schooling of the women was also very high for their generation, especially because, under the old system, women had far less
educational opportunity than men. Among two hundred thirty-

Table 7-2.   Men's Occupations

Occupation	Number	
Business executive and high public official	50	(37.3%)
Manager in business and public office	27	(20.2%)
Self-employed business and public office	15	(11.2%)
Nonmanagerial worker	13	(9.7%)
University professor	9	(6.7%)
Doctor of medicine	4	(3.0%)
Teacher (high school and junior high)	4	(3.0%)
Professional writer	3	(2.2%)
Lawyer	2	(1.5%)
Christian minister, Buddhist priest	2	(1.5%)
Not known	5	(3.7%)
Total	134	(100.0%)

eight women, twenty-eight (11.8 percent) had graduated from *joshi daigaku*, or women's college (about fifteen years of schooling), and fifty-two (21.8 percent) from women's higher schools (about thirteen years of schooling). Another one hundred twenty-nine (54.2 percent) had been to girls' high schools (about eleven years of schooling), and fifteen (6.3 percent) had only the compulsory primary school. The education of fourteen women (5.9 percent) was not ascertained.

In their day, the girls' high schools amounted to the highest school for liberal arts, and only a small portion of specializing women had training beyond this level. The social significance of the girls' high schools under the old system was roughly equivalent to university education today. The fact that over half the women had girls' high school education and 33.6 percent had even more shows that, like the men, they were the intellectual elite of seniorhood.

Educational level is a strong prerequisite for a successful career in Japan—far more so than in the United States. The occupations of the residents reflected their higher educations. Table 7–2 shows the distribution of seven occupational categories among men, including those who were not full-time residents and still had jobs. Shown are the highest occupational positions attained. Of one hundred thirty-four men, fifty (37.3 percent) reached executive positions in private corporations (usually major ones) or the top ranks in gov-

Table 7-3.   Women's Occupations, by Marital Status

Occupation	Married		Widowed		Never Married		Divorced		Total	
Housewife	80	(82.4%)	52	(66.6%)	0	(0.0%)	0	(0.0%)	132	(55.5%)
Nonmanagerial worker or public employee	2	(2.1%)	7	(9.0%)	21	(43.6%)	3	(20.0%)	33	(13.9%)
Teacher (high school and primary school)	8	(8.2%)	7	(9.0%)	10	(20.8%)	2	(13.2%)	27	(11.3%)
Self-employed (stores, restaurants, etc.)	2	(2.1%)	10	(12.8%)	1	(2.1%)	4	(26.7%)	17	(7.1%)
No job	0	(0.0%)	0	(0.0%)	6	(12.5%)	4	(26.7%)	10	(4.2%)
Nursery school teacher	2	(2.1%)	1	(1.3%)	2	(4.2%)	1	(6.7%)	6	(2.5%)
University professor	0	(0.0%)	1	(1.3%)	3	(6.3%)	0	(0.0%)	4	(1.7%)
Managerial worker	0	(0.0%)	0	(0.0%)	3	(6.3%)	1	(6.7%)	4	(1.7%)
Doctor of medicine	0	(0.0%)	0	(0.0%)	2	(4.2%)	0	(0.0%)	2	(0.8%)
Other or not known	3	(3.1%)	0	(0.0%)	0	(0.0%)	0	(0.0%)	3	(1.3%)
Total	97	(100.0%)	78	(100.0%)	48	(100.0%)	15	(100.0%)	238	(100.0%)

ernment bureaucracies. Twenty-seven men (20.1 percent) rose to mid-level managerial positions in business or government. Fifteen (11.2 percent) were the self-employed owners of businesses (stores, restaurants, etc.). Only thirteen (9.7 percent) ended their careers without reaching managerial positions. There were nine men who had been university professors. Four had been physicians—three administrators of large hospitals and one in private practice. Another four had been teachers in high schools and junior high schools, three had been professional writers, and two had been clergymen (one Christian minister and one Buddhist priest). The occupational backgrounds of five men are not known.

Women's careers by marital status are shown in Table 7–3. A career other than "housewife" and "no job" means at least fifteen years of full-time work. Overall, of two hundred thirty-eight

women, one hundred thirty-two (55.5 percent) had been housewives, followed by thirty-three (13.9 percent) in nonmanagerial private or public sector positions, twenty-seven (11.3 percent) teachers
in high schools or primary schools, and seventeen (7.1 percent) self-
employed in businesses. Ten had not held jobs—never-married
women and divorcees able to live without working. Six women had
been teachers in nursery schools, of whom four had been the directors of their own schools. Four had been university professors, and
four had been in managerial positions in private corporations.
There were two retired physicians. Occupations of three women
were not ascertained.

Given the norms of this generation, it is not unexpected that of
ninety-seven married women at Fuji-no-Sato, eighty (82.4 percent)
had been full-time housewives, and only fourteen (14.5 percent) had
had careers. Nonmarried women, of course, were more likely to have
worked. Among seventy-eight widows, fifty-two (66.6 percent) had
been housewives, seven had been regular workers in companies and
bureaucracies, and seven had been teachers in primary and secondary
schools. Ten had been self-employed in business—those who had
taken over ownership of the family business after their husband's
death. One widow had been a nursery school teacher and one a university professor. Naturally, those widowed early in their lives came
to have careers, whereas most late widows did not.

Six of the forty-eight never-married women lived on inheri-
tances; the rest had had various careers. Twenty-one had worked
for businesses or government as regular workers, only three rising
to managerial positions. There was also a strong tendency toward
educational careers: Ten had been teachers in primary or secondary
school; three had been university professors; and two had been
nursery school teachers. Two had been physicians, and one had
been self-employed in business.

Because women at Fuji-no-Sato had very high levels of education
(there was no significant difference between the never-married
women and others in this respect), the occupations of the never-
married women represent what was possible even for the best educated women in their time. There was little chance for promotion
to managerial positions in private corporations or government for
women; many never-married women in the sample had worked as
mid- and lower-level staff. The career of physician was also rare for

women; but the field of education was one in which women could find job security and social recognition. Although women in private companies usually had to survive explicit or implicit pressure to leave, teachers rarely faced such pressures. For better educated women, then, education, although a difficult career to enter, was a more secure one.

Lastly, of fifteen divorcees, four had no occupational histories. Three had worked as regular staff in companies or bureaucracies; one had reached a managerial position. Three had been teachers in high, primary, or nursery school. The remaining four had been self-employed, all of them apartment owners and managers. All fifteen women were divorced relatively early in their lives, and some had had only a short marriage.

THE PROCESS OF MOVING IN

Among married couples, it was predominantly wives rather than husbands who had been active and enthusiastic about moving to the community. The wives gathered the necessary information, studied various retirement communities, and took their husbands to visit potential choices. The husbands, however, made the final decision and settled the contract with the management.

The great majority of the residents at Fuji-no-Sato came from the Tokyo metropolitan area, particularly from the middle- to upper-middle-class suburbs. Although those residents who did not have children had mostly been living by themselves, as one would expect, the *dōkyo* model was rare even among those with children, especially sons. There was a strong tendency for those with adopted sons to have come to Fuji-no-Sato directly from *dōkyo* arrangements, indicating that there must have been some family conflict.

A strong desire to control their own fate was an underlying theme in the residents' decisions to move to Fuji-no-Sato. This was most evident among childless couples, childless widows/widowers, the never-married and divorced residents, as well as those with daughters only. These residents did not have the traditional resource, namely sons, a fact many of them spontaneously mentioned, along with thoughts on the unreliability of daughters or the fact that they were alone. They were also keenly aware of what would happen in the future as they grew older and more physically frail. As we pointed out earlier, "support" in these people's eyes meant total support in the form of *dōkyo*. They did not feel they could depend on nephews or nieces who had their own aging parents or parents-in-law to support. Such relatives may have helped them when they became dependent, but their assistance would be partial and intermittent, not total and continuous, taking such forms as help in finding a place to live. Faced with this uncertain future, these residents had taken action while they were financially and physically independent in order to be secure in their old age.

Couples and single residents with sons emphasized that they came to Fuji-no-Sato to avoid becoming a burden on their children. A seventy-six-year-old widow with two sons said,

> We never lived with our sons' families. After my husband died, I lived by myself, and I enjoyed the freedom. But I had a health problem, so I worried about the future. So, on New Year's Day of 1980 I met with my sons to discuss it. I told them I was anxious after the illness, and said, "I want you two to decide who I might live with." There was a pause, and then before the older one said anything, the second son said he would be willing to do it. I asked the second son to talk to his wife about it, and a few days later he called and said that since their children were still small, his wife wasn't too keen on it. That helped me decide to come here. Disappointed? Well, frankly yes, a little bit. But not too much, because I could understand why his wife said no.

The husband of a married couple with two daughters said,

> We have only daughters. When the younger one got married, my wife and I chose this way [of living] because the daughters now have their own families and parents-in-law. It may not have been necessary for us to come here while we're both okay, but we decided to do it anyway, thinking about the situation where one of us dies. It's better to come together, rather than waiting until one of us is alone.

Some wives said that because they had had such a hard time taking care of their parents-in-law, they wanted by all means to avoid being a burden themselves. A seventy-five-year-old widow with four married sons said,

> I lived with my mother-in-law and served her for a long time. My father-in-law passed away in his early sixties. He was a quiet person,

and I don't have any bad memories about him. But my mother-in-law was a difficult person, for me at least, and on top of that she was demented for her last three years. She would stray from the house, and several times we had to go to the police station for help in finding her. I was literally worn out psychologically and physically, having to watch her every minute. The police warned me that I had the responsibility for her safety, and she used to cross streets without looking. So I decided I would never become a burden on my children like that, especially on my daughters-in-law.

Residents with good financial resources were especially emphatic about this because they could still leave substantial money or property to their children. Those who had purchased old age security at the expense of their children's inheritance were more ambivalent. They came to Fuji-no-Sato because, we believe, their personal values placed independence, and the lightening of their children's burden of caring, over a dependency bought with financial conscientiousness.

In general, then, residents had a variety of worries that "pushed" them to select retirement community living. But there was also a strong "pull" factor where Fuji-no-Sato was concerned. The location of the community was by far the leading reason for choosing it over others. Many residents were familiar with the peninsula and some with the immediate area around Fuji-no-Sato.

PART III

SOCIAL INTEGRATION

8

Management and Residents: Communication Failure

In earlier chapters, we have shown the process of social and demographic change affecting the elderly. We have followed the complex and often confusing path of the development of institutional living for senior citizens. Against this background, we are almost ready to move to our main task: the description and explanation of social life at Fuji-no-Sato. First, however, we must deal with one more aspect of the wider social context within which our subjects' lives unfold, an aspect of the new phenomenon of Japanese retirement housing that has not yet been well understood by the Japanese themselves: cultural beliefs and expectations about "welfare" as it applies to the care of the aged. A lack of clear concepts that can guide expectations—specifically, the expectations that management and residents have of one another—has caused serious friction.

Fuji-no-Sato is an example of what we earlier defined as a "life-care" retirement community—a facility that provides, through a type of entrance contract, both living units specifically designed for the needs of the elderly and skilled nursing care for the duration of the resident's life. The relationship between Fuji-no-Sato and its residents is determined to a large extent by the terms of this contract. We have pointed out that the meaning of the word "welfare" (*fukushi*) is changing for the Japanese, and it is understood differently by different sets of users. The fact that the builders of this community advocate something called "new welfare" for middle-income people on the face of it does not clarify the situation, nor does the use of a new piece of industry jargon, *keiyaku fukushi*, which means "contract welfare."

"Contract welfare" really has no exact standard meaning. Its important connotations are poorly understood by the Japanese in general and the residents of Fuji-no-Sato in particular. The words "contract" and "welfare" have specific social meanings of their own

121

for the Japanese, but when they are combined to make a new phrase, that phrase at first lacks a clear and widely held set of associations of its own. It is ambiguous and subject to a wide range of interpretations. This terminology problem turns out to be far from superficial.

Soon after he began fieldwork, Kinoshita was surprised to hear strong criticism, sometimes even openly hostile remarks, from many residents about the community's management—those in the head office in Tokyo and the local director of the community. He was told with a sense of anger, disappointment, and betrayal about avoidable problems and inconveniences residents had experienced in the community. The management was at first bewildered by this criticism. Certain senior staff in Tokyo and some local management people, including the director, looked on the more outspoken residents as too demanding. The management felt that their own good intentions and strenuous efforts were not understood or credited.

To some extent, this problem set the stage for much of the social life we shall soon be describing. We must begin, however, by analyzing the negative images held by the management and the residents of each other and the residents' uncooperative attitude, stemming from conflicting interpretations of "contract welfare."

THE RESIDENTS' PERSPECTIVE

In their relations with the management, the residents perceived four chronic problems having to do with the building design, the physicians, the director, and the "money-making management policy." These were seen as major problems by almost all the residents, although reactions varied from open agitation to silent resignation. Their collective perceptions that emerged around these problems reveal a good deal about what the residents had expected and what they emphatically had *not* expected from Fuji-no-Sato.

BUILDING DESIGN

There were two problems with the building structure: the noise of flushing toilets and the heat in the second floor units in summer. The drain pipes from the upstairs toilets run directly through the toilet room in the downstairs units. The pipes are visible, and when the upstairs residents flush the toilet, the noise is very obvious to the residents in the lower units when they are using their own bathrooms.

There appeared to be three reasons why the residents perceived the noise as a major problem. First, the level and type of noise was unfamiliar to most of them. Japanese are used to other intrusive sounds, such as traffic noise, but not to this kind of sound. Although some other types of congregate housing in Japan have this architectural feature, most of the residents came from more traditional-style private houses. Drain pipes are usually hidden in the walls in such traditional housing. Second, the residents disliked the noise because it offended their sense of cleanliness—it was the auditory analog of visible human waste. Third, the problem occurred frequently. The elderly tend to use the toilet often, even late at night, when one most expects quiet and when, indeed, there are no other human sounds.

There was virtually nothing that the management could do to reduce this noise, because remodeling would have been too expensive. After much complaint, the director finally asked the residents not to flush the toilets during the night, with the result that meetings were held in several buildings and decisions made not to flush between about 10 P.M. and 6 A.M. But this was not completely satisfactory.

As for the heat problem, the buildings were constructed without air spaces between the roofs and the ceilings, so the sun raised indoor temperatures very noticeably in summer, and rooms did not cool off even during the night. Of course, this was desirable in winter, but the combined heat and high humidity in summer was, for many upstairs residents, difficult to cope with. Some said that on the worst days, the temperature would stay in the mid-eighties (Fahrenheit) all night. As a result, most of the upstairs residents had air conditioners installed at their own expense.

The management acknowledged the heat problem as a serious one and began at once searching for a solution. In May 1983, after a year of study, the management tried having special equipment installed on the roofs. According to tests, this should have lowered the temperature several degrees, but the residents' reactions to the renovation during the following summer were mixed. Some said there had been a marked improvement; others saw little difference.

The one thing they all agreed on was that it was good to see management finally respond positively to their problem. In their opinion, the problem had been management's responsibility in the first place.

In fairness to the management, recall that the planner had tried to make this community cheap enough for the middle-income elderly, setting guidelines aimed at an entrance fee within the range of the typical retirement bonuses of middle-income workers. Although the entrance fee was raised three times in four years beginning in 1982, the initial entrance fee still roughly meets this guideline. Better quality construction probably would have made this impossible.

This background reason was not well understood by the residents, partly because management had not made much effort to explain it to them and partly because the inconvenience of the outcome was more personal, concrete, and persistent than the abstract notion of equity that led to it.

PROBLEMS IN THE CLINIC

Resident complaints related to the clinic were also of two kinds: the unavailability of the physician on Sundays and the general quality of medical help.

The residents saw a serious problem in the fact that no physician was on duty on Sundays. They expected that any medical emergency should be promptly handled, an expectation promoted by the sales brochure, which says, "A physician is always on duty in the community." A full-time physician was actually living in Fuji-no-Sato from Monday through Friday; and on Saturdays, either a cardiovascular specialist from a nearby hospital or a family physician from the neighborhood came. However, from Saturday afternoon to Sunday evening, there was no physician in the community. Starting in the spring of 1983, the neighborhood doctor agreed to be on call throughout the week, including Sunday, and there are also both community-based and city ambulance services for emergency transport to any of several hospitals within a thirty-minute drive. But because Fuji-no-Sato is relatively far from the center of the city, many residents were worried about the emergency response system.

The residents claimed false advertising. Their criticism on this issue stemmed from their perception that the claims of the sales brochure were not being honored. The entrance contract does not state anything about the availability of the physician, only that the management undertakes to provide sufficient health care for the residents. But many residents made up their minds to come to Fuji-no-Sato largely on the basis of the brochure. Only a minority actually examined the contract before making the decision, and many are unaware of its terms, even after they have signed it and moved in. The residents admitted that the brochure is not a contract, but they felt betrayed, partly because they saw no reason to question its details and partly for other reasons to be discussed shortly. It did not help matters when, early one Sunday morning, a resident had a heart attack and died before a doctor could get there—an incident that reinforced for them the importance of the discrepancy.

The problem of physician quality arose from the difficulty of hiring a reliable doctor. The first full-time doctor quit after only seven months, and the one on duty during this study was the fourth in less than four years. The first doctor was seventy-five years old and apparently could not stand the work load. The second was sixty-three years old when she was hired, but she resigned after a year when she learned of the harsh criticism that some residents had made of her work. The third physician died at sixty-four after having served for seven months. The fourth physician came to Fuji-no-Sato in September 1981 and was still serving, aged seventy-two, at the time of this study.

Gender and age appear to be the main reasons why many residents did not think the clinic's physicians were reliable. In Japan, women physicians, except perhaps for obstetricians, are still viewed as less reliable than men, and this view appears to be held more strongly by the elderly than by young people. Dr. Miura, the current doctor, was not only a woman, but she was over seventy, having been hired by Fuji-no-Sato after she retired from her private practice as a family doctor in a large city. Dr. Miki, the part-time physician, was also old (seventy-four at the time of the study) and also a retiree who was persuaded by the director, Mr. Baba, to work for Fuji-no-Sato. Dr. Miki had been the director of a large general hospital in northern Japan, and he and his wife had come to the Izu Peninsula to spend their retirement years in a mild climate.

Generally speaking, the residents of Fuji-no-Sato had received better than average medical care before they moved to the community, and they undoubtedly expected at least a similar level of care at the clinic. How they viewed the abilities of Drs. Miura and Miki could be seen in their reaction to Dr. Shimoda, a cardiovascular specialist. Dr. Shimoda would come to the clinic on the first and third Saturday of each month. In his mid-fifties, he was an authority in his field and the medical director of a large hospital. When Dr. Shimoda was on duty for three hours on Saturday mornings, an unmanageable number of residents would clamor for appointments. On average, the full-time Dr. Miura saw twenty-three outpatients a day, and the number dropped slightly when the part-time Dr. Miki came (second and fourth Saturdays). In contrast, at least fifty people were seen by Dr. Shimoda during each of his three-hour visits.

The competition to see Dr. Shimoda took place as follows: The order of appointments is determined on a first come, first served basis. Like any medical institution in Japan, the clinic issues a name card to each regular outpatient. This must be put into a box at the reception desk on each visit. Appointments follow the order in which the cards are deposited. This outpatient service is open between 9 A.M. and noon, and when Drs. Miura and Miki were on duty, residents came around 9 A.M. Dr. Shimoda was so popular, though, that residents began to come earlier and earlier, leaving their cards and going home until opening time. Finally, some were coming as early as 6 A.M.

According to some residents, the management was simply incompetent in hiring doctors, but this seemed to us unfair for two reasons. First, Fuji-no-Sato could not afford to pay more than an average doctor's salary, let alone enough to attract someone the residents would admire. It is nearly impossible to have a clinic of this size and type sustain itself economically, and the Fuji-no-Sato facility continuously operates at a loss. The second reason will be familiar to rural people throughout the world: The community is located in a remote resort area where few young doctors want to live and practice.

Meanwhile, many residents appeared to expect a level of care that is unrealistically high for a retirement community. The residents association demanded that the management get a physician in on Sundays and even that they build a kind of geriatric hospital—the kind that must have at least three full-time physicians and more than twenty beds. That the latter is totally unrealistic for Fuji-no-Sato was something nearly all the residents knew—including, of course, the officers of the association. The association, however, stuck to its demand.

Several explanations seem likely for this unrealistic attitude. One is the better than average medical care most residents seemed to have been accustomed to on entrance. Another is the high priority given health care among the many attractions of Fuji-no-Sato and the encouraging information on this point contained in the sales brochure. Still another explanation is that the move to the community had the unexpected and upsetting effect of making it *more* difficult for some to get certain types of medical care. For example, Drs. Miura and Miki practiced only internal medicine, and the residents had to commute to outside clinics and hospitals for other specialties such as ophthalmology and orthopedics (although there are two dental clinics in the immediate neighborhood). Commuting is laborious for such residents because public transportation in the area is not well developed; in the summer, they have to take very early trains to avoid the tourism congestion. This last seems to be the chief reason behind the demand for a geriatric hospital. Lastly, the residents were not fully aware that acute medical care and long-term care are different, and they tended to misplace their concerns about future care in their demand for a better and larger acute care facility. This misperception is an easy one to have in Japan because the shortage of nursing home beds there has resulted in the use of acute hospitals for long illnesses. The average length of stay of elderly patients in Japanese hospitals in 1983 was eighty-eight days, as compared with eleven days in America.

In addition to hiring Dr. Miki, the management eventually responded to the residents' demands by building a new thirty-bed long-term care facility of its own.

PROBLEMS CONCERNING THE DIRECTOR

The director and the physicians are the most important staff people at Fuji-no-Sato, and it is not surprising that the continuity and competence of the directorship was also a major issue between the residents and the management.

The directorship had lacked continuity since the opening of Fuji-no-Sato. The first director was incompetent and was fired after only six months. For about the next two years, there was no real on-site director, an executive board member in the Tokyo head office holding the title *in absentia*. During this period, a section chief from the central administration acted in the directorial capacity. This person, Mr. Baba, was eventually promoted to the permanent post.

Residents interpreted the absence of a director as a lack of interest in them on the part of the management, not only because of the position's importance but, more to the point, because this hiatus coincided with the period when the residents were pressing for solution of the other three problems.

The residents' evaluations of Mr. Baba as the director were mixed. He was forty-one years old during the study and had no previous experience in serving the elderly. In fact, he had worked as a salesman for the construction company that built Fuji-no-Sato before being hired by the management of the community.

Mr. Baba was an energetic person and enthusiastic about his work. "He's so energetic," residents often said. "He doesn't sit in the office all day. He leads the staff in their work. He is so versatile. He and the maintenance staff can fix all sorts of problems. They even built a nice barbecue grill in the yard." In addition, Mr. Baba was an excellent supervisor, particularly of the younger staff. He would spend a good deal of informal time with them, which in turn made it possible for him to mobilize manpower outside of regular tasks. When one task group had too much work, staff from another section would help, so that, for example, maintenance staff usually helped when unscheduled drivers or ambulance assistants were needed.

On the negative side, people said, "He is too young to be the director. He has no family and no university degree. He is too impatient to listen to us. He isn't making enough effort to understand our feelings. We would like to talk with him more. He's only concerned with making money from us, and he can't understand what 'welfare' is."

At forty-one years of age, Mr. Baba was divorced and had only a high school diploma. Although these attributes would not be serious drawbacks for an American director, they were important to the residents. Age and education are markers of both technical and moral ability in the Japanese worldview. The ideal image of a director is a male in his mid-fifties or early sixties, a family man with at least a bachelor's degree. These criteria, lacking in Mr. Baba, would have indicated a mature man able to understand the residents' thoughts and feelings.

Maturity in this context means the ability to perceive nuances, to understand both what is said and what is left unsaid. The expression *rōjin no kimochi no wakaru hito*—a person who can understand what old people feel—was repeatedly raised by residents when they talked about Mr. Baba. *Kimochi,* usually translated "feeling," is a difficult word to render accurately in English; it generally means both thinking and feeling in a much broader sense than either English word. To understand *kimochi* means to grasp the whole spirit, to understand a person in his or her totality. Their use of this phrase indicates that the residents wanted their director to be not only sympathetic, not only attentive to their feelings and problems, but also able to interpret and carry out their unspoken wishes. This is the essence of an ideal dependent relationship in Japanese culture (see Doi, 1973).

It was impossible for Mr. Baba to understand and respond to the huge array of spoken and unspoken wishes of the residents, many of which were mutually contradictory; to try such a thing would leave the entire management in disarray. He was very capable as a personnel manager and fiscal manager, areas wherein he had training, but he did not have the interactional skills needed to deal effectively with the residents. Because he was trying to be as sensitive as possible, he simply did not know how to respond to the criticism of insensitivity. It was not that he did anything particularly wrong, but he was seen as doing too little, if anything, to show understanding of the residents' *kimochi.*

THE "MONEY-MAKING" POLICY

A major criticism that the residents had of Mr. Baba and the management in general was what they perceived as a profit-making policy, which seemed to contradict the "welfare service" policy. For instance, the residents believed that Mr. Baba demanded a profit from the store in the community center, whereas it should have operated as a break-even service. The barber would tell the residents that he had to give 10 percent of his fee to the administration, adding that he would prefer to give a 10 percent discount to his customers instead. And there were other accusations.

The perception of profit motive was an unfounded one, based on a serious misunderstanding about the principle of service charges. Although Mr. Baba tried to generate income from the shop, the barber, and other merchants who did business in the community, this income went into the operating budget of Fuji-no-Sato, helping to keep the monthly fee from being raised for four years. The misunderstanding was due to a lack of clarity about policy: whether the residents who use paid services should in so doing help subsidize the community or whether costs should come out of everyone's monthly fees. Fuji-no-Sato management had adopted the former policy without consulting the residents (a mistake, it seems) but later made efforts, largely unsuccessful, to explain its choice. Consequently, as other problems developed, the residents added their suspicion of this policy to what they thought of as evidence of profit-centered management.

The "telephone fee incident," as it is known by the residents, typifies the problem of misunderstanding and its consequences. It was an incident with major unfortunate effects on the thinking of both management and residents. Management perceived that their good intentions were totally misunderstood, and the incident more or less permanently cemented a negative image of the management in the residents' eyes.

As mentioned, Fuji-no-Sato has only one telephone trunk line connecting it with the outside, and all the phones in the community are extensions of this line—a system that has some advantages for the residents. The management initially charged the residents 30 percent more for phone service than the telephone company charged. No explanation of this rate was given the residents. After about two years of this, a resident who had worked for the phone company happened to discover the rate difference and brought the issue to the residents association. The association studied the issue, made inquiries to the phone company, and concluded that the additional charge was illegal. The association asked the management to stop this practice and to refund the extra that the residents had already paid.

Several mass meetings between the residents and the top staff of the Tokyo office were held, and the latter tried to explain the surcharge, which was paid into a fund to maintain the community phone system. Otherwise the residents would have to be charged a substantial fee for breakdowns. The attempted explanation failed because the residents were so convinced of management's wrongdoing—an interpretation that was supported by the phone company. In the end, the management gave in, dropped the surcharge, and refunded back payments. The residents rejoiced, thinking they had won justice. The refund was perceived as an admission by the management of its wrongdoing, and its image suffered accordingly.

COMMUNICATION PROBLEMS
WITHIN THE MANAGEMENT

Some of the these problems were caused by inexperienced administration. However, the management appeared to have good intentions toward the residents, and their response to such problems was positive and forward looking. Some problems, particularly in building design, have been avoided in the construction of their newer communities; and vigorous efforts have been made to explain the management system to the residents at these new communities to avoid similar misunderstandings.

It was perhaps inevitable that Fuji-no-Sato would have some of these problems, being a pioneer in the industry and something of an experiment. The managing organization itself was in a formative stage and experiencing communication problems among the staff. The head office in Tokyo was responsible for overall management, while the director was responsible for day-to-day community operation. Within the head office, there were communication problems between the Planning Department and the Administrative Department. Planning (1) proposed the "new welfare" philosophy for middle-income elderly, (2) formulated the sophisticated long-term management plan, and (3) supervised the actual architectural design and construction. But when Fuji-no-Sato opened, administration took on responsibility for running it while the Planning Department turned its attention to developing new sites. Administration staff apparently had not been properly included in the development process and did not thoroughly comprehend the philosophy or the highly mathematical long-term fiscal plan. These administration staff were unable to explain the system to the residents' satisfaction. The residents saw this as evidence of incompetence in the head office.

Two policies conceived by the head of administration, although rational enough in themselves, had major negative consequences. First, he thought it was essential for Fuji-no-Sato to achieve full occupancy promptly if the community were to survive financially, and he therefore emphasized an aggressive advertising strategy. Promotional brochures that contained some slightly exaggerated claims were approved, a factor that contributed to a climate of mistrust. His second problematic policy was to focus on the "safe" financial management of the community and, without consulting the residents, to have the director generate as much extra revenue as possible. Intended to protect the residents' investment, this policy ended up being seen as evidence of greed.

PROBLEMS AND CONSEQUENCES
OF "CONTRACT WELFARE"

Given that some major problems at Fuji-no-Sato appear to have been caused by well-intentioned but inexperienced management, the residents' reactions may seem somewhat uncompromising, rigid, and unrealistic. A sense of betrayal, disappointment, and distrust of the management prevailed among them. They were highly intellectual people and generally aware of what the management could and could not do in a realistic sense. Why, then, did they continue to make unrealistic demands?

Meanwhile, the management was bewildered that its good intentions could not be seen by the residents. The staff admitted their mistakes and took action to correct them. But the senior staff complained privately that the more they did for the residents, the more strongly they were criticized. The director and others sometimes tried to discredit the residents association and some of its outspoken residents, portraying them as too demanding. Mr. Baba and the staff did not seem to realize that this made further communication with the residents difficult.

During the early years of operation, the relationship between the management and the residents was deadlocked, each side interpreting events so as to reinforce its negative image of the other. For both sides, the issue was one of good faith—of sincerity—unfortunately, something that was nearly impossible to measure. The residents saw their attitude toward the management as one of self-defense, having come to the conclusion that the management was not sincere. The management, too, saw a lack of good faith in the residents' harsh criticisms and demands. In order to understand what sincerity meant for both sides, we must first understand what each expected of the other; these expectations grew partly out of the Japanese meanings of the words "contract," "welfare," and "contract welfare." Clear explication of this linguistic problem will help reveal some of the culturally based problems of retirement communities and other forms of contract welfare in Japan.

JAPANESE MEANINGS OF "CONTRACT"

"Contract" means something quite different for Japanese and for Americans. Wagatsuma and Rosett (1983:2) summarize this difference as follows: "While in the American mind the function of a contract is to predetermine strife and trouble in the future, pre-define dispute, and enunciate rights, a contract in the Japanese mind is a symbolic expression or reflection of mutual trust that is expected never to break down and that will work favorably for both parties in case of future trouble. . . . [The] 'confer-in-good-faith' and 'harmonious-settlement' clauses reveal the basic nature of the Japanese contract." Thus, for the Japanese, a contract means far more than what is stated on paper. It is a ritual, establishing a new relationship and a mutual commitment to that relationship on the basis of mutual trust. Mutual trust is not possible unless both parties take the relationship seriously—that is, unless they are "sincere." Put another way, the American style of contract may be excessively cut and dried and "cold" for the Japanese because, although it may be based primarily on the mutual trust of two parties, it also takes into account their possible distrust in the future.

The contract offered by Fuji-no-Sato is no exception to the Japanese style. For instance, it has only one short item each on such crucial issues as the management of the residents' health and their medical care:

Item 8: Health Management

The organization constantly monitors the health condition of the resident and provides professional consultations on health, and professional health checkups.

Item 9: Care

When the resident requires care due to illness, injury, or other reasons, and when the physician determines that care is necessary, the organization provides the necessary care at Fuji-no-Sato.

Although the contract is not specific, "care" in item 9 is taken to refer to both acute and long-term care and "the physician" to mean a physician on contract at Fuji-no-Sato, not other physicians. These items simply state goals and do not anticipate problem situations concerning the health management and medical care of the residents. There is no need for further specification because, like any contract in Japan, the Fuji-no-Sato contract includes the good faith and harmonious settlement clause at the end:

Item 35: Others

For issues not specified in this contract, and for interpretations of each item in this contract, both the organization and the resident, in accordance with relevant laws, will mutually confer and deal in sincerity.

Thus, both parties expect that the definition of health management and medical care, as well as whatever problems may arise in the future, are to be dealt with on an *ad hoc* basis and with mutual trust and sincerity.

Americans may be surprised that not one of the well-educated residents at Fuji-no-Sato was familiar with the terms of his or her contract. Many did not even bother to look at it. The residents felt there was no need to be familiar with its terms; they assumed they would be able to live at Fuji-no-Sato throughout their lives and would be taken care of in the community when they needed skilled nursing care as long as they were paying the monthly fee. The contract means to them the organization's commitment to these assumptions in exchange for their payment of the entrance fee and the monthly rate.

JAPANESE MEANINGS OF "WELFARE"

On the one hand, welfare for the Japanese still means public support for the needy. On the other hand, it is coming to include public well-being—the welfare of a "welfare state." Both meanings are reflected in social policies, but the term has an underlying cultural dimension that distinguishes the Japanese and Western meanings. The Japanese use the expression *fukushi no kokoro*, "the welfare spirit," a phrase that denotes an altruistic devotion of welfare workers to their clients. This is a highly emphasized cultural value among the Japanese, particularly when the clients are destitute. For instance, if a welfare worker is a young woman, she is often referred to as an "angel," serving the needy out of true devotion, usually working under inferior conditions and pay. Her self-sacrifice for others has strong cultural support, being one of the core values of the Japanese. If the worker is a middle-aged man, the Japanese expect him to be a highly moral person because they assume that anyone who devotes his life to the well-being of others does so out of desire and must have superior qualities as well.

These images may reflect an earlier reality, but today they are often stereotypes and mythifications. Still, images are important. Because of them, the working conditions of many welfare workers continue to be poor. After all, such outstanding people should be able to endure hardship!

The residents of Fuji-no-Sato like the phrase *fukushi no kokoro* very much. They perceive themselves as the beneficiaries of the welfare spirit. Fuji-no-Sato is a "welfare community," and the sponsoring corporation has the word "welfare" in its name.

But the builders of Fuji-no-Sato advocate something called "*new* welfare," which they take to be different from the traditional welfare and which does not entail the "welfare spirit." For the management, the new welfare defines the relationship between the service provider and the recipient in terms of a contract. It is an equal relationship in which the recipient is expected to be an independent individual. In short, a wide gap separates the residents' and the management's understandings of the word "welfare."

Intrinsic Problems of Contract Welfare

The lack of consensus on interpretations of contract welfare was an important reason for the poor relationship between residents and management. This issue is part of a larger cultural and historical problem for Japanese society. Using Western, individualistic suppositions rather than traditional Japanese ones, the management assumed that its relationship with the residents was ultimately determined by the terms of the contract that the residents had freely signed. Residents were taken to be intelligent people who comprehended the nature of their relationship with the management and were independent enough to take responsibility for their part in it. Management's responsibility was taken to be finite and based on reciprocity.

But the management was at first not successful in communicating this new notion, and the traditional meanings continued to dominate the residents' thinking. This communication failure can be seen in the language of the contract used by Fuji-no-Sato. It is a typical Japanese contract that simply states the commitment of the management to certain goals, with the assumption that they and the residents will negotiate, with sincerity and mutual trust, the best possible solutions of unforeseen problems. It can be read in the traditional way, and there is no wording to clarify nontraditional intentions.

The strength of the residents' position vis-à-vis management derived from their straightforward use of the traditional meanings of the terms. They viewed the contract as a symbol of the management's commitment to their comfort, health, and long-term care. They expected that because the management would respond to future problems with sincerity, it could not do anything contrary to their wishes. This expectation was amplified by their view that the contract is not merely a guarantee of good faith, but a *welfare* contract: namely, a contract that guarantees the "welfare spirit" on the part of the management. In other words, they did not perceive their relationship with the management as an equal one at all, but thought of themselves as the recipients of altruistic services, the traditional dependent position vis-à-vis the service providers. They thereby gained a moral upper hand, emphasizing their weak position and mobilizing moral rather than legal pressure. The residents' strength was further consolidated by their strong moral position as old people in Japanese society.

The residents, then, did not need to care too much about the terms of the written contract. Any information about Fuji-no-Sato, even the promotional brochure or a verbal explanation given by some staff member, was taken to be as legitimate as the contract itself, given the traditional "sincerity" interpretation. When they discovered that the management did not adhere to this assumed spirit behind what they had heard or read, the residents felt betrayed and became suspicious of all the management's motives. This suspicion grew through neglect and was seemingly confirmed when the management failed to respond satisfactorily to developing problems. The fatal blow to their trust was the imputed "money-making policy" because money making is exactly the opposite of the welfare spirit.

Once either side is convinced that sincerity has been lost in a relationship, its foundation has disintegrated, and it is extremely difficult to restore good faith. We believe this was the background of the residents' behavior, which had grown wary and demanding even to the point of irrationality.

This dilemma was just as much a hardship for the residents as for the management. The residents sought to exchange money for a kind of traditional, paternalistic goodwill. But can money buy the welfare spirit? Traditionally, devoted service by welfare workers was valued because its recipients were socially disadvantaged people; the welfare spirit was an altruistic spirit, directed toward the needy. The residents of Fuji-no-Sato are neither poor nor socially disadvantaged, but from a better than average social stratum. The question has a definite answer in Japanese culture: Money *cannot* buy the welfare spirit; it is an ethical value contradictory to the pursuit of money. The residents, who sensed this at some level, therefore felt uneasy in their self-righteous claims. They were not sure to what extent they could legitimately demand self-sacrifice in return for cash.

The very strength of the residents' logic on contract welfare, nonetheless, produced a kind of double-bind. The management felt they could not satisfy demands based on the traditional meanings of "contract" and "welfare" because such demands have no clear limits and could result in bankruptcy. But their sincerity would always be questioned if they rejected these meanings. As part of their effort to explain their operating policies and restore good relations with the residents, the management proposed the idea that the residents should send a representative to the board of directors during these negotiations. The residents declined the offer.

The difficulty for the management can be seen when one realizes that culturally rooted meanings are very difficult to change and that such changes take a long time. Unless and until a new generally accepted meaning of "contract welfare" emerges, problems like this will persist, and the management of Fuji-no-Sato will continue to bear not only its *legal* responsibility under the contract, but also its *social* responsibility as a welfare facility in the traditional sense.

9

The Residents Association

The Fuji-no-Sato Residents Association was the only formal organization among the residents. It was formal in the sense that (1) it formally represented the interests of all residents vis-à-vis the management and was recognized by both, (2) its membership was in effect mandatory, (3) representatives were selected in a systematic way, and (4) each representative was assigned a specific position on the Executive Committee. Here we examine the significance for social integration. During the course of Kinoshita's study, he was able to observe significant changes in the association's activities and functions.

HISTORY

The residents association was formed by the early residents in 1979, the first year of Fuji-no-Sato, to promote mutual understanding among themselves and achieve a harmonious life. It was not formed in the first place as a formal negotiating organization that would represent the residents' interests. The management initially proposed forming a three-part advisory council (five representatives from the residents, five from the management, and a few professional scholars in the relevant fields) to help coordinate policy with residents' opinions. This proposal never got serious attention from either side, partly because management failed to take initiative in such matters as recruiting qualified scholars and partly because, as major problems developed, the residents association simply became, in effect, the residents' negotiating organization.

Asked why the residents association was formed in the first place, a resident who had served during the first year of the association said:

> There weren't many of us the first year. We were very busy with ourselves in settling down. In the early fall of that year, I think,

someone suggested the formation of the residents association. This person had known that the residents at another retirement community had an organization of their own. All of us thought it a good idea. Because, you know, we were strangers when we came here, but we would be living here the rest of our lives. Fuji-no-Sato is our last place to live, so it was natural for us to have some kind of an organization in order to get to know one another well and to live harmoniously.

Two male residents then visited the other community to study how its association had been formed and what it was doing. The residents at Fuji-no-Sato modeled their association after the older one. However, aside from practical information like the method of selecting representatives and the amount of the membership fee, there was very little they could learn, their example being a rather inactive organization. Function was thus a problem for the Fuji-no-Sato Residents Association. They simply did not know what to do to promote mutual understanding. Various informal hobby groups were being formed independently by the interested residents, and trips and other general activities were planned by the administration. The residents association remained inactive for the first year.

Although the association was still doing little toward its original purpose in the second and third years, it began feeling pressure to take some action on the developing problems. There were, among the rank-and-file residents, growing concerns about some of the problems discussed in Chapter 8 and growing criticism of the management. Despite these pressures, the residents association maintained a cooperative and conciliatory position toward management. It simply suggested constructive steps to ease the problems, hoping management would respond. The Executive Committee of the association believed that if they openly confronted the management, the long-term repercussions would be serious, so they persuaded the residents to withhold their criticism and to take a wait-and-see attitude.

However, the management failed to respond as the Executive Committee had hoped, and pressures mounted. Particularly after the telephone fee incident, it became difficult to control the growing anger of the residents. The committee itself came under sharp criticism for its conciliatory position toward the management.

As a result, several outspoken residents were elected representatives in the fourth year, and the Executive Committee took the approach of confronting the management openly. The new committee was inaugurated in April 1982, and four months later Kinoshita began fieldwork. This committee established strong leadership for the first time, not only because it came to represent the frustrations and expectations of many residents, but also because it was headed by a president who introduced new ideas for promoting mutual understanding among the residents.

According to the bylaws, membership in the residents association was voluntary, but every resident was well aware that it was in effect mandatory. No one could openly dispute the association's purpose, and membership signified one's public support of that purpose. A member could safely refrain from active participation, but not joining was so problematic that even part-time residents belonged. Only a few independent souls refused to join. Membership meant essentially two things: a monthly membership fee of fifty cents, which was used to cover such association operating costs as copying the minutes of the meetings, and periodic service as a representative. A representative's tenure was in principle one year, but it could be extended for an additional year. Many early representatives served for two years because there were not enough permanent residents to take their places. In accordance with the Japanese fiscal year, the term of a representative was from April through the following March.

That nonmembers were subject to sanctions from members can be seen in the examples of Mr. Kadota and Mr. Komoto. Mr. Kadota was a strict isolationist; not only did he not join the association, he avoided any interaction with other residents and even with the staff. He told the representative who came to ask for his membership that he had nothing against the association; he simply wanted nothing to do with it. He never attended the meetings of his building, and his building mates saw Mr. Kadota as an uncooperative *kawarimono*, an oddball; but little was made of this fact outside their circle. Because his aloofness was passive, the residents of other buildings did not know of it.

The case of Mr. Komoto illustrates wider public sanction. Once a member, he had even served as a representative; but he withdrew in protest over a disagreement concerning the association's authority. Mr. Komoto argued that because each resident signed a contract with the management individually and there would always be opposing views among the residents, the association could not represent all residents. His view was rejected by the leadership, and he withdrew.

After this incident, Mr. Komoto began speaking up at public meetings between management and residents where major problems were being discussed, usually in a tension-filled atmosphere. On these occasions, he always drew attention to the fact that he was no longer a member of the association and thus had to express his opinion separately. Because the Executive Committee was trying to negotiate with the appearance of a united front, they saw Mr. Komoto's remarks as extremely uncooperative. Knowing this, the management too was obliged politely to ignore his views. As a result of his public action, other residents began to avoid Mr. Komoto—the strongest social sanction available at Fuji-no-Sato. He became increasingly isolated, and his dissatisfaction with living at Fuji-no-Sato steadily increased.

Mr. Komoto is the only resident we know of who has publicly taken a stand contrary to the residents association. Other residents either have passively remained silent at public meetings or have spoken in favor of the committee, but it is safer to be silent to avoid even the misperception of disagreement. Some residents thought the Executive Committee was demanding and irrational, even childish, but were afraid to speak out.

This kind of passive, self-protective attitude allowed the resident-management conflict to escalate to the point that some residents began worrying about the long-term impact. They feared the management would be driven into a corner and might lose interest in operating Fuji-no-Sato. But fearing accusations of disloyalty to the residents' cause, they remained silent, a concern that appeared often in interviews and private conversations with the researcher. One man, who served the association in the first year, said,

> When I was a representative, I learned that there are always opposing views to anything. Some residents, including [association] officers, are so self-righteous, and never try to see the [management's] point. No matter what it is, they're against it, even if it means paying more. They complain about the taste of the food, but I don't know what their standards are. My wife worked as a dietician in a company

restaurant, serving at least a couple of hundred meals a day. I asked her about the association's strategy of confronting the director and the dietician with these complaints, and she didn't get it either. Worse yet, they're trying to demand a meeting with everybody on the staff, not just the decision makers. I think Mr. Baba will refuse. The cooking staff will surely lose interest in keeping their jobs here if they have to face that kind of accusation themselves. My wife said just two words, "Premature infants!"

The association was led by an Executive Committee consisting of twenty representatives, two from each of the ten buildings. Although the selection of the building representatives was supposed to be done by secret ballot, all the buildings adopted an alternative method, namely, open consensus. In addition, every building adopted the policy that, unless a resident had special reasons such as ill health, he or she had to serve in turn. No resident could serve as building representative for more than two one-year terms. This policy was adopted not to share the honor, but to spread the burden because few residents wanted to do it. Each building was expected to have at least one male representative each term.

Generally, the residents in each building held a meeting in March, a month before the terms of office began. At the meeting, the outgoing representatives nominated new candidates for the coming year, the choices sometimes having been discussed with the nominees in advance. There has never been a case in which a nomination was opposed. Interestingly, after just four years, many buildings with large proportions of part-time residents were running out of candidates because most of the full-time residents had already served. In these buildings, those residents would have to serve a second time.

The residents of Fuji-no-Sato have never used voting because it is seen as public disclosure of the failure to gain perfect consensus, a situation to be avoided at all costs. Indeed, voting is incompatible with the traditional Japanese method of decision making; the Japanese try to resolve differences of opinion behind the scenes, informally, so that when an issue is brought up formally in public, there is always a consensus among the participants.

The method of electing the leadership of the Executive Committee followed this Japanese tradition as well. The committee consisted of a president, a vice-president, three treasurers, three secretaries for general affairs, and three standing committees: (1) the four-member Committee on Dining Hall Affairs, (2) the three-member Committee on Environment, and (3) the four-member Committee on Medical Care Problems. The leadership was completely dominated by men; the president, vice-president, chief treasurer, chief secretary for general affairs, and all chairmen of the standing committees were men. The female representatives supported the men by doing miscellaneous work, such as making copies for distribution, keeping notes of meetings with the management, and so forth. No female representative ever spoke at a negotiating meeting with the management. Both men and women took this division of labor for granted.

Electing the president and vice-president involved more delicate behind-the-scenes maneuvering because these positions were the core of leadership. The outgoing president would hold an informal meeting with the other leaders of his Executive Committee to discuss the matter, usually in late March, when they had the list of new building representatives. The outgoing president and some of the other leaders then met selected candidates to gain their consent to be nominated. The candidates usually declined the request (pleading incompetence), were pressed to reconsider, and accepted the request reluctantly. This process is a ritual often practiced among the Japanese; it has more than symbolic significance because anyone elected in this manner, that is, against his will, can save face if things go badly.

After the new president and vice-president were informally determined, the two of them would discuss candidates for the other leadership positions and meet with their choices for these positions to gain the nominees' informal consent. Only after this complex informal process was accomplished, usually between the middle and end of April, could a general meeting be convened and the new Executive Committee composition be approved by all the residents. There has never been a case of opposition raised at the formal meeting. The men were very skillful at this traditional method of selecting leaders, having been socialized to it throughout their careers. Recall that many of them had been executives in corporations.

A new pattern emerged in selecting building representatives, and consequently new leadership was established in the 1982–1983 Executive Committee. The leadership in the first three years took a conciliatory position vis-à-vis the management, despite the growing frustration of the rank-and-file residents over the handling of what they saw as major problems. The leaders came under criticism by the residents as being "too soft." Although these criticisms were never raised publicly, many buildings sent "hardliners" as representatives in March 1982. These hardliners were a handful of male residents who had usually spoken up at the negotiating meetings, demonstrating their ability to ask sharp questions or their courage to attack the management openly.

Another important characteristic of the Executive Committee was that the new president, Mr. Sonoda, unlike the hardliners, was a man who preferred a rational, task-oriented approach over the use of open hostility. When he spoke at the meetings, in contrast to the hardliners, he never seemed emotional, but always talked softly while pointing to the key questions. Although he was unable to lead the Executive Committee hardliners into his position, he gradually became respected by the other residents. He also gained respect by proposing and initiating new and welcome ideas about the association's activities for its members.

When this leadership group retired in April 1983, they became, so to speak, an "old guard." Thus, when the management proposed an increase of the monthly fee for the first time in June 1983, they were first consulted by the new leadership and eventually remobilized as active leaders in the negotiations with the management over this issue.

Despite the original purpose of the association, the Executive Committees in the first three terms did practically nothing to promote mutual understanding among the residents. The early leaders simply had few constructive ideas. Perhaps the most important thing they did was buy traditionally arranged flowers for members' funerals. Because the administrative staff routinely planned activities for the residents without consulting the Executive Committee, they naturally felt purposeless.

The 1982–1983 leadership introduced some new ideas and put them into practice. Soon after the Executive Committee headed by Mr. Sonoda was inaugurated, he proposed that, under the difficult circumstances of the time, the committee should keep members informed of their actions. This was adopted as a major policy, and the committee began distributing a monthly report to each resident instead of posting them on the association's bulletin board at the community center. The committee also proposed that residents regularly hold building meetings, led by building representatives and accompanied by tea and sweets provided by the association. The actual frequency of these meetings varied from place to place, being monthly in some buildings and less frequent in others. The purpose of the meetings was to enhance mutual understanding by providing an opportunity for the residents to meet and exchange views. Soon, however, the meetings started functioning as conduits for requests and information from rank-and-file residents through the representatives to the Executive Committee. The Executive Committee declined to arbitrate conflicting requests, but simply passed them all to the director.

The most important measure by Mr. Sonoda's committee was to start visiting hospitalized members on a regular basis. Over several meetings, the committee developed detailed bylaws on this practice so that it would continue as an official association activity. The bylaws state: "This bylaw provides that we visit our hospitalized members at regular intervals. Such members lead lonely lives at the clinic here, or in outside hospitals, and our contact with them is inclined to cease."

There were discussions over such issues as how often the visits should be made, what should be brought, who should go, how the traveling expenses should be covered, and whether lunch should be paid by the association. The most heated discussion was over whether hospitalized nonmember residents should be included in this system. Because nearly all residents were members, this was a somewhat hypothetical question, but the Executive Committee members were eager to make the bylaws perfect so there would be no ambiguities. In the end, it was decided that this was an official activity of the residents association, so nonmembers should be excluded.

Visiting hospitalized people, a traditional Japanese custom known as *omimai*, is common throughout Japan today. *Omimai* is an important national custom and one most relevant to life at Fuji-no-Sato. All the residents continue to be concerned about their health, and scme are frequently hospitalized.

The *omimai* system of trimonthly visits began in December 1982. A member of the Committee on Medical Care Problems would get the names of the hospitalized from the administration office, then the Executive Committee would ask either the patient's building representatives or friends to make the *omimai* visit. The visiting members would take flowers worth $2.

These three measures may seem fairly trivial, but for the Executive Committee and the residents of Fuji-no-Sato, they were the first steps toward forming a purpose for the association. They represented the new strength of the association and of its new president, Mr. Sonoda.

ASSOCIATION AND MANAGEMENT

The most important activity of the residents association was to represent its members' interests to the management, a fact that became clear during the 1982–1983 term. All standing committees were set up to deal with specific problems of the residents (medical care, meals, and environment), and there were no committees for social functions, such as the welcome committees for new residents one finds in American retirement communities.

When the residents had a problem, the president or vice-president and the chairman of the appropriate standing committee met with the director. The meetings were held *ad hoc*, not on a regular basis. Under the leadership of Mr. Sonoda, the Executive Committee made it a rule to submit requests to the director in written form and to get a written reply when appropriate. The Executive Committee wanted solid evidence of any agreements. Mr. Baba, the director, thought of this as a great nuisance, but he could not refuse to cooperate without a good excuse.

The Executive Committee was unable to settle conflicting requests from the residents and simply passed everything to the director. Not surprisingly, this often led to confusion. In one case, a building brought a request to cut some trees down to allow more sunlight, and there were similar requests from the residents in three other buildings. The president and the chairman of the Committee on Environment met the director and informed him of this request. Mr. Baba had his staff cut the main boughs (not the trees because that was prohibited) near the buildings in question. The following month, representatives of these buildings brought protests about the cutting, demanding protection of the environment. In another case, Mr. Baba was told that the women's spa at the center had too many faucets, and he asked his staff to remove some of them. When the opposite request came in, he had the faucets restored. Mr. Baba's pleas for consistency produced no noticeable results.

Obviously, the Executive Committee was unwilling to take the role of mediator, a job that would produce confrontation of differences and disturb the illusion of consensus. There was a strong emphasis among both the leadership and the residents on avoiding any kind of conflict, however minor. Disagreement on the tiniest issue, if made public, tended to be interpreted in a personal way. Accordingly, the residents were careful not to challenge others' views, but rather to maintain a noncommittal attitude. To leaders and residents alike, group harmony seemed to mean the mere absence of open conflict, rather than common goals that they should actively seek. This attitude drew further impetus from the negative relationship with the management because attempts to mediate residents' internal disputes could be seen as serving management interests and *ipso facto* possibly disloyal. Association buck passing was self-protective. Likewise, the association was incapable of resolving conflict among the residents, nor did the residents expect them to take such a role. Such conflicts were always brought directly to the director.

The key to association passivity lay in the residents' overall perception of their role at Fuji-no-Sato. They viewed themselves as the clients of devoted welfare workers and thought of Fuji-no-Sato as a place where they were entitled to a passive role. In short, it was a client model, the staff being the service providers and the residents, the recipients. As clients, they need not settle their own disputes because all community problems were to be handled by the director and his staff.

To clarify this, imagine a situation in which the staff is unable to provide many services, and the residents have to take an active role in community operation—that is, the client model is meaningless. (Whether or not the residents would have liked this is a different question.) The association's role in promoting social integration was greatly restricted, in effect, by the fact that the residents had sought to exchange money for responsibility—to buy the "right" to be passive. They had relinquished many possible roles that might otherwise have increased their sense of purpose and their solidarity. This may be a common problem in the social integration in many middle- or upper-class retirement communities, not just in Japan, but also in the United States.

In sharp contrast with the unwillingness and incapacity of the association leaders to mediate conflict among the residents, they demonstrated great skill in their negotiations with the management, the interactional skills they had learned in their careers. This was most vividly observed in a series of negotiations over the proposed increase of the monthly fee during the period of June to September 1983. This illustrates how lively these men could be when they had the rare opportunity to revive their old skills. During these negotiations, management took the initiative to improve its relation with the association.

In June 1983, the management proposed an increase in the monthly fee for the first time, setting the increase at 20 percent. Although the contract indicates the monthly fee may be raised or at least reevaluated every two years, the success of Fuji-no-Sato had made it possible for the management to hold the initial fee for nearly four years despite inflation and staff increases. The proposal was made at the annual meeting for disclosure of the accounts of the previous fiscal year, an event required by the entrance contract. About two weeks before the scheduled meeting, the management distributed the details of the previous and coming years' budgets, along with a letter of explanation for the increase.

The new association leadership had just taken office, replacing the influential group of 1982–1983. The new leadership was too green for this large issue. The new president consulted his Executive Committee and his predecessor and set up a Special Committee. In mid-June, about a week before the budget meeting, an emergency general meeting of all residents was convened to approve the formation of the Special Committee. The meeting was short, and the Special Committee was granted formal power to represent the interests of all members. The members of the Special Committee would be hand-picked by the current president, who quickly chose himself, the vice-president, the chief treasurer, and seven men from the previous year's leadership. The management representative nicknamed these "the seven samurai," a name that is still used to refer to the incident, even though most of them are now dead. The ten-member committee met several times and discussed strategies of interrogation and negotiation.

In late June, the two-day budget meeting was held in the large meeting room in the community center. The news about the formation of the Special Committee had been reported to the head office in Tokyo, so the head of the Planning Department attended as chief corporate representative of the management. This choice may have reflected a sense of crisis in the head office. Not only was the atmosphere among the residents extremely tense, but this was the first time the corporation had faced the task of negotiating a fee increase.

The meeting began in an extremely tense atmosphere. The room was packed with concerned residents, about ninety of them, and additional chairs were brought in to seat as many as possible. Those who could not get seats or who chose to stay in their apartments watched a telecast of the meeting through the community's cable T.V. system. The members of the Special Committee took seats in the front row, and other outspoken residents seated themselves near the microphone, their usual position at general meetings.

There was a sense of inevitability among the rank-and-file residents, the feeling that the monthly fee had to be raised. During the two weeks prior to the meeting, this had been the main topic of residents' conversations. All agreed that the increase should not be made, but if unavoidable, it should be kept to a minimum. They appeared to be waiting to see what concessions the Special Committee could get from the management.

At the outset of the meeting, the association vice-president, a retired public prosecutor, read as the official view of the association a prepared statement attacking the management's lack of sincerity by citing the previous major problems. The first day's meeting was concerned with the management's explanation of fiscal operations the previous year. It was a question-and-answer type of meeting. The members of the Special Committee took turns asking questions, as though they were following a planned strategy. The committee members seemed bent on discrediting the previous year's fiscal operations in order to argue that the proposed budget would be smaller if the community were properly managed, thereby obviating the need to raise the fee. This strategy was skillfully deflated by the corporate representative, and the session ended up identifying a few issues whose negotiability both sides agreed upon.

Meanwhile, during the dignified questioning by the committee, individual residents spoke in heated anger, some even shouting at the management representatives. Although their opinions were more or less ignored by both the committee members and the management representatives, the atmosphere grew tenser. As usual, no women spoke at the meeting.

Even the tone of the committee members' questions was sometimes harsh and accusatory—a remarkable contrast with the residents' extreme self-restraint in dealing with each other. The management appeared to be the only available target for whatever suppressed hostility they felt, and the audience, including women, seemed to relish as a catharsis the tense atmosphere and harsh words. In this sense, the confrontation with management may have been a necessary ritual for the residents as a group.

After a break of twenty minutes, the corporate representative (head of the Planning Department) spent two hours explaining the long-term fiscal management scheme, which he himself had developed. This was the first time it had been fully explained to the residents. Although it was very complex, the presentation was clear and impressive, and many residents felt relieved. Some felt they could begin to understand the system on which their livelihoods depended; others were relieved just to get an answer to a question that had nagged them for some time, namely, who was ultimately responsible for the overall plan? The corporate representative laid out a conceptual framework for the negotiations.

In the evening of the first day, the corporate representative invited the Special Committee to join him for informal discussion. It was a shrewd and appropriate next step, both sides being well aware that the actual negotiations would have to be held in private. The invitation was meant to be a cue to committee members that the management planned to conduct the negotiations according to the traditional Japanese way of handling issues *between equals,* and the cue was correctly received. In fact, this was the first time that the management had approached association leaders as equals, capable of serious negotiation. The invitation was welcomed by the committee, both sides got down to business right away, and the informal meeting lasted more than three hours that evening.

The general meeting was resumed the following day but cut short halfway through the schedule. At the end of the morning session, the association president made a motion that, because most of the residents' opinions had already been expressed, the meeting should be adjourned and further negotiations conducted by the Special Committee. The motion was approved. The framework of the negotiations had been established in the informal meeting the previous night, so management had used the second day not to discuss the issue, but to show sympathy by listening to the residents' views as much as possible.

After the general meeting, five meetings were held between July and early September. Each time, management representatives came to Fuji-no-Sato for the negotiations. After each session, the association reported progress on the bulletin board at the community center. It appeared that the negotiations were being conducted according to the accepted "hostile" attitude because the language used in these reports tended to be highly confrontational. But an important change was taking place in the actual negotiations, which had become highly task-oriented, without excessive emotion on either side. It was evident that the members of the Special Committee *liked* the corporate representative, who was both a skilled negotiator and a frank and honest person. Neither side seemed bent on outmaneuvering the other. Despite their respective official positions, mutual trust was being restored among them throughout the negotiating sessions.

The negotiations were concluded in the middle of September in a dramatic and very traditional way, typical of high-level negotiations in Japan. After the five meetings, it was virtually agreed that an increase of about 8 percent of the monthly fee was legitimate. But there remained some minor issues to be worked out—issues that appeared to have been intentionally left unsolved. A summit meeting was held to conclude the negotiations. Management was represented by the corporate representative, but the question of who would represent the Special Committee was extremely important because that person would have to be the real leader among the leaders. The person chosen was not the current president, who officially chaired the committee, nor the immediate past president, but rather the immediate past vice-president. He represented all the power of the Special Committee and thus of the residents as a whole.

It was typically Japanese that the representation of each negotiating side changed as the negotiations progressed from a group to one person on each side. Why the previous vice-president emerged as the leader of the committee members is not certain and was not predicted by Kinoshita or the management. Mr. Sonoda, the past president, was the most logical choice. But the vice-president was the only committee member who had a part-time job as a senior business executive in a large corporation. He was also one of the first committee members who accepted the sincerity and capability of the corporate representative, and his likeable personality might also have been a factor. At any rate, after this man's appointment as Special Committee representative, Kinoshita once overheard a couple of the other committee members addressing him in honorific speech—in this case, a sign of much greater respect than his age or status would have required.

The series of negotiations produced an outcome more important than the settlement of the fee increase itself. Most important, a pattern of representation for future negotiations had been established. Future problems would be dealt with differently; the corporate representative, acting as spokesman of the joint Departments of Planning and Management, had succeeded in defusing much of the hostility and let the committee know they would negotiate with him in the future. After the formal settlement of the issue, he said that his main objective had been to establish a sound framework within which the management could negotiate with the residents creatively and that the amount of the fee increase had been a secondary issue.

Another important outcome was the emergence of strong leadership among the residents. When serious problems have arisen in subsequent years, the Executive Committee of the association has been able to mobilize a pool of experienced leaders.

After the settlement of the issue, another emergency meeting of all residents was convened, and the committee reported the 8 percent increase of the monthly fee. It was approved without objection. Apparently the residents were glad the committee had succeeded in lowering the increase from 20 percent to 8 percent.

10

Group and Individual Activities

The age and class homogeneity of Fuji-no-Sato makes it a more or less egalitarian community and as such very unusual in Japan, where interpersonal relations are usually vertically organized. Like most other Japanese, the residents of this community have not been socialized to cultivate the unstructured, voluntary social relationships one usually finds in this kind of peer group–oriented setting. These facts give informal sociability at Fuji-no-Sato its own peculiar flavor, which may well add spice to Western ideas about social integration.

Here we are really interested in four kinds of informal activities: (1) hobby groups, (2) Christian groups, (3) volunteer groups, and (4) gardening. All these emerged spontaneously and are important in the residents' daily lives.

THE FORMATION OF HOBBY GROUPS

Hobby groups were the most common kind of informal activities, and a pattern quickly emerged for their formation. Kinoshita did not witness the formation or breaking up of hobby groups during the research because all had been formed earlier, but residents described it as a simple procedure. A group of residents (never a single individual) who planned to form a new hobby group would post an announcement on the bulletin board at the community center and consult with the staff about space and scheduling. When an instructor was necessary, the organizing residents usually found him or her before posting the announcement. In order to join the group, interested residents would simply show up at the meetings or talk with members. No group actively recruited new members.

The management passively encouraged all informal group activities; that is, they made every effort to provide accommodations for

Table 10-1.   Hobby Groups

Name of Group	Frequency of Meetings	Average No. of Participants	Men or Women	Need for Instructor
Japanese chess	Every day	10	Men only	Medium
Morning walking	Every day	8	Both	Low
Croquet	Every day	10	Both	High
Knitting	Twice a week	4	Women only	Low
Nagauta (traditional singing)	Twice a week	6	Women only	High
English	Once a week	7	Women only	High
Koto (stringed instrument)	Once a week	7	Women only	High
Chorus	Once a week	23	Both	High
Record concert	Once a week	10	Both	Medium
Discussion A	Once a week	10	Both	Low
Reading sheet music	Once a week	6	Women only	Medium
Discussion B	Once a week	10	Both	Low
Yōkyoku A (traditional music)	Once a week	5	Women only	High
Yōkyoku B	Once a week	4	Women only	High
Tea ceremony	Once a week	8	Women only	High
Japanese calligraphy A	Once a week	6	Women only	High
Japanese calligraphy B	Once a week	7	Women only	High
Painting/ drawing	Twice a month	10	Both	Medium
Wood carving	Twice a month	9	Both	Medium
Wood-block printing	Twice a month	10	Both	Medium
Haiku (poetry)	Once a month	18	Both	High
Doll making	Once a month	6	Women only	Low
Golf	Once a month	8	Men only	Medium

the activities but did nothing else to facilitate them. There was no activity coordinator on the staff.

There were twenty-three hobby groups in 1983, and their characteristics are presented in Table 10–1. The usual frequency of meeting was once a week, although there was some variation. The number of participants ranged from four (in the knitting group and one of the *yōkyoku* groups for traditional music) to twenty-three in the chorus, with the majority of the groups having around ten people. The number of participants in each group appeared to be determined not only by the group's popularity, but also by the size of the available room and the size that is ideal for a given type of hobby—for *yōkyoku*, for instance, seven people would be the maximum for an ensemble. There were thus two *yōkyoku* groups and two calligraphy groups.

Women were clearly more active in hobby groups than men. Only two groups were solely men—Japanese chess (*go* and *shōgi*) and golf. Eleven were women only, and ten were of mixed gender. Eleven groups were ranked high in need for an instructor, which meant that their activities would be difficult without recognized experts as instructors. A male member of the croquet group was officially qualified as a referee, and he not only interpreted the rules during the games, but also coached members and was recognized as the semiofficial instructor. Likewise, the instructor of the English group had been a high school English teacher; the other members were all beginners.

The availability of these semiformal instructors was usually important for group formation. With the exception of the chorus instructor and the *haiku* poetry instructor, who came from the surrounding neighborhood, all instructors were residents of the community.

Some groups lacked recognized instructors but had skillful or knowledgeable members who acted as *ad hoc* instructors as needed. This happened when the activity did not require very skilled instructors or when the skill level of the members was already high. In the record concert group, a few members who were particularly knowledgeable about classical music gave short explanations, but the group sometimes functioned without them. The wood carving group had several very skillful members whose technical abilities were almost indistinguishable from one another. Any skillful member could give advice to the beginners, and they also exchanged advice among themselves.

Five groups had little need of instruction at all. The morning walkers simply met at 6 A.M. and took about an hour's walk together around the community.

There were many traditional hobbies—Japanese chess, *nagauta*, *koto*, *yōkyoku*, tea ceremony, Japanese calligraphy, and *haiku*—supporting the Japanese stereotypical view that old people enjoy traditional hobbies. Most hobby group members had pursued their hobbies for a long time, and some of them were semiprofessional. This was particularly true among female participants in traditional arts, and all the instructors in these groups had high-level official certificates. Instructors or otherwise, all these women started taking lessons when young, a practice typical in upper-middle-class families.

On two occasions each year, the hobby groups demonstrated their activities or exhibited their works: the May 15 anniversary festival commemorating the opening of the community and the community festival on Respect the Elders Day, September 15, a national holiday. Activity groups such as chorus, *nagauta*, *yōkyoku*, and tea ceremony held demonstrations in various rooms in the community center; craft groups exhibited their works, such as knitting, wood carving, wood-block printing, or Japanese calligraphy, in the craft room.

PATTERNS OF PARTICIPATION

Of 121 residents for whom interviews were completed, overall 71 (58.7 percent) belonged to at least one hobby group. Among 40 men, 27 (67.5 percent) had at least one membership; 13 (32.5 percent) had none at all. Among 81 women, 44 (54.3 percent) belonged to at least one group, and 37 (45.7 percent), none. Thus, in simple proportion, men, although a minority in the community, appeared to be slightly more active than women. However, men's and women's participation patterns were distinctly different.

Table 10–2 illustrates patterns of participation by sex. No residents had more than 7 memberships. Among active men, the number of memberships clustered in the range of 1 to 4 groups, with a mean of 2.8. Nearly half the active women had only 1 membership, and the mean was 2 groups. In terms of individual participation, men were more active than women. Thirteen of the 40 men (32.5 percent) and 37 of the 81 women (45.7 percent) belonged to none at all.

The unaffiliated men's reasons for their nonmembership are categorized into six groups. Four mentioned declining health, and another four said they preferred to use their time with complete free-

Table 10-2.   Male and Female Memberships in Hobby Groups

Number of Groups	Men		Women	
0	13	(32.5%)	37	(45.7%)
1	8	(20.0%)	21	(26.0%)
2	5	(12.5%)	11	(13.5%)
3	5	(12.5%)	7	(8.6%)
4	5	(12.5%)	4	(5.0%)
5	2	(5.0%)	0	(0.0%)
6	1	(2.5%)	0	(0.0%)
7	1	(2.5%)	0	(0.0%)
Total	40	(100.0%)	81	(100.0%)
Mean gps/actives	2.8		2.0	

dom. Three said they were not good in groups. One man mentioned that he had no particular reason, one said no group matched his interests, and one said he had to take care of his dependent wife. In other words, nonparticipation was a situational necessity for five of the thirteen men (38.4 percent)—either declining health or need to care for a wife.

The reasons given by thirty-seven unaffiliated women fall into seven categories. Nine said they found the social interaction in hobby groups annoying, and another nine mentioned that they preferred freedom of time use. Eight women said that because they were not yet completely settled down in the community and could not regularly attend, they felt their participation could disturb the group activities (*meiwaku ni naru kara*). Seven women mentioned their declining health, two mentioned they had to take care of their dependent husbands, and one said she had been indirectly refused membership. One said she was still studying which group to join. Thus, nine out of thirty-seven nonparticipating women (24.3 percent) mentioned either declining health or care of dependent husbands, and eight others had situational reasons for their nonparticipation.

These findings provide some insight into the residents' social attitudes. First, the unavailability of interesting hobby groups was not the main reason for nonparticipation—only one man gave that reason. Second, refusal to grant membership was exceptional, applying to only one woman, who, when she asked about participating, was told indirectly that the instructor of the group was not eager to have more members. Third, external reasons such as declining health and dependent spouses were important for both men and women, an understandable finding considering the advanced age of some residents. Fourth, many men and women stressed that they enjoyed personal freedom more than participation in the groups, and this characteristic appeared to be related to their lifestyles. Fifth, a significant number seemed to feel uncomfortable or shy in informal group situations. Men used the expression that they were not good at such things; women said they found the social atmosphere of groups annoying. They emphasized the costs of participation rather than the benefits of nonparticipation.

Although one may think that points four and five are opposite sides of the same coin, Kinoshita's impression from the interviews suggests otherwise. Those men and women who stressed personal freedom spontaneously used the same word, *jiyū,* to explain their nonparticipation. They appeared to mean what they said. Put another way, they appeared to emphasize the perceived benefits of their nonparticipation.

INTERACTIONAL CHARACTERISTICS

Three closely related attitudinal tendencies emerged from the study of hobby group behavior. First, none of the twenty-three hobby "groups" were actually groups in the sense of being closely coordinated or team activities. Rather, they were loosely organized and individual centered—really parallel, not interactive, activities. Attention seemed distributed serially or simultaneously to the individual members, rather than focused on the group, and this tended to be true even in groups that had a high need for instructors. For example, the *koto* group had to be completely reorganized after its initial members quit in a body, protesting the instructor's insensitivity to individual needs. The instructor was a semiprofessional artist and tried to have members play her original compositions. She assigned each a specific part and gave intensive lessons. This was apparently much more than the members wished to do; they simply wanted to play *koto* as a "light" hobby. Because the instructor did not change her view, the members decided to dissolve the group.

Second, many participants seemed to regard their relationships as primarily instrumental, not social, as evidenced in the wood-block printing group incident. At first, the group would give a small gift to the instructor twice a year, summer and winter, following, as other groups did, the Japanese custom of seasonal gifts to teachers. During the course of this research, however, many members became as skillful as the instructor, and in the late fall, some of the members met to discuss whether they should give him the usual gift now that there was little he could teach them. In the end, they decided to discontinue the custom and did so without giving any explanation to the instructor. Of course, it was obvious to him why he did not get a gift.

The third attitude has to do with gender differences in participation, and here we must introduce two key concepts for the analysis of social interaction among the residents: "situational specificity" and "additional significance." Situationally specific interaction, a concept derived from role theory (Parsons, 1951), means that behaviors, artifacts, people, places, or utterances have different meanings in the various social situations in which they occur or participate. A room used for a specified hobby group activity, for example, becomes the boundary of a "situation," and the meaning of all activity that takes place there is specific to that situation. A social interaction based on specific formal roles is interpreted specifically to the performance of those roles, that is, in terms of what is expected of each person in those roles. In the context of this discussion, this notion refers to interpersonal behavior in the context of various hobby activities. Additional significance is a concept similar to Levy's (1952:281) "functional diffuseness." It means the development of other meanings as a result of interactions that stem from functionally specific situations. For instance, a woman in the tea ceremony group participates in the group's activity, and interactions in this group have situationally specific meaning. However, as she engages in the activity, she is able to cultivate a sort of intimacy with other members, whom she comes to perceive as her "friends." This is referred to as the development of additional significance.

These two notions are useful in understanding residents in interaction in general and in gender differences in hobby group participation in particular. Although the objective data showed that more men participated in groups, and the participating men belonged to more groups on the average than women, the meanings men attached to participation were quite situation specific, whereas the women's style tended to generate more additional significance.

Hobby groups could be all male, all female, or mixed (Table 10–1). The Japanese chess group and the golf group were made up of men only. The golf group was a special case, and we discuss it in Chapter 11. Behavior in the chess group was typical of pure situation-specific interaction and had virtually no additional significance. This group met every day, with ten players or so at any given meeting. The members simply came into the room, found partners, played a game or two, perhaps watched others play for a while, and left the room. In both kinds of Japanese chess, *go* and *shōgi*, a game is played by only two persons, and both players remain silent most of the time, concentrating on thinking. Spectators also remain silent in order not to disturb the players. Conversations were rare and usually about the strategies of games. The meanings the men attached to their interactions were completely circumscribed by the situation. Although tournaments are enjoyed by such clubs outside the community, no Fuji-no-Sato member was willing to plan and organize a tournament, and there had never been one here.

Ten groups were composed of both men and women. In these, the meanings of both heterosexual and male-to-male interactions were situation specific also, although the women in these groups formed among themselves small circles that continued to associate outside the group.

The possibility of generating additional significance was most frequent in the eleven women-only groups, particularly in small groups whose membership was stable. In these groups, incompatible members were gradually filtered out, and regular interaction over several years generated intimate sentiments among the members. The *yōkyoku* A group was a good example of this. It had only five members, taught by a former professional. All the members valued each other and the instructor. They occasionally ate out together and held gatherings—a year-end party, for example—at an outside restaurant.

We are not aware of any detailed studies of hobby group participation among the elderly in Japan. An international survey by the

Prime Minister's Office (1982:136) showed that Japanese aged are much less likely than Americans to take part in volunteer activities outside the home and that only 16 percent of those over sixty take part in a hobby group. It is therefore our impression that both men and women at Fuji-no-Sato were highly hobby oriented for Japanese elderly. Although men's participation was situation specific, many were very active. Perhaps the men enjoyed hobby activities but are unwilling or unable to generate additional significance in their relationships; cultural attitudes are also involved here. Moreover, both men and women were active in hobbies they had enjoyed throughout their adult years. This was more true among the women, but many men also had been active in their hobbies while they were working. Finally, solitary hobby orientedness was discernable among those not active in groups, although this seemed far more characteristic of women than men. Many nonactive women took correspondence courses in such topics as Japanese classics, history, or *tanka* poetry.

The hobby orientedness becomes clearer if we look at Japanese cultural attitudes toward leisure activities. In America, leisure activity is culturally valued for its own sake, the so-called "fun morality" (Henry, 1963). Furthermore, a high activity level *per se*, leisure or otherwise, has cultural support in America—the healthy elderly are eager to show their vigor—and hobbies are probably more available than paid work to most. Some American social gerontologists support this idea by equating activity with adjustment. The notion is called "activity theory" (Maddox, 1964), and many American retirement communities advertise "an active way of life" as an attraction.

In contrast, all Japanese retirement communities emphasize medical and nursing care rather than an active way of life in their advertisements. The fun morality simply does not hold for the Japanese, especially those who are currently elderly. Throughout their lives, the stronger value has been the "work morality." Given their generation's attitude toward leisure, the residents' hobby orientedness must be related to their decision to live in a retirement community, probably partly as cause and partly as effect.

CHRISTIAN GROUPS

Among the interviewees at Fuji-no-Sato, there were at least forty-nine baptized Christians (eleven men and thirty-eight women); and there were others who, although not baptized, were philosophically Christian. The existence of these formal and informal Christians was in part due to the fact that although the managing organization of the community has no religious basis, it is an outgrowth of a Christian organization, a very large nonprofit social welfare corporation. In fact, the parent organization's president was a very famous charismatic Christian in Japan, and he was also the board president of Fuji-no-Sato's managing organization. Christian residents who knew of him appeared to trust him and thereby to judge Fuji-no-Sato as a reliable enterprise.

Many of the Christians had been believers all their lives, something that marked them as special in their generation and strengthened our perception that they were originally from intellectual, upper-middle-class family backgrounds. In the late nineteenth and early twentieth centuries, as Japan was undergoing modernization, Christianity first spread among the socially privileged, intellectual class. Only in subsequent generations did it become popular with other segments of society.

There were five Fuji-no-Sato groups organized by Christians: a morning prayer group, a discussion group, a hymn group, a sermon group, and a Bible study group. The morning prayer group met every Monday morning and was attended by about fifteen residents. The meeting was chaired by an eighty-three-year-old retired minister. This person also chaired a small discussion group every Saturday in which about six people participated regularly. Although this group was meant to be a free discussion group, the retired minister usually talked much of the time, as if he were giving a sermon. The hymn group was the only one headed by a nonbaptized Christian, and it was the most "secular" group of all; it had many informal Christians and even some non-Christians who simply liked the hymns. About eighteen residents gathered every Sunday. The sermon group was the largest, about twenty-three people who met three times a month to listen to tapes of famous sermons. The Bible study group of about twenty residents held meetings twice a month. The minister of a nearby urban church would come to chair the meetings.

The five groups were open to all residents, but except for the hymn group, their regular members were Christians. Nor were all the community's Christians, baptized or otherwise, regular members of these group activities. In fact, there was a great deal of membership overlap in the five groups, and many Christians belonged to none of them.

Three group organizers had acquired recognition as leaders among the Christians. Among these was the retired minister, the only resident from that profession. He was greatly respected by the other Christians, but his advanced age (eighty-three years) and declining health limited his activity; he was seen as a symbolic leader. Second, the leader of the sermon group happened to be Mr. Sonoda, the popular president of the residents association in 1982–1983. His modest, mellow character was admired not only by the Christians but by the residents in general. The third leader was a woman who organized both the Bible study group and the only volunteer service group at Fuji-no-Sato.

Individualism and functional specificity characterized social interaction in the Christian groups. Participants came to the scheduled meetings, engaged in scheduled activities, and departed when meetings were over. There was no active soliciting of non-Christians, no group socializing, and no outside scheduled meetings. The mere fact of Christian belief seems to create strong interpersonal bonds.

THE VOLUNTEER SERVICE GROUP

In Chapter 6, we mentioned that within the estate there is a fifty-bed nursing home operated by a separate Christian welfare organization, and a group of women volunteers helps at this facility. This group, the only volunteer service group at Fuji-no-Sato, was started by the Christian woman just mentioned. The group was loosely organized, with the leader simply assigning a group of three or four women to visit the home each day, Sundays excepted. Each group thus constituted took one turn a week, so there were six small groups, which never met jointly. Participants were not necessarily Christians. Whoever wanted to participate could contact the leader, who in turn would assign the new member to an appropriate day. No participant served more than one day a week, and no men participated. Their volunteer work, which never varied, consisted of folding and sorting the nursing home's large volume of laundry.

Participants usually met in the community and walked together to the home, where they would work for two to three hours in the afternoon. Their interaction was relatively functionally diffuse: They talked informally and exchanged information about the community while working. Doing the same thing regularly with the same people appeared to help them structure their lives and cultivate friendly relations. Although this was also true for some members of hobby groups, it seemed more applicable to this group for two reasons. First, because of the low functional specificity, small group size, and routine nature of the work, each volunteer could observe the others' personalities easily through informal conversation.

Second and more important, this was the only group that regarded its activity as a kind of "work." They called it *oshime tatami*, which literally means folding and putting away diapers, although the laundry at the *toku-yō* home included linens, clothes, towels, and other things in addition to diapers. It seems that the word "diaper" had symbolic meaning for them because a diaper symbolizes the work of intimate personal care, the culturally prescribed work of women. Although the work of personal care generally refers to motherhood, it does include the care for dependent aged parents, as in the traditional *dōkyo* arrangement. By calling the activity diaper folding, these women located it perceptually within their familiar framework of significant "work," a perception reinforced by two additional factors: (1) Unlike leisure activities, this service was seen as a *helping* and thus productive activity. (2) They drew a perceptual line between themselves and the aged in the home. As one woman said, "We are helping the pitiable (*kawaisōna*) old people." Engaging voluntarily in helpful group work stimulates sympathetic social feeling. Activity and talk are likely to be of a helpful sort, the commonality of goals supersedes mutual differences, and people see each other at their best.

When the right opportunities were there, the residents of Fujino-Sato eagerly took part in informal groups and felt good about their engagement. The problem in Japan is that such opportunities are extremely few. The volunteer group was successful because it took little effort to organize, and the activity was a familiar one. To the extent that the staff at similar facilities is able to help find other activities like this and encourage the organization of groups around them, community life might be richer. Indeed, the residents at Fujino-Sato were an enormous human resource; they had varied abilities and experience with which to help others.

GARDENING

Gardening was the most important solitary activity at Fuji-no-Sato. The physical effort, time, expense, and interest that many residents poured into gardening was remarkable. Within a couple of years of opening, almost every available space in the community had become a garden, neatly demarcated by volcanic rocks.

Gardening was the first spontaneous common activity among the residents, having begun within a month or so after the community's initial occupation. As these early settlers testified in story after story, this was enjoyable but physically hard work for them. The volcanic soil is thin and rocky, and the residents had to begin by removing most of the rocks. They recalled nostalgically those early days, when they enjoyed the natural friendship of adventurers, and neighbors would come together for mutual aid. Many of them first got to know their neighbors through this collaborative work.

Hard work was not the only investment they made in this venture. Once the rocks had been removed, the residents bought soil and fertilizers at the store in the community center. Because there was little natural soil in the beginning, the amount of topsoil they bought was enormous. Some residents hired professional gardeners to design the planting.

Initially, gardening space was claimed on a first-come, first-served basis, and the early residents naturally occupied the best spots in their neighborhoods. By the end of the second year, nearly the whole grounds had been claimed and developed; but in spite of their emotional and financial investment, early residents listened to the needs of later settlers to participate. Gradually, a pattern of setting aside some garden space for new residents emerged.

Gardens represented the residents' taste in plants. Some had only trees in their gardens, others preferred less colorful wild plants, but the vast majority liked to plant flowers in such a way that their gardens were rarely without blooms. Growing vegetables was practically unheard of. Instead of buying bedding plants, most residents would order seeds through the mail, germinate them by hand (usually in their rooms), then transplant them in the gardens. For this, they had to acquire some knowledge and technique. The most important part was planning: What kind of flowers should be planted in which seasonal order? What kind of care would they need?

Women were more active than men in gardening. Among married couples, wives were generally in charge of gardening, although their husbands sometimes helped with heavy work. There was also a tendency toward scaling down one's engagement in gardening as one's health declined, either by planting relatively carefree plants or trees or by giving up gardening and passing the space to someone else. Meticulous care and constant attention were showered on growing particular kinds of flowers.

Gardening had six important meanings in the context of Fuji-no-Sato. First, it was a hobby. Even those residents who were not involved in gardening often mentioned that they liked plants and gardening. The lush natural surroundings of Fuji-no-Sato were one of its attractions to many. Because gardening is a hobby that one can do alone, it also seemed to suit the individualistic life-style of many residents.

Second, gardening may have effectively compensated for one of the most serious problems in this community: the limited social stimulation and consequent boredom. Gardening provided constant change for the residents. Plants never stay the same, and their life cycle is often less than a year, allowing residents to observe the cycles of growth, peak, and decline.

Third, the constant demands of the plants meant never-ending "work" for the residents, who conceived a sense of social responsibility for the look of things, especially if many colorful flowers were involved. The best known resident in this regard was Mr. Tsuruno, a sixty-five-year-old widower who was known as "Mr. Gardener." Dressed in work clothes, his habit was to toil in the gardens every day. Not only had he the most extensive "private" gardens, he received from the staff custody of the "public" gardens near their administrative offices as well and even persuaded the director to build a small greenhouse. Because of his special status, Mr. Tsuruno could ask the staff to water the plants or monitor the temperature in the greenhouse when he was not available. Although he often complained of the burden of his responsibilities, there was no denying that he enjoyed both the work and the status.

Fourth, gardening was also a form of competition for some of the women, who competed to produce the first flowers each season. Mrs. Fujita, a seventy-four-year-old widow, was one of the keenest in this competition. She ordered her seeds by mail, germinated them in her room according to a careful schedule, and planted the seedlings in her garden even before the seasonally safe moment. If she was successful, she would have flowers sooner than other residents; if she failed, she always had some reserve seedlings in her room. Like other residents involved in the competition, she never talked about her motives, but it was obvious to those interested in gardening that her success would be widely recognized. All the true gardeners knew the seasonal timing of the various plants; and of course, gardens are a highly visible arena for competition.

Fifth, due to certain interactional problems at Fuji-no-Sato, gardening may have been a socially "safe" activity for the residents. As a point of mutual interest, it could generate socially neutral conversation and interaction. People could exchange their knowledge and techniques or trade young plants without getting too personally close. It gave functional specificity to interaction.

Finally and most important, gardening appeared to be a sanctuary for many residents, particularly women. The formality of relationships, and the gossip, created stress. Residents could feel at ease and be themselves when gardening. When asked what they liked most about gardening, many said, "Plants respond to us in a *shōjiki* way." *Shōjiki* means "honest," "upright," or "straightforward," generally referring to the human character. In this context, it meant that, unlike in interpersonal relationships, where one's genuine intentions were often misunderstood, gardening produced results that were faithful, for better or worse, to one's true ability. The plants were "straight" to one's intentions and skill, thereby giving one a sense of control that was lacking in interpersonal relations. Although this problem is a chronic one throughout Japanese society as a whole, it was particularly troublesome at Fuji-no-Sato.

11

Patterns of
Social Interaction

Our study of social interaction is implicitly comparative, seeking to juxtapose Fuji-no-Sato with age-homogeneous settings that have been described in other cultures. In this sense, we are interested in characterizing this community as a whole—as a particular kind of social entity whose patterns are determined by the rules of its parent culture, by its demographic and physical structure, and by its unique history. Previous chapters have been devoted to the details of these constraining factors and have laid the groundwork for the discussion that follows.

We also found a good deal of internal complexity at Fuji-no-Sato, a variety of interaction styles and problems, depending on the details of the interpersonal event—the setting, the actors, and the purpose of the interaction. Rather than discuss the variety of interactions, we focus on the cross-cultural level of analysis, therefore underlining those features of background and setting that make Fuji-no-Sato stand out as a unique whole. Other analytic strategies—a focus on residents' personalities, for example—would produce other impressions of the community.

The first task in presenting Fuji-no-Sato as a culture-specific set of social patterns is to show, in broad strokes, its typical *kinds* of interaction. Under what circumstances do people usually come together and why? What features of the setting distinguish this from other communities and give it internal consistency? The second task is to explore in some detail those cultural *norms* governing interpersonal behavior that are especially relevant. Only then can we examine the characteristic social problems and processes that result: the problem of controlling social interaction, the socialization of new residents, and the establishment and maintenance of friendship.

SETTINGS

We distinguish between "interaction" (a structured sequence of behaviors that results as two or more residents mutually react to each other directly) and "encounter" (people's mere coming into close proximity). We use the word "setting" to refer to the socially defined space in which interaction occurs, including the physical space (room, path, courtyard, bench, etc.) and the broad meaning of the behavior occurring in that place at that time (chance meeting, lesson, medical consultation, meal, etc.).

There are two important broad classes of settings. "Functionally specific" settings are those in which participants share a fairly specific purpose. In "nonspecific" settings, shared or recognized purposes are minimal or absent. For example, when a group meets in the craft room for wood carving lessons or when a resident shows up in the clinic waiting room, the setting is functionally specific. Nonspecific settings include casual encounters or agglomerations of people in open areas like the lobby of the recreation building or one of the neighborhood streets. The importance of this distinction results from the importance of mutually shared expectations and mutually accepted rules of conduct as catalysts for social interaction in Japanese culture. The culture is relatively poor in rules for the formation of goal-free, diffusely gregarious interactions among new or distant acquaintances, with the result that nonspecific settings rarely lead to the formation of real relationships.

One way to explain this is to say that interaction outside the first-level sphere of *amae* (see Chapter 2) is usually regulated by the performance of well-known social roles; the intrusion of personal material—feelings, opinions, needs, attractions, and aversions—into such second-level relationships is generally avoided. Having a formal purpose provides the role structure within which interaction has socially accepted meanings and predictable outcomes while deflecting attention away from the participants' personal actions and motives. These characteristics thus allow smooth interpersonal relations with a minimum of intrusion from the personal sphere. This in turn allows functionally diffuse first-level relationships to develop gradually among the participants through "side interactions" ostensibly related to, or permitted by, the main purpose of the setting. We referred to the possibility of these side interactions (which, incidentally, can be the main motive behind forming the setting in the first place) in Chapter 10 as "additional significance" of functionally specific settings. However, additional significance does not automatically appear in functionally specific settings.

Social interaction at Fuji-no-Sato is limited compared with age-homogeneous communities in other cultures because (1) functionally specific settings are few, (2) interactions in such settings often do not generate additional significance, and (3) nonspecific settings have very limited possibilities for forming ongoing relationships.

Functionally specific settings at Fuji-no-Sato can be divided into two groups. First, membership groups engaged in activities that occurred in the activity rooms or outdoor hobby areas and were structured by their scheduling (time and place) and attendance (members only). Second are settings where residents pursued individual aims in a common public space.

It was difficult for membership groups to meet spontaneously or schedule additional events because the community lacked appropriate space for such things. However, even if the opportunity were there, it is doubtful that many of these groups would have evolved much additional significance. Because their interactions were defined by their *members' choice to engage in a specific activity,* the overall contribution of each participant's conduct in meeting this group goal was constantly at issue, leaving the typical participant with a keen sensitivity to his or her responsibility, and thereby damping spontaneity.

The major functionally specific settings where residents came together in common space to pursue individual aims included the dining hall, the hot spring bath, the clinic waiting room, and the shop/office at the community center. These settings tended to generate whatever additional significance residents found in their community interactions and encounters because participants had relatively little choice about being there as opposed to somewhere else. The contribution of each person's behavior to some accepted *group* goal (other than general politeness and affability) was therefore not at issue. At the same time, certain constraints tended to structure interaction among casual acquaintances (the need to wait; the time needed to eat, bathe, or shop; taking turns; respecting personal space and other needs; etc.).

The importance of these settings was great. Many residents, especially the newer ones, would have had trouble finding any occasion for conversation with others if the communal settings had not existed. Many residents made a point of having at least one meal a day at the dining hall, mainly because of the sociability this provided. The opportunities these settings provided were limited, of course, by the infrequency of their use. One cannot spend much more than an hour a day bathing, and the clinic waiting room provided only a few minutes of casual interaction every few weeks for most residents. Even in the dining room, the time actually required to eat was less than the scheduled one hour for breakfast and hour and a half each for lunch and dinner.

The exception to this limitation was the shop/office, which was open from 9 A.M. to 5 P.M., with an hour break for lunch. Residents could go there any time of day for a variety of purposes—checking the mail, buying sundries, reporting maintenance problems, requesting services, reserving guest rooms, signing up for meals, and so on. The functional specificity of the setting permitted casual interaction, and the relatively wide variety of functions reduced mutual expectations among patrons and disinhibited light interaction while multiplying opportunities for any given resident to meet others.

The lack of willingness to inject personal values and needs into nonintimate social interactions resulted both in residents' failure to use *unstructured* public space for casual interaction and their failure to use existing nonspecific settings to develop relationships. A few places, like the porch of the community center and frequently used streets, did produce a great many encounters, but these tended to be very brief and superficial.

A corollary of the sharp division of Japanese social interaction patterns into first- and second-level types is that the sphere of personal life, symbolized by one's dwelling place, is sharply set off from the sphere of public life. Japanese do not "drop in" on each other unless they are already intimate. The traditional home is separated from the street by a formal entryway or *genkan*, which marks the transition from the public to the private space. Unless a visitor is an intimate of the household, he or she must be greeted by the resident in the *genkan* and formally invited to cross the private threshold. This ceremony obligates both parties to show formal courtesy and is seldom incurred unless important business is at hand. Consequently, there was relatively little visiting from apartment to apartment.

BUILDING INFORMAL TIES

Although residents shared many characteristics and spent most of their time on the premises (which are surrounded, after all, by deep woods), little informal interaction developed. A Westerner is tempted to conclude from this that the residents were lonely and bored, but this is not quite what our research indicated. In his interviews, Kinoshita gave people ample opportunity to express their private feelings about their social lives, and their answers were often surprisingly candid.

On the whole, few residents had any regrets about the shallowness of their neighborhood interactions. Many spontaneously commented that they didn't want deep or close relations with their neighbors. One typical way of justifying their lack of close friendships was to say, "My relations with other people here are strictly *tatemae.*" The expression *tatemae* refers to one's social self, as opposed to one's private, idiosyncratic self, or *honne*—the self one reveals (if at all) only to intimates. The *tatemae* and the *honne* are the selves expressed in the *enryo*-laden second level and the *amae*-laden first level, respectively. Although the latter is far more desirable, it is foolish to expect it from ordinary acquaintances.

This finding of low motivation for close neighborhood relations is also common in other types of planned communities in Japan (see Kiefer, 1976), but it is not easy to explain. There are probably several reasons for it.

One reason may be a kind of self-fulfilling prophecy. Knowing the difficulty of establishing deep relationships under such circumstances, the residents simply distributed their energies to other needs and expected little from their neighbors. This would help keep the rewards for casual interaction minimal, which in turn would confirm the prophecy. Such expectations may have been strengthened by the fact that many residents, especially the men, had achieved a rather high level of social status during their work careers and therefore presented a daunting prospect to anyone who would want to be their friend.

Expectations for neighborhood intimacy were also lowered, it seemed, by the fact that many residents would have preferred to live with children if their family relationships had been stronger. Many saw themselves as deviants in this respect—as people who failed to found a "normal family" and therefore less than admirable neighbors themselves. It was obviously different for never-married residents (who, of course, had social problems of their own), but those who did have children, especially sons, tended to be defensive about this. They perceived a certain stigma attached to their living at Fuji-no-Sato as a result of the nontraditional character of that choice.

Another likely explanation actually supports disengagement theory. Having spent their productive lives deeply involved in many taxing relationships, they had had enough and looked forward to some solitude and autonomy in late life. Residents would say that they had spent sixty or seventy years developing their own personalities and saw little need to change to accommodate others. The other side of the status question comes in here as well. Many of them may have felt they would stand to lose status by associating with less accomplished neighbors. This dynamic was probably supported by the relative formality of ordinary second-level relations and by the fact that Fuji-no-Sato is a small, relatively isolated community where it is difficult to avoid people one does not like once one has established a relationship with them. Although this last may also be true of some Western age-homogeneous communities, it is particularly serious in Japan, where the consequences of social mistakes are relatively severe and permanent.

Two final reasons for the lack of motivation to form close bonds were the gossip problem and the sheer unfamiliarity of the setting. Lacking a traditional hierarchical social organization and set of neighborhood institutions, Fuji-no-Sato residents found themselves rather vulnerable to destructive gossip. Because the great majority of them had lived in traditional independent housing most of their lives, they were also on the whole unfamiliar with apartment or condominium living and therefore naturally insecure about how to get along with their neighbors here. *Tatemae* was a means of imposing a familiar structure on an unfamiliar situation.

GENDER DIFFERENCE

So far we have been discussing interaction at Fuji-no-Sato as though it were gender-neutral, but this is far from true. Men tended to maintain considerable distance in their interactions through the use of formality and self-restraint, whereas women tended to be much more socially active, both in the beneficial sense of friendly interaction and in the destructive sense of gossiping. Interactions between the sexes were relatively few and tended to be highly functionally specific. Both men and women tried to avoid much contact with the opposite sex, not only because the culture as a whole tends to restrict heterosexual contact to certain very specific role sets but because the residents (especially women) had a profound fear of gossip.

On the whole, interaction among men was so limited and shallow that one sometimes had the impression that friendship did not exist among them. They typically chose their vocabulary from the highest levels of politeness and formality, for example. This linguistic habit is difficult for a non-Japanese speaker to visualize; but some of the flavor may come through if one imagines a conversation between two English bankers, each of whom believes the other to be a member of the royal family. Favored conversation topics were very general political and social issues or problems with the management of the community. Men often characterized their mutual relations simply by saying, "We respect one another."

Casual interaction among women, although problematic, was much more evident (more frequent, diverse, and intimate in tone), probably because women's socialization and adult roles permit somewhat less formal interactions at level two.

KEY NORMS

Close observation of the regularities of social interaction at Fuji-no-Sato revealed a number of widely shared but unstated, and perhaps often unconscious, rules about appropriate behavior, which we can call *norms*. Norms are the evaluative standards against which behavior is judged. Although they are often implicit and must be inductively derived from the observation of behavior itself, they can often be stated explicitly by the more self-conscious and articulate members of society, and they are necessary for learning patterned social behavior. Rosow says: "The sheer presence of norms is a *necessary but not sufficient* condition of effective socialization. While there can be little socialization without norms, the converse does not inevitably follow—that the existence of norms assures effective socialization" (Rosow, 1974:71, original emphasis). In a similar vein, we are claiming that norms are necessary but not sufficient for regulating and structuring, or patterning, social interaction.

In Chapter 2, we examined Rosow's contention that age-homogeneous communities in America often provide opportunities for elderly residents to develop norms peculiar to their own neighborhoods and to develop positive self-images and strong interpersonal relationships on the basis of these new norms. We mentioned that this might not work well in Japan because of the division of norms into first- and second-level types and the importance of age grading and other forms of social hierarchy in the role sets generated by these norms. In America, then, the isolation of a class- and culture-homogeneous group of elderly from other groups—particularly younger age groups—actually fosters the development of new roles and the socialization of residents to the performance of these roles. In Japan, homogeneity may have the opposite effect: The absence of younger generations in the community may prevent the socialization of the aged to normal (which is to say, familial) roles and may fail to provide the social distinctions (age, prestige, etc.) out of which normal relations, which are typically hierarchical, and their supporting norms can grow.

At Fuji-no-Sato, this situation was compounded by the newness of the neighborhood. Lacking traditional institutions like businesses, churches, families, and self-government, the community offered few traditional roles, or role-norms, upon which social relations could be based. But this does not mean Fuji-no-Sato was normless. There are many general norms available in Japanese culture from which people can and do choose in constructing a sensible social life. The residents had modified and enlarged this hypothetical list to produce the orderly interactions we saw in the community. Of the many operant norms at Fuji-no-Sato, we have chosen three that seem particularly useful in understanding the quality of life there, recognizing that this list is by no means exhaustive.

"Don't Cause Trouble (*Meiwaku*) to Others"

By far the most important norm at Fuji-no-Sato was the need to avoid imposing on others' comfort and freedom. This was usually expressed as the avoidance of "causing *meiwaku*"—a concept that is difficult to translate but overlaps the ideas of "trouble," "annoyance," "bother," "nuisance," and "inconvenience." This idea is probably familiar in all cultures in one form or another, but it had acquired special significance at Fuji-no-Sato, to the extent that it seemed to color almost every act of at least some of the residents.

The Japanese tend to use *meiwaku* as a gauge of the closeness of relationships. The closer or more intimate two people are, the more they can expect of each other, and thus the less likely a given act is to be classified as *meiwaku*. Put otherwise, a given request may cause *meiwaku* if asked of someone at the outer edge of level two, but not of someone in level one. The objective magnitude of the request is of course also relevant, so there are some things one cannot ask even a relative to do.

In general, though, the concern over causing *meiwaku* is characteristic of second-level relationships. Where one cannot expect a high tolerance for dependency, yet where there is enough of a relationship that the other would have difficulty simply refusing a favor, one must strive to assess accurately the amount of *meiwaku* in a request before making it. If there is danger one has exceeded the limit, one is likely to add to the request *meiwaku o kakete, sumimasen* (I'm sorry I'm causing you [this] trouble). Conversely, one should not be *over*concerned with causing *meiwaku* to intimates for fear of being accused of overformal (*mizu-kusai*) behavior.

Those familiar with Takeo Doi's writings on dependency in Japan will notice that there is great overlap between indulgence in *amae* (dependency behavior) and in causing *meiwaku* when the *meiwaku* is a request for self-gratification. In this case, *meiwaku o kakete sumimasen* is almost synonymous with *gokoi ni amae sasete itadakimasu* (I will indulge myself in your kindness). There are strict limits on the range of situations in which one may get away with a mere apology of this kind.

The central significance of the *meiwaku* norm at Fuji-no-Sato can be explained on the basis of the unusual role of *dependency* in the residents' life-styles. Briefly, most of these people seemed to have been unusually independent throughout their lives, the decision to come to this community was itself a statement of this independence, and the maintenance of an appearance of self-sufficiency was crucial to residents' self-esteem. We examine this analysis beginning with two examples.

First, as we mentioned in Chapter 7, many residents answered the question about their motives for moving to Fuji-no-Sato by saying, "In order not to cause *meiwaku* to our children (daughters-in-law, siblings, etc.)." The degree of apparent *meiwaku* avoided in this way varied according to the family situation, so some residents could have elected the traditional three-generation living arrangement (still a widely accepted level of *meiwaku*), but others would have had to depend on other kin (less acceptable). In any case, the residents' ability to choose a low-*meiwaku* alternative, living at Fuji-no-Sato, apparently gave them a profound sense of control over their own fate.

Second, one of the hobby groups was studying *yōkyoku*—traditional songs accompanied by the *shamisen*. When one of the group reported that her neighbor had complained about the noise of her home practice, the entire group immediately voted to give up home practice altogether in order to avoid possible widespread *meiwaku*. They did not ask their own neighbors how they felt about the practicing or suggest that practicing could be done carefully. The report of the single member engendered the assumption that all their neighbors may have been enduring unacceptable *meiwaku* and that this was a chance the students dared not take. This was, in effect, a kind of self-*meiwaku* because the group had access to the community center only one day a week, and their homes were the only other place they could practice. Their behavior, though, was typical here.

This analysis seems to fly in the face of the American belief that Japan is a society that encourages dependency, especially in the aged; but we are not really suggesting that dependency in general was mistrusted by our residents. Rather, Americans tend automatically to link particular kinds of behavior with particular moral attitudes; and when they do not find a particular behavior associated with the expected valuation, they assume they have found a *reversal* of the Western set. As Margaret Clark (1969) puts it, in studying other cultures, we must conceptually separate dependent behavior and the evaluation attached to it.

Japanese values are not a mirror image of American with regard to dependency. The Japanese elderly are not mysteriously permitted the very things American elderly are denied. True, there are forms of interdependency accepted in Japan that are rejected in America, but this does not mean the Japanese elderly enjoy a blissful irresponsibility vis-à-vis their children. *Meiwaku* upon children is better avoided if possible, just as is *meiwaku* upon anyone else. Dependency is more easily accepted when it is inevitable, not when it clearly can be avoided.

Consider the famous group centeredness of the Japanese in this context. The quality of interpersonal relationships has an unusually high priority in their value system, but this quality depends on *mutual* concern. The fact that one realistically *can* depend on one's children when necessary does not change the importance of one's concern for their well-being. As an objective measure of this, we offer three statistics: (1) About the same percentage of Japanese (44 percent) and Americans (42 percent) over sixty say they need to work for money. (2) Of the Japanese elderly, 39 percent, versus 24 percent of the Americans, work. (3) Although only 14 percent of working older Americans say they feel *obligated* to work, 38 percent of working Japanese elderly say this (Prime Minister's Office, 1982:117–119).

Given these observations about the structure of dependency in Japan, our analysis of the *meiwaku* norm makes sense. The fact that the residents at Fuji-no-Sato were able to live largely without first-level relationships shows that they had achieved a remarkable degree of independence for people their age. This achievement was not motivated, as it might be in the West, by a high priority on independence itself—mutual interdependence is still a yardstick of value in interpersonal relations—but because it allowed them to avoid causing *meiwaku*. This value was purchased at considerable cost to themselves, and it would simply be inconsistent for them to tolerate high levels of mutual expectation—high tolerance for *meiwaku*, if you will—in their new community.

Whether this preference for self-sufficiency grew out of innate character traits or was imposed by circumstances is difficult to say for most residents, but we believe it was the latter for the childless and those who had never married, especially women. Given that a family life, centered on raising children, is the prototype of intimacy among the Japanese, the absence of it from one's experience probably results in the development of habits of autonomy. Granted, there were individuals at Fuji-no-Sato whose past lives reflected more normative patterns of dependency, but the prevalence of self-sufficient types among the residents was enough to produce this extreme emphasis on the collective ethic of "no *meiwaku*."

"Exchange Respect"

The exchange of traditional forms of respect is another nearly universal Japanese norm that acquired special meaning at Fuji-no-Sato. One such form is the simple greeting, usually a bow and a few polite words. Greeting is especially important for older people in Japan, and it generally signifies that the greeter recognizes the identity of the other. Strangers are rarely greeted in casual situations.

The Fuji-no-Sato norm, which specified that every resident should always greet every other at each encounter, resulted in mutual verification of community membership. To the extent that Fuji-no-Sato was seen as a physical territory, this mutual greeting, which usually excluded visiting strangers, amounted to recognition of territorial boundaries. If a resident was not sure if someone was a resident, he or she gave the minimal greeting given to the most distant acquaintance: a short, silent bow.

This function of the greeting was especially clear when the norm was violated. The accusation, "She doesn't even return a greeting," was one of the harshest criticisms residents made of each other. Such a breach implied that the nongreeter did not want to share in the mutual acknowledgment of community membership. The person whose greeting was not returned experienced this as a stinging humiliation. It was as if the lack of acknowledgment amounted to a rebuttal of a strongly held, or at least strongly expressed, value—that residence itself implies a bond, perhaps tenuous but nonetheless crucial. Once a greeting had gone unreturned, it would never be offered again, and the possibility of a relationship between the two would be lost, apparently forever. The importance of returning greetings was so great that residents who had vision or hearing impairments worried a good deal about accidentally violating the norm. But their worry soon faded because the community evolved ways of greeting that were too conspicuous to go unnoticed or misunderstood.

The importance of this norm elevated the custom of greeting to a kind of yardstick of personal character among the residents. When they wished to criticize a young person for callowness or a daughter-in-law for a lack of filial feeling, they often metaphorically used the expression "doesn't even return a greeting."

This emphasis on small matters of etiquette is not unique to the Japanese setting. We have noticed it in American retirement communities as well, and it seems related to the relative *scarcity of media of exchange* that can be used to foster relationships in such settings. In more traditional communities, where people occupy a greater variety of roles, many things not only *can* be, but *must* be exchanged in the course of everyday life; and these exchanges build and cement relationships. Money, goods, information, advice, services, in-kind help, honors, thanks, even sex are all in daily circulation in a traditional community. But in a community where everyone's needs are fairly well met by a paternalistic staff and where there are few significant status differences or role specialties among residents, genteel deportment and kind speech are among the few things that can be exchanged. Under these circumstances, even small differences in manners among residents assume great significance, and major breaches of etiquette are disastrous.

This principle, which we might call *maximizing the available media of exchange,* also applied to other expressions of respect and concern appropriate among socially homogeneous neighbors sharing second-level relationships. Three important examples were attendance at funerals, use of personal names, and preservation of anonymity.

In a traditional Japanese neighborhood, everyone who knows the family of a deceased person usually attends the funeral ceremony, dressed in formal clothes. At Fuji-no-Sato, funerals of residents were usually held at the community center, and they were the best attended unplanned social gatherings in the community. Nearly every resident attended every ceremony, dressed with traditional formality. This custom appeared spontaneously with the first funeral in the community and has continued ever since. An attempt by the director to lower the level of formality by having staff attend funerals in ordinary work clothes with mourning bands was strongly criticized. Residents also rejected the director's suggestion that they themselves should dress less formally.

The only departure from traditional funeral etiquette had to do with the payment of funeral donations, or *koden*. This custom in a traditional community has the dual function of helping the bereaved meet funeral expenses and acknowledging long-standing relationships between the families in the community. Ordinarily, the recipient family keeps strict records of how much money is given by whom, and this exact amount (plus an inflation rate adjustment) is returned each time a member of the donor family dies. However, neither the economic nor the ritual function of *koden* was important at Fuji-no-Sato because the family of the deceased was usually able to pay funeral expenses without difficulty and because long-standing family relationships did not exist among residents. The custom of *koden* was willingly dropped after the first couple of funerals because it added nothing to the expression of respect; in fact, it could have been interpreted as a detraction—an implication that the deceased was not well-off.

Memorizing and using one another's proper names was another example of maximizing the medium of respect. In traditional Japanese communities, the necessity of learning everyone's name is eased by the custom of using kin terms for both address and reference. Thus, old people are generally called "grandmother" (*obaa-san*) or "grandfather" (*ojiisan*), people of a certain age are called "aunt" or "uncle," younger people are called "older sister" or "older brother," and so on. At Fuji-no-Sato, this was somewhat impractical to start with because everyone would be *obaasan* or *ojiisan*. It is also more formal and respectful to use names. As a result, kin terms were never used, either by the residents or by the staff, to refer to residents; names were used instead. It was therefore important to learn the names of as many residents as possible as quickly as possible, ideally until one could recall everyone's name on sight.

This has some peculiar side effects. For one thing, kin terms are age specific, whereas names are not. Using names helps eliminate considerations of age as status markers and thus works as a social leveller. For another thing, substituting personal identity for social role as a term of address may have encouraged psychological individualism and contributed to some of the self-assertive tendencies we have mentioned. Third, it resulted in a loss of age-related identity among the residents, so they sometimes actually seemed to forget their social identities as elders. On one occasion, when Kinoshita had accompanied an elderly resident to the hospital, she was called by a nurse in the usual way, "*Obaasan, obaasan,* this way please." Later the resident said, "You know, Kinoshita-san, I was a bit surprised at the hospital today. When I heard the nurse call '*Obaasan,*' at first I didn't know who she meant. The next moment I told myself, 'Why, it's me! I'm an *obaasan!*' But I haven't thought of that in some time."

There was another peculiarity of the community that produced a special type of respect behavior: the *preservation of anonymity.* In a typical Japanese community, the long association between neighbors produces a fund of shared information about many details of one another's life history, but Fuji-no-Sato society not only lacked this fund, it upheld norms that interfered with the sharing of such information.

There were two main reasons for residents' reluctance either to give or to request information about one another's background. First, because everyone's life had been lived outside the community in mutual anonymity, there was no way of verifying what people said about themselves. As a result, there was a lack of trust among residents, either that self-disclosure would be believed and accepted or that it would be given honestly. Some of the early residents apparently tried to establish a prestigious standing at Fuji-no-Sato by giving exaggerated descriptions of the wealth and luxury of their earlier lives. This attempt succeeded at first, but in the long run, it led to a *loss* of social acceptance among their uniformly high status neighbors, who saw their boastful attitude as somewhat crass and common. In the course of the first couple of years, this evolved into a norm whereby residents tended to withhold information about their former blessings and achievements and even regard an interest in their achievements as a kind of nosiness.

Second, there was a shared assumption that the move to Fuji-no-Sato might have been a second-best alternative for many. As a culturally deviant choice, so they thought, residence itself carried the suggestion that there might have been something slightly shameful about a neighbor's past. Mutual respect demanded that such secrets be carefully avoided in conversation.

"Dress to Impress!"

Although age norms regarding dress and grooming are more rigid in Japan than in the United States, two facts about Fuji-no-Sato led to innovation in this area. First, the age homogeneity of the community removed some of the pressure for conformity to the usual dress norms. There were few young people around to serve as contrasts to the residents' dress styles. Second, the relative homogeneity of social class and life-style eliminated many of the usual means of indicating wealth and social status (such as housing, neighborhood, and occupational cues), thereby shifting status competition to more subtle levels. We have mentioned the key role of gardening in this respect, but dress was equally important.

The residents took great care of their appearance. They wore clothes that were simple but of good quality. They were well groomed, and many women also dyed their hair. On the whole, the women used cosmetics more often and more heavily than other women their age, with the result that one noticed a "youngness" in the self-presentation. They did not look much like typical Japanese elderly.

Two revealing expressions of Japanese dress norms are *hade* and *jimi*. Although these terms are used to refer to one's overall format, including personality and life-style, they are often expressed in clothing. *Hade* is the term used to describe people who are a bit flamboyant—showy, zestful, youthful—perhaps to a fault. *Jimi* refers to the opposite, one who is a bit too sober, subdued, old for one's age. Younger Japanese women are more careful about avoiding an excess of *jimi;* older women shy away from a *hade* image.

Personal preference in clothes and grooming is generally subordinated to a strong set of norms that regulate one's impression on others. A women over seventy, for example, might feel that her own appearance is a bit too *jimi*, but will prefer to sacrifice her personal taste to create the desired social image. The norms are strong enough that Japanese who come to the United States for the first time are usually astonished by the appearance of American women, especially older ones, because the brightness of their clothes and the amount of makeup are much too *hade* by Japanese standards. If an elderly Japanese woman were to groom and dress like many American elderly, her sanity would be questioned.

The combination of age homogeneity and status homogeneity at Fuji-no-Sato led to a relaxation of these norms, so the typical woman resident would usually appear to an outsider too *hade* for her age, and many seemed to enjoy this freedom. There was a kind of competition to see who could get away with the most *hade* image. Because a person who went too far became the object of gossip, the range of *hade*ness was limited. For example, bright pink clothes were not acceptable, but some residents wore a soft, muted pink that appeared a bit *hade* by outside standards. Women also said that, at Fuji-no-Sato, they could again wear clothes they had discarded five or more years earlier as being too *hade* for their advancing age.

The residents talked a good deal about the importance of "proper appearance" in public places. This was probably a lifelong habit among these upper-middle-class people, but the freedom and leveling of their situation both strengthened its importance and added to it a flavor of adventure. One woman said, *"Jimi* clothes sometimes make me depressed. When I'm in a gloomy mood, like on rainy days, I try to wear something a bit *hade* and a bit more makeup. I don't think I'd have this freedom if I weren't living here."

GOSSIP

Gossip—the exchange and critical evaluation of more or less private information, often rumor and often negative, about a third party—was almost exclusively women's business and was especially common among those with a housewife's career. One common example of gossip was *speculation* about "suspicious" behavior or changes in behavior, as when a woman who usually ate with her husband in the dining hall happened to appear there alone or when two women who used to be seen enjoying walks together stopped doing so. This speculation was often the content of small group conversation. A second common example of gossip was *personal criticism*, usually between close friends: "This is only between you and me, but. . . ." For instance, Mrs. Akimoto bitterly commented to Mrs. Taga that Mrs. Maki should not have been allowed to perform a traditional dance at the community festival. Mrs. Akimoto, who had taken lessons for years, felt Mrs. Maki's amateurish performance was embarrassingly clumsy.

Gossip was a serious problem for many women at Fuji-no-Sato. Shortly after Kinoshita began fieldwork in the community, one woman said, "This is a frightening place [*kowai tokoro*]." It later became clear that she was referring, as many other women did in the course of the study, to the danger of character assassination through gossip. The women's fear seemed to stem from three conditions: (1) the absence of privacy, leading to their inability to control their public image; (2) the lack of a system of social control, whereby gossips and rumor mongers could be called to account; and (3) the lack of a system of information control, whereby false public belief could be corrected.

Mrs. Ogino and Mrs. Yosue, for example, were members of the same hobby group and formed enough of a friendship that the younger Mrs. Yosue often visited the apartment of the older and slightly disoriented Mrs. Ogino. It happened that Mrs. Ogino had mislaid some money and, as forgetful people often do, suspected someone had stolen it. She told the director. When the money did not turn up, she began to suspect Mrs. Yosue, who was the only other person regularly in her apartment. She mentioned this to the director and to some of her friends. Soon it became a widespread rumor, and Mrs. Yosue overheard it. Naturally, she was extremely dismayed and went to the director to protest her innocence. The staff and residents who knew Mrs. Ogino were fairly certain the whole thing was an artifact of her chronic confusion, but the news soon spread beyond this circle. Even though few residents gave any credence to this unlikely story, it made good conversation. Mrs. Yosue felt very strongly that she had to prove her innocence, but she did not know what to do.

A good example of the ease with which information was distorted could be seen in the rumors about Kinoshita himself. In the introductory notice he posted on the community bulletin board, Kinoshita mentioned that he had studied at the University of California for three years. He soon learned, to his amazement, that in the residents' eyes, he was the son of a wealthy family whom the president of the managing organization had met on a study tour in the United States, where he had invited him to come to the community. Kinoshita had to spend a great deal of time canceling these impressions as he got to know the residents.

The moral wrongness of gossiping was universally acknowledged, but residents' ability to resist the temptation was uneven.

Most women with work careers considered it a nuisance and avoided it. As one of them said, "I don't like hearing gossip, so I quickly switch the topic when conversation about other residents starts." Men were also self-controlled in their talk about each other. When asked their opinion about women's weakness for the vice, most men said something like, "Those women [usually meaning the housewife element] have never killed the self [*jibun o koroshita koto ga nai*]."

"Killing the self" is an expression meaning the attainment of mature self-control, especially control of the emotions, and it was well known by the men that this is necessary for cooperative work in a hierarchical setting. Not only are the demands of corporate work often stringent, but one's behavior must reflect a keen awareness of one's place in the pecking order of a bureaucracy or corporation. Gossip is, among other things, a form of status competition and as such is usually out of place in a setting where all statuses are well known and powerfully protected. Career women also have apparently had to learn to kill the self.

In contrast, the work of most housewives requires less close coordination of effort. The housewife may have to "kill the self" when it comes to appetites for comfort, luxury, and ease, as well as yearnings for unconventional forms of self-expression. In a neighborhood of housewives, although there is usually a fairly clear status hierarchy, the ranking system is likely to be less rigid than that of the work world in Japan, thereby inviting competition of all kinds, including gossip.

The gossips at Fuji-no-Sato were the commonest victims of their own art and the most anxious about the practice. Like any other Japanese, they were personally highly vulnerable to criticism. In a traditional neighborhood, the participant in gossip is buffered from the cruel world of wagging tongues by the fact that she has some control over the opinions of those within her first-level circle. The tattler knows who, among her own acquaintances, must not hear a particular piece of gossip from *her* lips: One can identify the friends of the victim. Thus, overlapping circles of intimacy provide a mechanism whereby gossip is kept under control. But the relative newness of acquaintances, and the relative inability of the Fuji-no-Sato women to form first-level relationships, greatly weakened this mechanism of control. The gossips, like everyone else, were unable to establish a defensive front against criticism aimed at themselves. They were also more likely to hear rumors about themselves than

others, and as experts, they had a precise appreciation of what the
system does to victims.

THE LACK OF MUTUAL
KNOWLEDGE AMONG MEN

If gossip was the chief problem among the women, the men's
problem was a lack of information about each other. Men maintained formality and distance from one another; they avoided conversation about personal backgrounds or anything that could be
construed as gossip. In their own words, they respected one another. They generally accepted the prevailing assumption, namely,
that their neighbors were uniformly successful in respectable careers (which was on the whole quite true), and they took the attitude that the decent way to deal with one another was as social
equals in any case.

One important result was that men knew very little about each
other—almost nothing, in fact, other than names. Some were frus-
trated by this because it made even casual conversation difficult.
Politics, economics, the news, and the management of Fuji-no-Sato
practically exhausted the list of possible topics. After interviewing
a retired physician, Kinoshita was asked by the man to disclose the
former occupations of some of the others. He stressed that he just
wanted to know who among them might have some interests in
common with him. He was also unsure of how to approach these
men even if he knew this.

In their work lives, the men had taken part in formal role sets
that had structured their interactions. The lack of such role sets
at Fuji-no-Sato created for them a kind of normative vacuum in
which interaction was difficult. In order to avoid embarrassment,
men were therefore required to treat one another with respect appropriate to the outer edge of level two, and they thereby entered
a vicious circle in which mutual ignorance perpetuated mutual
ignorance. The possibility of fairly continuous interaction is provided in the culture at large by formal role sets but was greatly reduced in the roleless situations characteristic of Fuji-no-Sato. This,
of course, interfered with the slow development of informal relationships too.

THE MANAGEMENT OF DISTANCE

Managing interpersonal distance was an important feature of social life at Fuji-no-Sato. Avoiding people one does not want to see is difficult in this small community. The residents evolved elaborate ways of doing so, and if those methods failed, they at least kept unwanted interaction to a minimum. For women, this was largely a problem of managing physical distance because their relationships lacked the formal distance typical of men's.

One method of distance management was the strict division of space into public and private—a practice illuminated by Goffman's use of the term "region." A "region," says Goffman (1959:106), "may be defined as any place that is bound to some degree by barriers to perception." He speaks of "front" and "back" regions, referring roughly to public and private space.

We have mentioned that mutual apartment visiting was very limited at Fuji-no-Sato; residents understood implicitly that mutual visiting was not an option except among fairly close friends. Women would say, "Our relationships here are only up to the doorstep (*genkan*)." Any place outside one's unit was therefore "front region," or public, and the apartment took on added meaning as *the* inviolate place, the one area in which one had complete control of encounters.

Events that could bring chance assortments of residents into close contact had to be planned with great care. When the staff planned a bus trip, for example, residents tended to avoid signing up until the last minute so they could make their decision on the basis of who else would be going. There was a fair amount of last-minute canceling as the list neared completion. Changing directions to avoid an encounter in the street was also common, as was "waiting until the coast is clear" if a resident spotted an undesirable encounter in the making.

However, due to the physical layout of the community, it was impossible completely to avoid unwanted encounters, and the strict rule on returning greetings precluded the possibility of ignoring someone who was obviously in the line of sight. Distance management was therefore found in the variety of greeting styles used in the frequent chance meetings. There was a fine gradation, ranging from the most distant (a silent, short bow while maintaining maximum physical space) to a mutual approach and a friendly chat. Even in the most distant greeting styles, residents were careful to make eye contact and to acknowledge the other's greeting. The former was necessary in order to interpret the other's greeting: Was this really a greeting and not (let's say) ducking under a tree branch? Was it really meant for me and not someone else? The necessity of returning greetings is obvious.

The extremely complex exchange of cues in these greeting styles would make an interesting study but is something we did not undertake systematically.

NEW RESIDENTS:
THE INFORMALITY OF SOCIALIZATION

Although he did not make a detailed study of the process by which new residents learned community norms, Kinoshita noticed a dramatic absence of formal procedure or ritual that might convey this kind of knowledge. This was important because it both exacerbated and drew attention to the lack of formal structure we have been talking about throughout this chapter. As Rosow (1974:28) says, "The general categories or referents of socialization and [social] integration are the same, so that socialization becomes one major mechanism of integration."

During Kinoshita's stay in the community, six new full-time residents actually moved in, although several others signed the entrance contract. Kinoshita interviewed four of the new residents about their moving-in experience.

The administration did little to introduce these new people, simply listing their names and apartment numbers on the administrative bulletin board when they had signed the contract. This had little effect, partly because there was typically a time lag between the signing and the physical moving in, or at least the taking up of full-time residence. As a result, new residents seemed to appear suddenly and unanticipated, without formal introduction from the management or anyone else.

In more traditional communities, of course, new neighbors occasionally appear as well, and often without formal introduction. There the custom is that one pays a call on the neighbors on each side and on those across the street, offering a small friendship gift.

But the fact that Fuji-no-Sato was *not* a traditional-style community either socially or in its physical makeup seemed to create some confusion about even this simple custom. New residents typically asked other residents what the custom was here, but the answers were not uniform. There was confusion not only about proper etiquette toward neighbors, but about the *definition* of a neighbor.

Two of the four new residents interviewed, having spoken to people who had not observed the traditional formal visit, decided that the custom was not observed here and simply introduced themselves informally to those who shared the stairs or walkways of their units. Each of the other two (one a widow, the other a widower) made formal visits to their neighbors, but differently. The widow, on the advice of a nextdoor neighbor, visited all the residents on her floor with a small box of candy. The widower, following the suggestion of a member of the residents association, visited the neighbors on each side and the one upstairs, but did not offer gifts.

Early interactions typically occurred around the problems of moving in and getting settled. Although the staff provided a good deal of help, the new residents had to learn from the older ones such practical information as where to get the best goods and services at the best prices. A certain number of female friendships usually formed as a result of this process between women who were neighbors or who found each other congenial in their chance encounters in public areas like the dining room or the baths.

One might expect that the residents association would have taken on some of the responsibility of introducing new residents, but this was not the case. Building representatives had no such official role, and there was no welcoming committee for the community as a whole. The community was not a formal institution, and the lack of a regular induction ceremony paralleled the attitude of individuality we have discussed.

None of the membership groups (hobby, religious, volunteer organizations) actively recruited new members. Newcomers were on their own in finding out from the bulletin boards, the staff, or other residents what social opportunities there were. They then had to muster the poise to seek membership on their own—something that deterred a fair number from taking part in group activities.

FRIENDSHIP

Friendship, that informal bond between people who simply find each other's company pleasant, is as difficult to study as it is essential for an understanding of social life. Individuals in any culture differ widely in the criteria they use for assigning the label "friend" to another, and any study of social networks reveals that the label is not always reciprocated. Rather than attempt a detailed study of the semantics of friendship, in this research, we simply chose to look at all kinds of sustained informal interaction among residents in search of typical patterns we could discuss under the broad heading.

There is little systematic research on friendship among older people in Japan, but even casual knowledge indicates that it differs somewhat from American patterns. As we mentioned earlier, both sexes, but especially men, tend to form strong lifelong bonds with peers from school years and early adulthood and to make few really close friendships thereafter. The tendency can be clearly seen in this segment from an interview with Mr. Oki, a seventy-four-year-old high-status retired business executive:

> The moment my friends and I meet at the reunion, we are brought back to our school days. Then we exchange news and ask about other friends who didn't make it. It's very sad to hear of the death of old friends, and it makes me realize my time is also running out. . . . Even after I started working, it was always these school friends—even though we were scattered—that I turned to when I had real personal or family problems. We can confide in each other down to our bones. . . . So, compared with my school friends, my relationships here [at Fuji-no-Sato] are only superficial.

Mr. Oki went on to say that the closeness and centrality of these old school relationships continued even though they did not meet very often. Unlike his neighbors, they were a network that stood ready to be mobilized on short notice, any time he needed them. There is, however, often an easy familiarity among men and women who share roughly the same level of social status and who are brought together by some mutual or parallel task.

At Fuji-no-Sato, we saw a marked difference between the sexes in the friendship patterns of older people who have not known one another long. This situation produced a mutual diffidence among

Table 11-1.   Extent of Men's and Women's Acquaintances

Number of Names and Faces Recognized	Men	Women
1–10	7 (14.6%)	11 (13.6%)
11–20	15 (31.2%)	20 (24.7%)
21–30	4 (8.3%)	20 (24.7%)
31–40	4 (8.3%)	3 (3.7%)
41–50	8 (16.7%)	13 (16.0%)
51–99	3 (6.3%)	3 (3.7%)
100+	7 (14.6%)	11 (13.6%)
Total respondents	48 (100.0%)	81 (100.0%)

men that almost completely precluded true friendship among them, but not so among women. We have already alluded to differences in roles and normative expectations of the two sexes throughout life that might help account for this. How, then, did the typical man or woman living at Fuji-no-Sato experience the community as a source of friendship?

One cannot be friends with people one does not know at all. Table 11–1 shows that both men and women tended to fall into two groups: those who knew few others (fewer than twenty for men and fewer than thirty for women) and those who knew many (more than forty). On any given day, about two hundred thirty to two hundred fifty residents were living at Fuji-no-Sato. Many of those with circles of recognition over one hundred had served as officers of the residents association, so on the whole, the typical politically inactive resident had a rather limited circle. The question is why. Although community norms (not causing *meiwaku*, not asking about background, etc.) and the fear of gossip restricted residents' freedom to get to know one another, our overall impression was that most residents were simply not interested in having a lot of friends or acquaintances, for reasons we have discussed.

Moving to a level deeper than mere recognition, Kinoshita distributed questionnaires asking residents to name three people with whom they were "familiar" and how they got to know these people. The Japanese word used was *shitashii*, which is more distant than a true friend (*tomodachi*), but closer than a mere acquaintance. The equivalent in America might be someone you know pretty well. As

Table 11-2.   Bases of Men's and Women's Friendships

Basis of Friendship	Men		Women	
Hobby groups	31	(35.2%)	54	(30.3%)
Neighbors	16	(18.2%)	49	(27.5%)
Dining hall	14	(15.9%)	8	(4.5%)
Christian group	7	(8.0%)	10	(5.6%)
Residents association	3	(3.4%)	2	(1.3%)
Same place of origin	3	(3.4%)	5	(2.8%)
Gardening	1	(1.1%)	4	(2.2%)
Graduates of same school	1	(1.1%)	8	(4.5%)
Hot spring bath	2	(2.3%)	7	(3.9%)
Common friends elsewhere	0	(0.0%)	6	(3.4%)
Previous acquaintances	2	(2.3%)	5	(2.8%)
Other	8	(9.1%)	20	(11.2%)
Total friendships	88	(100.0%)	178	(100.0%)
Total respondents	48		81	

a more general category than "friend," *shitashii* relationships include friendships. Table 11–2 summarizes the results.

Many people could not name three *shitashii* relationships, so the mean number for men in this survey was 1.8 and for women, 2.2. Hobby groups and neighboring clearly produced the largest number of friendships at this level, followed by use of the dining hall and the communal baths. If a resident did not join a hobby group, did not eat in the dining hall, and bathed at home, his or her chances of meeting people would have been small, other things being equal. This underscores the earlier point; that functionally specific settings tended to generate the most agreeable social interaction, although functional specificity was neither a necessary nor a sufficient condition for friendly contacts. This point is also emphasized by the fact that common background factors, like Christianity, were rarely enough by themselves to create social bonds. In fact, the lack of active mutual curiosity among the residents meant that they tended to be unaware of common backgrounds. Kinoshita's interviews and examination of the entrance applications revealed, for example, that some residents were fellow alumni of the same big universities and that many of the men had had similar occupations.

THE GOLF GROUP

Men, then, not only tended to know little about each other, but tended to classify low levels of knowledge and interaction—levels Americans would describe as "acquaintance"—with the term *shitashii*. The peculiar formality and distance of most informal relationships among men could only be overcome, apparently, when ready-made models of male solidarity could be transferred from the men's earlier lives to fit the circumstances of Fuji-no-Sato. This was clearly demonstrated by the golf group.

There were eight men in the golf group. They played at a nearby course once a month. The arrangements were made for the group by some staff members (including the director), who also played, although they were not regular members of the group. After each outing, the members and staff held a dinner party at a nearby restaurant. The interaction included drinking, singing, joking, and intimate talk about the attractive women at Fuji-no-Sato. The choice of vocabulary and conversational style was casual, contrasting sharply with the highly formal language ordinarily used between men in the community.

All the men in the group said in private that they liked the company of the others very much and that the relationships among them were different from those they had with other men in the community. There was remarkable agreement about their expectations of each other, and they all agreed that this was not close friendship, but rather "good company." Golfing had been a long-term social activity of all these men, and it was the only long-term social activity any group had brought with it into the community. Golfing, as a pastime of a certain type of upper level businessman, has developed a definite subculture of its own in Japan that includes well-known norms, among which is the expectation of easy sociability and informality among golfers on an outing. A similar atmosphere can be found in the frequent group minivacations that Japanese companies sponsor for their executives and the after-hours drinking behavior of men's peer groups of all kinds.

Here we had a form of informal sociability that resembled friendship in many respects but was specific to a limited kind of interaction. However much they may have liked each other's golfing company, the relationship between golfers did not really generalize to everyday life. It was a kind of *situational intimacy* that had many parallels to the *ritual* affirmation of social bonds in other societies. In the "new age" literature of post-1970s America, this behavior is referred to as "male bonding."

Ritual intimacy, or the "rite of renewal," generally functions to strengthen relationships that have other more important or more economic functions, such as cooperative action among neighbors or workmates. Here, these economic functions seemed to be absent, and the ritual seemed to have the sole function of providing sociability in an atmosphere where other forms of pleasant informal interaction were not able to develop. This is an example of the flexibility of the relationship between form and function in social behavior—the way a ritual pattern can be detached from its traditional function and used to fill a different need in another situation. The example of the golf group also serves as evidence of one of the main theses of our study: that the scarcity of cultural norms supporting casual sociability among relative strangers was a problem for the residents at Fuji-no-Sato.

FRIENDSHIPS AMONG WOMEN

In contrast to the men, the women appeared eager to make friends. Although most of their interactions were shallow, they observed one another closely in search of cues that a friendship might be possible. This was partly because sociability among women in traditional settings is less closely tied to formal roles and partly because these women were more likely than the men to be without a marital partner and hence perhaps more likely to suffer from loneliness.

In looking for potential friends, the women searched not so much for shared experience or formal similarity of status or background as for a general *feeling* of compatibility. They said they wanted to find *aishō no au hito*—"people who are compatible [with me]." *Aishō* is a common word in the language and simply means an unspecified "fitting together" of two personalities. It is a word used in describing the art of marital matchmaking as well as the feelings of friends for each other. The women at Fuji-no-Sato felt no need to specify what it meant to them, but it apparently included personality characteristics, life-styles, tastes, and expectations of the relationships.

Women spent a good deal more time than men in informal socializing and chatting and did so in more kinds of settings. This activity was of a more genteel and subdued kind than what one often sees in groups of elderly women in traditional Japanese communities, where sexual joking and bawdy singing are not rare. For one thing, the women of Fuji-no-Sato are quite refined in all their behavior. For another, they lack the lifelong acquaintance among themselves that supports disinhibition in late life. We can convey some of the flavor of female friendship at Fuji-no-Sato by offering an example of a more or less ideal relationship between two women, a true first-level bond between a pair of confidantes.

Mrs. Imamiya, age seventy-five, lived with her ailing husband. Her friend Mrs. Funaki was a seventy-six-year-old widow. They met for the first time at the dining hall soon after both had moved in. When the calligraphy group was formed, they both joined and thereby were able to meet in a functionally specific setting once a week.

At first, the two kept a cautiously polite distance as they gradually accumulated knowledge about each other's character, feelings, and habits. Each one told Kinoshita privately how she had learned that the other was neither a boaster nor a gossip. Still, neither took the initiative in establishing a deep friendship for a long time.

A year and a half after their initial meeting, Mrs. Funaki sent Mrs. Imamiya an invitation to come to her apartment for tea. This was correctly perceived as an invitation to enter a new kind of relationship. Mrs. Imamiya could have declined at this point if she had not been sure of their *aishō*, but she chose to accept the invitation. From this time on, Mrs. Imamiya could look forward to occasional visits to Mrs. Funaki's apartment. The two never met at Mrs. Imamiya's because her ill husband was usually there, but this was not a serious obstacle to the friendship.

Once the initial friendship had been formed, the two were often seen together in the community. They helped each other with shopping and other chores, and they spoke separately to Kinoshita about the pleasure they got from simply being together. Each said she respected the other, could confide in her, and would ask her for advice and help if necessary.

There did not seem to be many such close friendships at Fuji-no-Sato, but there were several, indicating that first-level relationships could develop between women, but they required time and favorable circumstances.

On the whole, social life at Fuji-no-Sato was what one would expect in a newly created environment of unrelated, habitually independent adults in a kin-based society where casual relationships tend to remain casual. Intimate acquaintance was neither common nor expected, for the most part. Smooth social relations were easiest in situations where minimal emphasis was placed on group norms and where the activity was familiar from other settings. The lack of clear rules for conduct and clear channels of communication interfered with the residents' ability to find close human contact when they wanted it and even to feel secure from the threat of isolation and status loss. Efforts to manage this situation led to heightened formality and heightened sensitivity to one's own and others' needs for privacy and respect.

12

Conclusions

This has been essentially a cultural gerontological study of an age-homogeneous community in a non-Western society. Through it, we have sought, first, to refine Western ideas about the social integration of the aged and, second, to look into the future of retirement communities in Japan. Other scholars and service workers will undoubtedly want to take other lessons from this study of Fuji-no-Sato, but we summarize what we see as the contributions of our work to our own guiding questions.

A FAMILY SUBSTITUTE?

In order to locate Fuji-no-Sato in the larger context of Japanese society, we examine again why retirement communities are emerging in Japan now. The aged population has been growing explosively; yet the traditional support mechanism, the *dōkyo* family living arrangement, seems to be losing its popularity and effectiveness. Expectations of filial support on the part of aged parents, and the sense of obligation on the part of adult children to give support, are changing, but no clear new norms have yet emerged. Meanwhile, the nation prospers, and many elderly have attained financial independence of their children, at least while they remain healthy. Although the Japanese government has been making a great effort to supply the needs of the dependent ill elderly by building *toku-yō* homes and increasing services like home care and adult day care (see Chapter 5), the long-term care system for the aged is still inadequate.

These factors mean that the elderly have little control over their own fate, even when they are physically and financially independent. The middle class, who cannot count either on their children or on admittance to *toku-yō* homes when they become dependent, are especially ill at ease about their future.

199

The retirement community is a new alternative to the fading tradition of the three-generation household, and it is the only really acceptable choice for the elderly without children. Quite naturally, "safety and security in old age" (*rōgo no anshin*) is the overwhelming concern of both developers and residents of these communities throughout Japan. But the retirement community is so new in Japan that it is only beginning to demonstrate itself as a reliable alternative to traditional care. Whether or not one's safety and security in old age in fact *can* be guaranteed through one or another of the many new retirement community models is still the key question here.

Given this crucial *economic* question, most developers at first largely neglected residents' social and psychological needs. Nor did the new tenants know how to create a pleasant and supportive society once they moved to a retirement community. Both sides shared the assumption that care would be provided for the physically and mentally dependent. Although the results are only beginning to show up, in our view, many retirement communities may prove unable to fulfill their claims, even with respect to basic care services. Further, the long period during which residents would remain independent got little attention from either clients or providers. Metaphorically speaking, the Japanese have been so busy building the container for a comfortable and secure old age that they have only begun to think what should be put inside.

The Japanese retirement community is, among other things, an experiment in *family* change. The traditional *dōkyo* arrangement has many advantages in its ideal form because it is a *total* support mechanism in which the financial, social, physical, and emotional needs of the aged are handled in one setting, albeit at the expense of heavy work that usually falls on the shoulders of one family member—most commonly a daughter-in-law. The ideal is in most cases far from the reality, and even the reality of *dōkyo* care is growing scarcer all the time. At the same time, no one, including the elderly and their children, expects the retirement community to become a family substitute in the traditional sense of total support. The expectation is that these communities will replace the physical care functions of the family, that is, that the elderly will be cared for when they become "bedridden" (*netakiri*) and/or "demented" (*boke*), two terms that always crop up in the speech of the Japanese aged when they talk of their anxieties for the future. This leaves the overall question unanswered: Who should bear the onerous responsibility for the overall well-being of the physically and mentally dependent elderly? If the retirement community is given this role by default, its future in Japan depends heavily on the extent to which it can live up to the challenge.

Still, the idea of care in a family setting lingers, especially among those with living children, even among the Fuji-no-Sato residents. Their most poignant dilemma is the double-bind of having exercised their autonomy by choosing an alternative that is somehow second best. It is as if their bodies and their minds have parted company, the former choosing to remain autonomous while the latter drifts elsewhere, looking for a now unattainable "home." Residents tend to express this dilemma in their idiosyncratic and inconsistent demands on the staff.

This kind of behavior might be more typical of the present generation of elderly than of later ones because of the tremendous social changes they have traversed in their lives. But retirement communities must develop a philosophy that somehow recognizes the lingering ideal of the family, even though they cannot replace it as a total support system. This philosophy must be clear and acceptable to the residents, their families, and community staff. Fuji-no-Sato had not fully developed and articulated such a philosophy at the time of our research. Since 1983, however, this problem has been given a high priority by the management in an effort to restore good relations with the residents. They have made promising strides toward a workable philosophy, making them apparently unique among Japanese retirement communities.

ESTABLISHING SECOND-LEVEL
RELATIONSHIPS

Like other "new towns," Fuji-no-Sato is an unusual social setting in Japanese society in the sense that it began as a purely informal and peer group society. To its residents, the community is still an unfamiliar, unstructured, and newly constituted social situation in which they have few guidelines for appropriate behavior. It lacks two of the three core social institutions of Japanese life: Although it contains the seeds at least of community, it does not and cannot contain the family or the workplace. These two missing institutions help locate the Japanese formally in their society, with roles governed by accepted norms. Naturally, family and job take their place alongside community as the bases of the Japanese sense of belonging. Through these institutions, Japanese social relations have their fundamental two-level structure; and the first level, embodied in the family, is the more important.

Family remains the core institution throughout one's life and meets the whole range of one's needs at various times during the life cycle. One is born and grows up in the natal family, creates one's own life-style through the procreative family, and eventually dies in the extended family. At Fuji-no-Sato, this primary structure is largely irrelevant, as is the main second-level structure of normal adulthood: work.

The residents of Fuji-no-Sato coped with their unstructured situation by employing behavioral guidelines adapted from traditional repertoires. The principal guidelines they used were those of formal interaction, those characteristic of the outer edge of level two. With very few ties carried over from previous experience, this was the only way they could at first live in a geographically isolated, small, face-to-face community.

In the absence of biographical experience or cultural techniques for forming close relationships under these circumstances and given restrictive conditions such as status competition, the scarcity of exchangeable goods and services, and gossip, they in effect *consolidated* their relationships at the formal level. Patterns of sociability characteristic only of new or distant relationships by normal Japanese standards appeared to have become stabilized as the dominant ones at Fuji-no-Sato. The functionally specific social interactions, the polite and shallow *tatemae* relationships, the great importance attached to avoiding *meiwaku*, and other characteristics of Fuji-no-Sato life indicated this routinization of social distance. Closer friendships were rare, and development of true first-level relationships was found among only a few women.

There may have been a factor contributing to the routinization of social distance that had little to do with the residents' age or the newness of the community, namely, their image of "resort living." The area around Fuji-no-Sato was one of Japan's most famous resorts, and this fact played a major part in attracting residents. It may also have given the community something of the image of a vacation retreat in the residents' eyes, that is, a place where people come to enjoy themselves, not to form close personal relationships and networks of mutual support. Even those who wanted closer contact with others may have felt this as a restraint on their sociability.

This overall picture of interpersonal distance and mutual alienation is part of the answer to the question of Japan's relevance to the Western model of social integration in age-homogeneous communities with which we started this inquiry. In many Western societies, especially the United States, lifelong group memberships and ascribed social roles, although important, are thoroughly supplemented by short-lived, flexible relationships and statuses that are achieved or acquired temporarily, often by choice. In such societies, which Fredrik Barth (1975) called *contract* societies, interpersonal norms tend to be somewhat vague and flexible, and interactions tend to be *negotiated* in a somewhat *ad hoc* fashion. Under these circumstances, it may be possible for age-homogeneous communities of elders to create their own definition of community and construct comfortable roles and relationships accordingly. The difficulties of Fuji-no-Sato's residents underline the importance of these cultural features in understanding the aging process in the West.

When we turn to our other main interest, the implications of such communities for the well-being of Japan's elderly, we find this a difficult evaluation to make. In this book, we did not directly raise the question of whether retirement communities are a good thing, a question that simply cannot be answered at this stage. Retirement living is still in its infancy. The social forces that created it are still rapidly evolving, as are the images and expectations of it held by residents, developers, and the public at large. What seems positive today might produce negative effects in the long run, and vice versa. Because Fuji-no-Sato was one of the first such communities, even though we have been observing it for nine years now, we must be careful about generalizing to other communities, most of which are much younger and therefore evolving in a context that Fuji-no-Sato itself has helped alter. We must await in-depth studies of other communities, a research effort that has not yet begun. With these reservations in mind, we address the crucial question: Are the social shortcomings of the retirement community an acceptable price to pay?

One way of answering this question is to ask the residents of places like Fuji-no-Sato themselves. We have seen that many of them actually showed little inclination to seek closer relationships with their neighbors, a fact that suggests there may be nothing to worry about. In portraying the community as weakly integrated, and therefore socially impoverished, are we not committing the ethnocentric sin of applying Western standards of integration where they are out of place? Are we peddling romantic notions of the ideal community, dredged up from a mythical golden age and applied to a culture where it has rarely if ever really existed?

We reject such suggestions for several reasons and insist that the need for stronger social bonds is real. First, many of the residents at Fuji-no-Sato actually did seek closer relations with their neighbors, and many expressed anxiety at the difficulty of doing so. First-level relationships are the ideal in Japanese society under most conditions, and their loss was generally seen as a high price to pay, even for the freedom and autonomy enjoyed by many of our residents. In a closer knit community, it might have been more difficult for some residents to find the privacy and liberty they sought, but this simply suggests that the ideal would be a *balance* between the availability of cozy intimacy and that of liberating isolation. In our view, isolation now has a decided edge.

Second, the formality and distance of social relationships created several practical problems in the community. If residents had known one another better, they would have been able to exchange all kinds of information and help, for which they had to rely on the staff as things stood. This of course raised the costs of management (which the residents ultimately had to pay) and led to delays and errors as the complex formal chain of communication between staff and residents was brought into play. Again, was this too high a price to pay for self-determination? For some people, it probably was. Our impression was that it would not have been for the majority.

Third, although most of the residents at the time of the study were still healthy enough to be fairly self-sufficient, they have grown less so as they have aged. Observation of communities of frail elderly in the United States (Hochschild, 1973; Perkinson, 1980) shows how important resident-to-resident support and help can be and how important deep mutual knowledge and caring among the residents is in ensuring this kind of support.

In pointing to the need for a greater range of social options in communities like Fuji-no-Sato, then, we are not suggesting that the ideal would be a single, great, first-level fellowship, or even that such a thing is possible. We are suggesting that more sensitivity to the social barriers that keep elderly strangers separate in Japanese culture and more creative approaches to breaching those barriers *for those who want and can benefit from friendship* would not be a bad idea.

To this end, we have seen that the development of friendship in this culture depends on the accessibility of regular, structured relationships of the formal, second-level type—that is, it depends on something we can call community integration. We have seen that community integration by this definition was relatively poor at Fuji-no-Sato, and consequently first-level relations were quite difficult for most people to manage. Further, as in any such alienated group, there is a vicious circle linking the inaccessibility of first-level relationships to residents' lack of interest in seeking them.

POSSIBILITIES FOR CHANGE

The lack of familiar tasks, roles, and hierarchical relationships meant that peer group activities at Fuji-no-Sato rarely generated the kind of meaningful, ongoing interactions that could lead to friendship, particularly among the men. One way of looking at this is to say that the lack of structural or external formality led to an *ad hoc* or internal self-imposed formality. What may be needed is the relative formalization of these peer relations, the formation of a new set of "intermediate" roles that are neither as culturally fixed as occupational and familial roles (which are largely unavailable anyway) nor as amorphous and spontaneous as the casual contacts available in the community at the time. These intermediate roles, although lacking the familiarity and clarity of more traditional ones, would nonetheless resemble work roles in being (1) functionally specific and task oriented, thereby directing attention away from individual differences and personal choice, and (2) specialized, creating meaningful interactive role *sets* with mutual obligations and rights, like teacher-student, worker-manager, and so on, thereby generating stable ongoing interactions.

Roles in the residents association, for men, and the volunteer group, for women, are good examples of "intermediate" roles that already existed in Fuji-no-Sato society but were clearly available to only a few. One possibility for generating more roles like this would be to organize groups that provide some kind of service to others— various kinds of organized volunteerism. Such groups would probably not serve the residents themselves, partly because this would generate social hierarchies within the community (which the residents would probably resist) and partly because there is a definite limit to the number of meaningful tasks that could be done this way. Volunteer services for people *outside* the community, however, would avoid both these limitations and would seem to be a possibility. There is the obvious question of whether many residents would be willing to join such groups or whether they could be motivated to do so, and here we can only guess. The possible benefits for social integration within the community would suggest it is worth a try.

If and when a certain level of social integration has been achieved, it would also make sense to increase the number and variety of settings for nonspecific social interaction. Although such settings rarely generate meaningful interactions among relative strangers, as we have explained, once people are engaged in ongoing, meaningful, second-level role sets, the availability of settings for casual interaction can promote the gradual transition to friendship. This is especially important in a community like Fuji-no-Sato, where living space is highly privatized.

THE QUESTION OF LONELINESS

Loneliness is one of those maddening ideas that is too complex and ambiguous to measure well but that nevertheless persists in attracting the attention of gerontologists because it seems to promise important understandings about the aged. One does not have to be a gerontologist to know that many old people in any culture love to talk, love to be touched, love to see their children and grandchildren, love the stimulation of social events and entertainments. It came as a surprise when Cumming and Henry's famous Kansas City study showed a surprisingly good adjustment level among middle-class elderly with relatively few close social contacts (Cumming and Henry, 1961). Clark and Anderson (1967) also found some people who had been fairly happy lifelong loners and continued to be in old age. Studies like these, which suggest that loneliness and social isolation are not necessarily linked in old age, seem to contradict a certain common sense. The difficulty of measuring the key variables leaves the question of loneliness an open one in gerontological debate.

Like most other researchers, we have not done a thorough study of the concept of loneliness and have little confidence that the simple measures we used actually put the question to rest. But given this caveat, our data on loneliness suggest some insights into the life-styles of the residents. Low levels of reported loneliness and high levels of overall morale (using a Japanese version of the Philadelphia Geriatric Center Morale Scale) (Lawton, 1975) indicate that emotional pain related to the deprivation of human contact was not much of a problem for the people at Fuji-no-Sato. This finding makes sense in the light of two facts, one having to do with the nature of loneliness and one having to do with the life histories and adaptive styles of the residents.

Loneliness (and this applies to the famous hunger of the elderly for certain kinds of company) arises not from the simple absence of human contact, but from the frustration of one's *expectations* about certain kinds of contact at certain times and places. We are not lonely when we are satisfying our urge for a solitary walk in the wilderness or a solo trip to a distant place or sitting in front of our computer behind a closed office door. We *are* lonely, even in the midst of people we know and like, when we want to share something with a particular absent person or to hear reassurance from a particular absent voice. The old are lonely because key faces and voices have left their lives and no longer appear in those places and at those times when they were most expected. It is not the hermit who misses human contact; it is the fully social person, one who has come to anticipate it.

It was therefore the unusual person who was lonely at Fuji-no-Sato, the person who made strong associations between the scenes, settings, and events of his or her new life and those of an earlier milieu where close fellowship was the rule. Most people saw the new community for what it was: a place away from familiar faces, family, old friends, colleagues, and even casual acquaintances of the past; a place of unfamiliar sights, sounds, and smells that rarely even evoke memories of situations where a particular face should appear. Having chosen this place, they may have found themselves disappointed about its stuffiness or the boredom of its routines, but they would rarely feel lonely.

This was especially true of the average Fuji-no-Sato resident, whose character was more self-sufficient and less gregarious than the average in other communities. The residents here were self-selected individualists, seekers of privacy and self-determination. Moreover, for many, these traits were probably lifelong strategies, not mere *ad hoc* adaptations to the dilemmas of aging we have discussed elsewhere in this book. A significant number of them were never married, childless, or divorced—those who had not lived in a typical family situation for some time, perhaps not since they had left their family of childhood. Because marriage and parenthood are usual bases of intimacy in adulthood, many of these residents probably had not fully developed the usual habits and skills that go with social bonding in Japanese society. Perhaps many of them had to suppress needs for *amae* and other forms of intimacy or to divert such needs in other directions.

Here is another reason, less cultural and more idiosyncratic than the lack of friendship-promoting social organization, why work-centered volunteerism might help foster interpersonal ties in communities like Fuji-no-Sato. For these particular people, work might be one of the few acceptable ways of expressing social feelings. In this connection, it is interesting that instead of the high rates of loneliness we expected to find, we found high rates of *boredom* instead.

Still, the residents of Fuji-no-Sato have shown courage in their struggle to find meaning in an unfamiliar environment. They are the planners of the highly complex enterprise of growing old in today's Japan, the explorers of new social frontiers. For some, it has been an unintended and even an unwanted expedition, but they have made their contribution and deserve to be called the honored.

Hiroshige, wandering through the final scenes of feudal Japan in the nineteenth century, with an artist's prescience labored to capture in his "fifty-three stages" the essence of the ancient Tokai Road. Though lacking Hiroshige's genius, we are likewise engaged in documenting a journey, hoping the record of the elders' struggle will be appreciated by coming generations of travelers, both serious and curious. Our caravan has passed perhaps a dozen of the fifty-three scenes, and we still have much to depict. We conclude this book with a sense of our responsibility to follow and understand the further stages of this unique journey.

Bibliography

Achenbaum, Andrew W., and Peter N. Stearns. 1978. "Old Age and Modernization." *The Gerontologist 18* (3), pp. 307–312.

Barth, F. 1972. "Analytical Dimensions in the Comparison of Social Organizations." *American Anthropologist 74* (1,2), pp. 207–220.

Butler, Robert N. 1975. *Why Survive? Being Old in America.* New York: Harper and Row.

Clark, Margaret. 1969. "Cultural Values and Dependency in Later Life." *In* Richard A. Kalish (ed.). *The Dependencies of Old People.* Ann Arbor: University of Michigan-Wayne State University, pp. 59–72.

Clark, Margaret, and Barbara Anderson. 1967. *Culture and Aging.* Springfield, Ill.: Charles C. Thomas.

Cowgill, Donald O., and Lowell D. Holmes (eds.). 1972. *Aging and Modernization.* New York: Appleton Century Crofts.

Cumming, E., and W. Henry. 1961. *Growing Old: The Process of Disengagement.* New York: Basic Books.

DeVos, George A. 1973a. "Introduction." *In* G. DeVos and H. Wagatsuma (eds.). *Socialization for Achievement.* Berkeley: University of California Press, pp. 1–9.

———. 1973b. "Role Narcissism and the Etiology of Japanese Suicide." *In* G. DeVos and H. Wagatsuma (eds.). *Socialization for Achievement.* Berkeley: University of California Press, pp. 438–485.

Doi, Takeo. 1973. *The Anatomy of Dependence.* Tokyo: Kodansha.

Geertz, Clifford. 1973. *The Interpretation of Cultures.* New York: Basic Books.

Glaser, B., and A. Strauss. 1969. *The Discovery of Grounded Theory.* Chicago: Aldine.

Goffman, Erving. 1959. *The Presentation of Self in Everyday Life.* New York: Doubleday Anchor Books.

Hamaguchi, Eshun. 1982. *Kanjin shugi no shakai—Nihon* (Japan: The contextual society). Tokyo: Tōyō Keizaisha.

Health and Welfare Statistics Association. 1983. *Kokumin no fukushi no dōkō* (Annual report on general trends in welfare). Tokyo: Kōsei Tōkei Kyōkai.

———. 1990. *Nihon no kōsei tōkei* (Health and Welfare Statistics in Japan). Tokyo: Kōsei Tōkei Kyōkai.

Henry, J. 1963. *Culture Against Man*. New York: Random House.

Hochschild, Arlie R. 1973. *The Unexpected Community: Portrait of an Old Age Subculture*. Berkeley: University of California Press.

Japan College of Social Work. 1982. *Yūryō rōjin hōmu ni kansuru juyō chōsa hōkokushō* (Report on the social demands of yūryō homes for the aged). Tokyo: Nihon Shakai Jigyō Daigaku.

Johnson, Sheila K. 1971. *Idle Haven: Community Building Among the Working-Class Retired*. Berkeley: University of California Press.

Kawashima, Takenori. 1957. *Ideorogii to shite no ie seido* (The family system as an ideology). Tokyo: Iwanami Shoten.

Kayser-Jones, Jeanie S. 1981. *Old, Alone, and Neglected: Care of the Aged in Scotland and the United States*. Berkeley: University of California Press.

Keith, Jennie. 1980a. "Old Age and Community Creation." *In* Christine L. Fry (ed.). *Aging in Culture and Society: Comparative Viewpoints and Strategies*. New York: J.F. Bergin, pp. 170–197.

———. 1980b. "Participant Observation." *In* Christine L. Fry and Jennie Keith (eds.). *New Methods for Old Age Research*. Chicago: Loyola University, pp. 1–20.

Keith-Ross, J. *See also* Ross.

Kiefer, Christie W. 1974. *Changing Cultures, Changing Lives: An Ethnographic Study of Three Generations of Japanese Americans*. San Francisco: Jossey-Bass.

———. 1976. "The Danchi-zoku and the Evolution of Metropolitan Mind." *In* L. Austin (ed.). *Japan: The Paradox of Progress*. New Haven: Yale University Press, pp. 279–300.

———. 1987. "Care of the Aged in Japan." *In* M. Lock and E. Norbeck (eds.). *Health, Illness, and Medical Care in Japan*. Honolulu: University of Hawaii Press, pp. 89–109.

———. 1990. "The Aged in Japan: Elite, Victims, or Plural Players?" *In* J. Sokolovsky (ed.). *The Cultural Context of Aging*. New York: Bergin and Garvey, pp. 181–195.

Kinoshita, Yasuhito. 1981. "Now You See It. Now You Don't: Free Medical Care for the Aged in Japan." Paper presented at the thirty-fourth annual meeting of the Gerontological Society, Toronto, Canada, November 8–12.

———. 1984. "Social Organization in a Japanese Retirement Community." Ph.D. diss., University of California, San Francisco.

———. In press. "The Political-Economy Perspective on Health and Medical Care Policies for the Aged in Japan." *In* S. Ingman and D. Gill (eds.). *Geriatric Care, Distributive Justice, and the Welfare State*. Albany, New York: SUNY Press.

Laird, Carobeth. 1979. *Limbo: A Memoir About Life in a Nursing Home by a Survivor*. Novato, California: Chandler and Sharp.

Langness, L. L. 1974. *The Study of Culture*. San Francisco: Chandler and Sharp.

Lawton, M. P. 1975. "The Philadelphia Geriatric Center Morale Scale: A Revision." *Journal of Gerontology 30*, pp. 85–89.

Levy, M. J., Jr. 1952. *The Structure of Society*. Princeton, New Jersey: Princeton University Press.

Maddox, G. L. 1964. "Disengagement Theory: A Critical Evaluation." *The Gerontologist 4*, pp. 80–83.

Mendelson, Mary A. 1975. *Tender Loving Greed*. New York: Random House.

Ministry of Health and Welfare (Kōseishō). 1986. *Future Population Estimates for Japan*. Tokyo: Institute for Population Problems.

———. 1990. *Health and Welfare White Paper, 1989*. Tokyo: Kōseishō.

Miyajima, S. 1986. "Combatting Elderly Disability." *Kosei no Shihyo 33* (11), pp. 31–39.

Myerhoff, Barbara. 1978. *Number Our Days*. New York: Simon and Schuster.

Nakane, C. 1972. *Japanese Society*. Berkeley: University of California Press.

National Welfare Association (Zenkoku Shakai Fukushi Kyōgikai) (ed.). 1982. *Kōreisha mondai sōgō chōsa hōkokushō* (Summary report on surveys of aging problems). Tokyo: Zenkoku Shakai Fukushi Kyōgikai.

Neugarten, Bernice. 1975. "The Future and the Young-Old." *The Gerontologist 15*, pp. 4–9.

Nikkei Business. 1991. "*Keieinan kakugo de zoku-zoku shunyū: Sore demo gambaru hontō no riyū*" (Expecting financial problems, they keep coming: But the real reason is the long term). *Nikkei Business 582*, pp. 195–196.

Ogasawara, Yuji. 1982. "*Rōjin hōmu no taikei to seido*" (The system and institution of welfare homes for the aged). *In* Fumio Miura and Yuji Ogasawara (eds.). *Gendai rōjin hōmu ron* (A study of welfare homes for the aged). Tokyo: Zenkoku Shakai Fukushi Kyōgikai.

Palmore, Erdman. 1975. *The Honorable Elders: A Cross-Cultural Analysis of Aging in Japan*. Durham, North Carolina: Duke University Press.

Palmore, E., and D. Maeda. 1985. *The Honorable Elders Revisited*. Durham, North Carolina: Duke University Press.

Parsons, T. 1951. *The Social System*. New York: Free Press.

Perkinson, M. 1980. "Alternate Roles for the Elderly: An Example from a Midwestern Retirement Community." *Human Organization 39*, pp. 219–226.

Plath, David. 1972. "Japan: The After Years." *In* Donald O. Cowgill and Lowell D. Holmes (eds.). *Aging and Modernization*. New York: Appleton Century Crofts, pp. 132–150.

———. 1980. *Long Engagements: Maturity in Modern Japan*. Stanford: Stanford University Press.

Prime Minister's Office (Sorifu) 1980. *Kōreisha mondai no genjō* (White paper on aging). Tokyo: Ōkurashō Insatsukyoku.

Prime Minister's Office, Bureau of Aging. 1982. *Rōjin seikatsu to iken: Kokusai chōsa sho* (Lives and opinions of old people: Report of a cross-national survey). Tokyo: Ministry of Finance Printing Office.

Quadagno, J. 1982. *Aging in Early Industrial Society*. New York: Academic Press.

Reynolds, D. 1976. *Morita Psychotherapy*. Berkeley: University of California Press.

Rosow, Irving. 1962. "Old Age: One Moral Dilemma of an Affluent Society." *The Gerontologist 2*, pp. 182–191.

———. 1967. *Social Integration of the Aged*. New York: Free Press.

———. 1974. *Socialization to Old Age*. Berkeley: University of California Press.

Ross, J. K. 1977. *Old People, New Lives: Community Creation in a Retirement Residence*. Chicago: University of Chicago Press.

Senior Welfare Development Center (Rōjin Fukushi Kaihatsu Sentā). 1982. *Kōreika shakai ni taiōshita kyojū chiiki no seibi ni kansuru chōsa hōkokushō* (A research report on housing in the aging society). Tokyo: Rōjin Fukushi Kaihatsu Sentā.

Slater, Philip E. 1970. *The Pursuit of Loneliness: American Culture at the Breaking Point*. Boston: Beacon Press.

Smith, Robert J. 1974. *Ancestor Worship in Contemporary Japan*. Stanford: Stanford University Press.

Soda, Takemune, and Fumio Miura (eds.). 1982. *Zusetsu rōjin hakushō* (Illustrated white paper on aging). Tokyo: Sekibusha.

TMIG (Tokyo Metropolitan Institute of Gerontology). 1981. *Tokubetsu yōgo rōjin hōmu oyobi riyōsha jittai chōsa hōkokushō* (Research report on *toku-yō* homes and their residents). Tokyo: Tokyo Metropolitan Institute of Gerontology.

Ushio, M. 1989. "The System of Health and Medical Services for the Aged in Japan." *Japan Hospitals*, no. 8, July, pp. 9–20.

Vladeck, Bruce C. 1980. *Unloving Care: The Nursing Home Tragedy*. New York: Basic Books.

Wagatsuma, Hiroshi. 1982. *Nihonteki shūdanshugi no kokusaika wa kanōka* (Is internationalization of Japanese group-centeredness possible?). *In* Eshun Hamaguchi and Shupei Kumon (eds.). *Nihonteki shūndanshugi* (Japanese group-centeredness). Tokyo: Yuhikaku.

Wagatsuma, Hiroshi, and Arthur Rosett. 1983. "Cultural Attitudes Toward Contract Law: Japan and the U.S. Compared." Unpublished manuscript.

Webb, Eugene J., et al. 1966. *Unobtrusive Measures: Nonreactive Research in the Social Sciences*. Chicago: Rand McNally College Publishing.

Weber, Max. [1904] 1930. *The Protestant Ethic and the Spirit of Capitalism* (Trans. T. Parsons). New York: Scribner.

Weiss, Robert S. 1973. *Loneliness: The Experience of Emotional and Social Isolation*. Cambridge: MIT Press.

Yuzawa, Yasuhiko. 1970. *Rōjin fuyō mondai no kōzō to tenkai* (The structure and development of the problem of elderly dependency). *In* Shoichi Nasu and Yasuhiko Yuzawa (eds.). *Rōjin fuyō no kenkyū* (The study of elderly dependency). Tokyo: Kakiuchi Shuppan.

Index

Acquaintance. *See* Casual relationships
Activity theory, 162
Additional significance, 160–161, 171
Adjustment, 207
Aesthetics: arts and crafts, 92, 156–158, 208; dress and grooming, 93, 182, 184–185; gardening (*see* Leisure: gardening); music, 155, 156, 157, 163, 178, 185; nature, 83–85, 117; noise, 122–123; poetry, 155, 156, 157
Aids to daily living, 70, 72, 101
Alienation, 205
Altruism, 135, 137, 146, 154–165, 206, 208
amae, 17, 28–29, 177, 208. *See also* Dependency
Americanization, 25
Ancestor worship, 48, 51
Anderson, B., 207
Anthropology: methods, ix, x, 1, 10–15, 204, 207; research, 100, 199
Architecture: of Fuji-no-Sato, 85–95, 122–124, 131; regulations, 73; and social interaction, 174; of *yōrōin*, 66–67
Arranged marriage, 109, 196
Associates, 28–29

Back region, 189
Barth, F., 203
Bedfast elderly, 58, 67, 70, 99, 200. *See also* Health: chronic illness
bekkyo, 54–61
boke. See Dementia
Boredom, 167, 208
Buddhism, 47, 62, 92, 112, 113
Bushi, 47

Capitalism, 6
Casual relationships, 27, 170–173, 188, 193–194, 205, 206, 208
Childlessness. *See* Parenthood

Christianity, 47, 62, 92, 112, 113, 154, 162–164, 194
chū. See Filial piety
Citizenship, 48
Civil code, 46–52
Clark, M., 179, 207
Climate, 84
Clinic. *See* Hospital care
Clothing. *See* Aesthetics: dress and grooming
Comfort: bathing, 93; incentive to move, 77, 117, 125, 202–203; as part of "welfare," 136; problems, at Fuji-no-Sato, 123–24
Communications: advertising, 77, 78, 79, 104, 124, 127, 132; bulletin board, 13, 93, 94, 95, 136, 152, 164, 186, 191; data systems, 95–98; failure, 121–138, 168, 183, 186, 188, 204; language, 71–74, 77–78, 121–138, 175, 182–183, 195; loudspeaker, 94; mail, 92; news media, 10, 14, 40, 74, 79, 92, 95, 105; in research, 14; telephone, 71, 91, 95, 130–131; television, 95, 97, 150
Community: creation, 1, 9, 22, 26, 87; integration, 204–205; meaning of, 16; theory of, 22–26; traditional characteristics, 181, 183, 190, 196, 202
Community center. *See* Public space
Competitiveness, 28, 94, 126, 167–168, 185, 202
Conditional *bekkyo*, 35
Condominiums, 8, 74
Conflict: avoidance of, in research, 14; in families, 58, 115, 116, 174; intergenerational, 6; between residents and management, 2, 121–138, 140, 142, 145, 147–153; in residents association, 143, 144, 145, 146, 147, 148
Confucianism, 48–49
Consensus. *See* Values
Consociates, 28–30

215

216   *Index*

Continuum-of-care. *See* Health care
Contract: Japanese meaning of, 133–135; residential facilities, entrance, 76, 77, 102–105, 121, 125, 133–138, 190, 194
Contract societies, 203
Contract welfare, 121–122, 132–138
Convoy, 28, 30
Cultural lag, 52
Cumming, E., 21, 207

Day care, 70, 199
Death: and bodies, keeping of, 99; fear of, 125; of former respondents, x; funerals, 181–182; inevitability, 4; public records, 45; rates, 61; in war, 108–109
Definition of the situation, 19
Dementia, 68, 95, 117, 186, 200
Demography: aging of Japan, 2, 37–41, 78, 199; based on households, 47; Fuji-no-Sato, 107–117; health facilities, 65–69; living arrangements, 52–61; senior housing, 74
Dependency: activities and, 158; aging and, 6; avoidance of, 92, 174, 177–180, 198, 199, 201, 204; family and, 3, 41–45, 54–61, 110–111, 115–116, 199; health care policy and, 70, 102; housing and, 60, 64, 76; stereotype of Japan, 178
DeVos, G., 17, 24
Disability. *See* Health: chronic illness
Disengagement, 21, 174
Distance. *See* Intimacy: avoidance of
Divorce, 25, 47, 107, 110, 114, 115, 208
Doi, T., 28
dōkyo, 54–61, 115–116, 165, 199, 200

East Asian culture, 16, 19, 25, 199
Economics: aging and, 68–71, 199–200; health care, 4–5, 68–71; housing, 76; prices, 74; retirement, 41–45
Education, 14, 55, 111–115, 128, 194
Emperor, 48, 50
Employment rates, 179
enryo, 28–29, 173
Entryway, 172–173, 189
Environmental Protection Agency, 85
Epistemology. *See* Objectivity
Ethnography. *See* Anthropology: methods
Exchange, 181, 202, 204

Family: burden of elderly on, 111, 115–117, 178–179; change, 45, 69, 200;

conflict, 58, 115–117, 178–179; and household, 74; in-laws, 110, 116; law, 49–51; registration, 46–47; roles in, 25, 205. *See also ie*
Fees. *See* Fuji-no-Sato: finances
Filial piety, 17, 37, 48
Finances: of families, 47–48; Fuji-no-Sato, 103–110; independence, 41–45, 70, 116–117; security in old age, 4, 8, 18, 20, 41, 43–45, 49–51, 63–65, 72–73, 77, 78, 104–106, 138, 200–201
Food and eating, 70, 72, 91, 92, 93, 94, 142–143, 146, 161, 172, 195, 197
France, 22–23, 26, 38, 94
Friendship: aging and, 21; barriers to, 173–174, 205; collective work and, 166, 192, 196, 206, 208; durability, 192; formation of, 160, 192, 194, 205, 206, 208; functions of, 27; meaning of, 192; men and, 195–196; personality and, 165; social integration and, 169; women and, 196–197
Front region, 189
Fuji-no-Sato: Administrative Department, 131, 153; compared to other communities, 7–10, 16, 76, 169, 203; demographics, 9, 107–117; description, 83–106; directorship, 122, 124, 127–129, 147, 148; entrance requirements, 103; example of Japanese culture, 17–19; finances, 8, 102–106, 124, 130, 145, 149–153; history, 8–9; management, 9, 32, 121–138, 139–152; operating system, 102–106; Planning Department, 131, 150–151, 153; research method, 10–15; social integration in, 23–24, 30–33, 203; social interaction in, 169–198
Functional diffusion/specificity, 27, 160, 165, 170–171, 194, 205
Funerals, 93, 181–182

Gardening. *See* Leisure: gardening
genkan. *See* Entryway
Geriatric health facilities, 70
Gerontology, ix, 2, 11, 199, 206
Gifts, 147, 160, 190–191
giri, 28–29, 32
Glaser, B., 17
Goffman, E., 189
Good faith, 133–138
Gossip, 93, 174, 185–188, 193, 197
Graying of Japan. *See* Demography
Great Britain, 4, 39, 42
Great Depression, 63
Greeting, 180–182, 189–190

Groups: group-centeredness, 17, 136; meaning of, in Japan, 24–25; nonparticipation, 157–158; voluntary, 154–168, 191, 194

hade, 184–185
Health: as admission criterion, 64, 69; beliefs, 83, 93; chronic illness, 59, 61, 64, 66, 67, 101, 115, 197, 199–200; demographics, 4, 37; group participation and, 157–158; mental, 207; tuberculosis, 109
Health and Welfare Statistics Association, 65, 66, 67
Health care: at Fuji-no-Sato, 96–102, 124–127; continuum of care, 100–102; costs, 66, 69–70, 100; emergencies, 97–98, 125; expectations, 77, 87–89, 124–127; preventive care, 99–100; in retirement housing, 75–77, 162; social policy, 8–10, 18, 62, 70–71; standards, in Japan, 5, 105, 126
Health professions: helpers, 101; *kaigo fukushishi*, 101; nurses, 96, 97, 98, 101; physicians, 98, 99, 112, 113, 114, 124–127; social workers, 101; status of, 126–127; teams, 102
Henry, J., 7, 162
Henry, W., 21, 207
Hiroshige, 208–209
History: aging and, 19, 46–61; industrialization, 5–7, 46; of retirement housing, x, 3, 62–79, 203
Hochschild, A., 11, 20, 22, 205
honne, 173
Hospital care, 68, 69, 70, 99, 124–125, 127, 146
Household: extended, 52–61, 178; headship, 47–49, 62; legal definitions, 47–52; nuclear, 52–61; privacy, 172–173; structure, Fuji-no-Sato, 107–111; structure, Japan, 41, 52–61, 74
Housing: co-residence and, 55, 60; modern types for aged, 64–68; modernization and, 55; and population aging, 4, 7, 18; traditional types for aged, 62–64
Humor, 21, 32, 149

Identity, 25, 27
ie, 46–52, 62–63, 111
Illness. *See* Health
Income, 10, 41–45, 64, 124
Independence. *See* Dependency: avoidance of

Individualism: residents of Fuji-no-Sato, 141, 167; in United States, 24–25, 136
Industrialization, 5, 7
Informal interaction, 154–168
Inheritance, 47, 50–51, 106, 111, 117
Interaction: actors, 169; control of, 169; meaning of, 161, 170; preconditions, 158–161, 165, 169, 171, 202, 206; purposes of, 169; settings, 169–173; side-, 170; styles, 169
Interviews, 12, 103, 108, 109
Intimacy: avoidance of, 168, 173–174, 183, 188–190, 202, 204; example of, 197–198; expectations of, 173–174, 198, 207; preconditions, 31, 160, 161, 171–173, 192–198, 204–205; sphere of, 27, 28 (*see also* Level-one relationships)
Izu Peninsula, 83–84

Japanese Americans, 34
Japanology, ix
jimi, 184–185
Johnson, S., 11, 22

kaigo fukushishi. See Health professions
Kansas City Study, 207
Kawabata, Y., 83
Kayser-Jones, J., 7, 11
keihi hōmu: characteristics, 65–66, 72; defined, 64, 71; numbers, 66, 78; terminology, 78
Keith, J., 11, 23. *See also* Ross, J.
Kiefer, C., 11, 16, 24, 65, 173
kimochi, 129
Kin terms, 182–183
Kinoshita, Y., 10–15, 74, 94, 122, 139, 154, 186, 188, 190, 193, 194
Kinship. *See* Family; Household; *ie*; Parenthood
kō. See Filial piety
koden, 182
kokka, 48
koseki, 47

Laird, C., 7
Law, 46–52, 133–138
Law for the Health of the Elderly, 69, 70
Lawton, P., 207
Leisure: desire for, 158; gardening, 86, 166–168, 184; hobbies, 92, 154–162, 171, 194; sightseeing, 83–84; sports, 83–84, 155, 156, 195–196; vacations, 83–84, 110, 195

Level-one relationships, 27–33, 170, 172, 176, 177, 204–205
Level-three relationships, 27–33
Level-two relationships, 27–33, 170, 172, 174, 176, 177, 181, 201
Levy, M., 160
Liberal Democratic Party, 68
Life-care communities, 8, 9, 78, 100, 102, 121
Life cycle, 29
Life-guarantee communities, 8, 74, 78
Loneliness, 20, 146, 173, 196, 206–208
Longevity, 4–6, 37–41, 77, 164
Long-term care. *See* Nursing homes

Maddox, G., 21, 162
Maeda, D., 16
Management: of Fuji-no-Sato, strategy, 76; relations with residents, 94, 121–138
Marital status: effects of war on, 25, 196, 208; of Fuji-no-Sato residents, 107–111, 114–115; and social integration, 25, 196, 208; and social status, 129. *See also* Divorce; Widowhood
Marriage, 47
Maturity, 128–129
Meaning. *See* Values
Meiji Period, 46–47, 49–50
meiwaku, 177–180, 193, 202
Mendelson, M., 7
Methods. *See* Anthropology: methods
Middle age, 70, 129, 135
Ministry of Health and Welfare, 8, 53, 65, 66, 72, 73, 101
Miura, F., 67, 74
Miyajima, S., 66, 70
Money-making policy, 122, 129–131, 137
Morale, 207
muko-yōshi, 50, 110
Music. *See* Aesthetics
Mutual aid, 51, 52, 103, 136, 166, 179, 191, 196, 197, 203, 204–205
Myerhoff, B., 11, 22

Nakane, C., 17
Names: memorizing, 13; use of, 181–183
National Retirement Housing Association, 73
Needs: feelings, 110, 129, 200; living arrangements, 3; privacy, 198; psychological, 200; respect, 198; roles and, 27

Neighborhood: friendship and, 166, 173–174, 183, 192; functions, 48; and living separately, 58; meaning of, 16–17; new members, 190–191
netakiri. See Bedfast elderly
News media. *See* Communications: news media
Norms: distance, 183; dress, 184–185; etiquette, 181, 189, 191, 195, 205; at Fuji-no-Sato, 175–188, 198; household structure, 48–51, 58; importance of, in Japan, 177, 198; interaction and, 169–172; *meiwaku*, 177–180; respect, 180–183, 198; saving face, 144; theoretical value of, 23, 31
Nursing homes: availability, 65–67, 78, 87–89, 127; cost, 68, 69; at Fuji-no-Sato, 87–89, 100, 102, 164–165; social policy, 64–68

Objectivity, 1–2, 204
Occupations, 16, 24, 45, 105, 112–115, 202, 205
Ogasawara, Y., 63
"Old old," 38
Older Americans Act, 63
omiai. See Arranged marriage
omimai, 146
oya-kokō. See Filial piety

Palmore, E., 16
Parenthood: childlessness, 16, 25, 62, 105, 110, 111, 115, 179, 208; legal meaning of, 47–52; support, 55–61, 110–111, 199
Parsons, T., 160
Part-time residents, 109
Patriarchy, 47, 62
Pensions, 41–45, 60, 61, 106
Perkinson, M., 11, 22, 205
Personality: of authors, x, 2; conflict resolution and, 152; of director at Fuji-no-Sato, 128–129; friendship and, 165; leadership and, 145, 153; social acceptance and, 141
Plath, D., 16, 29–30, 31
Politics, 25, 68, 78
Postmodernism, 2
Poverty, 62–65, 68, 78, 135
Prime Minister's Office, 54, 162, 179
Privacy, 17, 66, 172–173, 186, 197, 204
Property, 105–106
Public space, 13, 87, 92–95, 171, 172, 189, 194

Quadagno, J., 20
Questionnaires, 12

Reciprocity. *See* Mutual aid
Rehabilitation, 69, 70
Religion. *See* Ancestor worship; Buddhism; Christianity; Confucianism
Relocation, 91, 110, 115–117, 190–191
Residence patterns. *See* Household
Residential care, 100–101
Residents association: activities, 140, 145, 146–147; bulletin board, 94, 146, 152; bylaws, 141, 146; committees, 139, 140, 142–153; compulsory nature of, 141–142; conflict with management, 2, 126–127, 130, 132, 140, 142, 145, 147–153; elections, 143; fees, 140, 147; friendship networks and, 193; hardliners, 145; history, 139–147; internal conflict, 143, 144, 145, 146, 148; male domination of, 144; mediation, 148, 149–153; officers, 144–153; representatives, 140, 141, 143, 144; "seven samurai," 149
Respite beds, 70
Respect the Elders Day, 157
Retirement, 41–45, 105–106
Retirement communities: in crosscultural perspective, 7, 11, 18–19, 20; financing, 72–79; history and characteristics, 8, 9, 71–79; philosophy of, 201–209; social integration in, 21–23, 24, 200–208; as solution to elderly housing, 200–209
Reynolds, D., 25
Ritual: absence of, at Fuji-no-Sato, 190, 191; form and function in, 196; funerals, 93, 181–182; male bonding, 195–196; Respect the Elders Day, 157; saving face, 144; year-end parties, 161
rōjin byōin, 69
rōjin hōmu: defined, 63; stigma of, 78, 87
Role. *See* Social roles
Role narcissism, 24
Rosett, A., 133
Rosow, I., 6, 21–23, 31, 176
Ross, J., 2, 11, 20, 22–23, 26. *See also* Keith, J.
Rules of conduct. *See* Norms

Safety, 91
Scandinavia, 70
Schutz, Alfred, 29
Self-esteem, 18, 174, 176, 178
"Seven samurai," 149

Sex: and interaction patterns, 175, 195–198; segregation, 95, 181; sexuality, 21; and voluntary groups, 155–158, 160–161. *See also* Women
Shopping, 13, 84, 93, 94
Silver business, 74–77
Situation: and casual interaction, 197; defined, 160
Situational specificity, 160–162
Skilled nursing care. *See* Nursing homes
Social attitudes, 159
Social class: aristocracy, 51; homogeneity, at Fuji-no-Sato, 154; and housing, 67; lower middle class, 14; middle class, 14, 41, 45, 64, 67, 68, 70, 106, 163, 184–185; peasants, 51; warrior class, 47, 51; wealthy, 105, 163, 183, 186
Social control: lack of, at Fuji-no-Sato, 186–188; residents association and, 141–142; in traditional communities, 187
Social distance. *See* Intimacy: avoidance of
Social integration: at Fuji-no-Sato, 87, 110, 117–118, 154–168, 190, 191, 204; methods of studying, 12; preconditions, 201–206; theory, 18, 20–23, 190
Social mistakes, 174, 180–181, 185–188
Social networks, 192–194, 203
Social norms. *See* Norms
Social property, 103
Social roles: in contract societies, 203; in Japan, 26–33, 202, 203; and interaction, 170–171, 176; lack of, at Fuji-no-Sato, 188, 196, 202; of researcher, 13–14, 21–24; theoretical value of, 23–26, 31, 176; work and, 202
Social services. *See* Health care; Welfare
Social status: community role and, 167; dress and, 184–185; friendship and, 27; of Fuji-no-Sato residents, 111–115, 137, 188; hierarchy, 174, 175, 205; importance of, for childless, 16; interaction and, 174, 176; loss of, 174; occupation and, 105, 128; preservation of, 175, 183, 202; terms of address and, 175, 182–183, 195
Social welfare. *See* Welfare
Social Welfare Agency, 65, 87
Socialization, 22, 25, 110, 190
Soda, T., 67, 74
Standard of living, 41, 61, 74
Stigma, 9, 47, 78, 86, 109, 174, 183
Strangers, 13, 27, 180, 190–191, 196
Strauss, A., 17
Sweden, 4, 39

Taisho Period, 63
tatemae, 173, 202
Taxes, 47
Telephone fee incident, 130–131, 140
Territoriality, 86, 180
Tokugawa Period, 46
toku-yō hōmu: availability, 66, 71, 199–200; characteristics, 65–68; defined, 64; at Fuji-no-Sato, 89
Tokyo Metropolitan Institute of Gerontology (TMIS), 67
Transportation, 71, 83, 84, 85, 93, 124, 127

United States: concept of roles in, 31; contract law in, 133; customs, 94, 184; employment of aged in, 179; health care costs in, 68–69; individualism in, 24–25, 136; living standard, 91; retirement housing in, 7, 20, 21–23, 24, 70, 72, 76, 181, 204–205; social integration in, 24, 147, 176, 203; social policies, 5–6, 63
Unobtrusive measures, 10–11, 194
Urban-rural differences, 55, 58, 126
Ushio, M., 54, 69

Values: and aging, 3–7, 46–52, 129, 137, 164; and gossip, 186–187; group consensus as, 143, 148; intimacy, 204; and meaningfulness of life, 4; of researchers, 1; sensitivity, 129; in sociological theory, 21–23; and welfare, 135–138, 148; work, 162, 165, 167, 179
Visiting, 172–173
Vladeck, B., 7
Volunteerism. *See* Altruism

Wagatsuma, H., 133
"We" feeling, 23, 25, 31, 32, 87
Weber, M., 6
Welfare: contract welfare, 121–122, 132, 138; Japanese meaning of, 9, 16, 62, 68, 78–79, 128, 129, 135–138; policy, 38, 41–45, 62–65, 68; welfare spirit, 135; in Western societies, 4–5
Welfare Act for the Aged, 63, 64, 65–66, 72, 74
West Germany, 39
Western culture: age homogeneous communities in, 3; aging in, 18, 37, 203; individualism in, 136, 179; industrialization, 37; and social integration, 26, 28, 154, 203; social interaction style of, 174
Widowhood, 46, 107, 108, 109, 114, 115, 116
Women: in community leadership, 144, 151; demographics, 37–41, 107–111; discrimination against, 125; education of, 111–114; employment of, 59–60, 109, 113–115, 187; gossip, 185–188; hobbies of, 155, 156, 157; interaction habits of, 175; legal rights, 47, 49, 50; roles, 167
World War II, 3, 46, 105, 108–109

yōgo homes: defined, 64, 71; numbers, 66, 78; terminology, 78
yōrōin, 62–64, 66
yūryō homes: characteristics, 72–79; defined, 71; Fuji-no-Sato as, 86; terminology, 78
Yuzawa, Y., 50, 52

Compositor: Recorder Typesetting Network
Text: 10/13 Palatino
Display: Palatino
Printer: Thomson-Shore, Inc.
Binder: Thomson-Shore, Inc.